Two Native Narratives
of the
Mutiny in Delhi

Two Native Narratives *of the* Mutiny in Delhi

Charles Theophilus Metcalfe, C.S.I.

of the Bengal Civil Service

ABI Prints & Publishing Co.
New Delhi

TWO NATIVE NARRATIVES OF THE MUTINY IN DELHI

ISBN-978-81-86787-20-5

First Published: 1898

Reprinted in **2016** by:
ABI Prints & Publishing Co.
Pooja Apartments, 4B, Ansari Road, New Delhi-110 002 (India)
Tel.: 23287589, 23255799; Fax: 91-11-23270385
E-mail: aryanbooks@gmail.com
www.aryanbooks.co.in

Designed and Printed in India by
ABI Prints & Publishing Co., New Delhi

THE EMPEROR BAHADUR SHAH,
King of Delhi in 1857

After a miniature painted for the late Sir Theophilus Metcalfe, 1844.

PREFATORY NOTE.

My husband, in the introduction to this book, has explained how these native narratives of the Siege of Delhi came into his possession. The translation and arrangement of the originals were to him an endless source of interest and enjoyment, during the last years of his life, and his task was only completed a few weeks before his death in 1892. Accounts of the Indian Mutiny by Englishmen, and from an English point of view, have flooded the literary world, but feeling strongly, as he did, the intense interest of this (so far as he knew) the only *native* narrative, its publication was one of the dearest wishes of his heart. Death prevented his seeing the fulfilment of his desire; and it has remained for me to carry it out as best lay in my power. If the British public evince as much interest in the reading as he did in the translating and compiling, his work will not have been thrown away.

ESTHER G. METCALFE.

THE BEGUM ZURAT MAHAL.
Chief Wife of the King of Delhi.

Taken when she was a prisoner after the Mutiny, 1857.

INTRODUCTION.

ON the 1st of February, 1885, I received from Hyderabad the following telegram: "Mainodin Hassan Khan died yesterday morning." This event releases me from a promise, made so far back as 1878, that I would not, during the lifetime of Mainodin, publish the contents of certain papers which he had given to me under circumstances hereafter stated. I now offer a translation in English of those papers, as a contribution to the history of the Indian Rebellion of 1857-8. The chief interest of the narrative is confined to the events as they occurred in and around Delhi. So much has already been written about the so-called Indian Mutiny, that I feel some hesitation in offering this book to the public. In the interests of India and England it is best that the bitter memories of that cruel rebellion should be forgotten. On the other hand, a lasting historical interest is attached to that great event. The generation that saw the Mutiny of the Indian Army is fast dying out. Many of the principal actors have passed away. The rising generation, which is to govern our greatest dependency, knows but little of the details of the stirring scenes. Each corner of India where the soldiery mutinied had a special history of its own; but around Delhi and Lucknow the greatest interest was centred. Upon one of these two centres in Northern India the rebel soldiery gradually converged, as regiment after regiment mutinied, and it was at Delhi that the question of English supremacy was virtually decided. I hesitate in recalling painful scenes, the thought of which stirred up the feelings of Europeans at the time, to an extent which can now be hardly realized. A side of native character was shown which few Europeans had ever fully realized to be existent. No men had more faith in those they led than the officers of the Company's Army—often up to the last moment when the deadly blow was given. Amidst the bloodshed and violence of those times, however, there were found natives loyal and true, whose minds remained unaffected by the madness of the times. The writer of one of the narratives which is here given was an example of this constancy. Munshi Jíwan Lall was an educated native gentleman, closely associated with the court life of the King of Delhi for many years before the Mutiny, and during the time of the outbreak. His father, Girdharí Lall, a lineal descendant of Rajah Rogonath, Prime Minister of Aurungzebe, had been Munshi or writer, first to Sir David Ochterlony and afterwards to Sir Charles Metcalfe, when Agents to the Governor-General at the Court of the Mogul. Jíwan Lall, in younger days, had been present both at the siege of Bhurtpur and at Jeypur, when in June, 1835, Mr. Blake, the Assistant to the Resident, was killed. Later in life, being appointed as Accountant of the numerous pensions paid by the British Government to the King's family, he became a kind of go-between, taking confidential messages from the Governor-General's Agent to the Mogul. He for many years lived in daily contact with the King and his family, and was thoroughly familiar with all the various characters about the King, and with the Palace intrigues. During the actual Mutiny at Delhi and the siege of the city, he was resident within the walls; a careful observer of every event and acquainted with every incident that occurred; often in fear of his life, but protected by Palace influence. A writer by caste and profession, he recorded each day's events as they happened, and has thus preserved a valuable detailed record of what occurred in the city during the siege. After British power was re-established, Jíwan Lall was made an honorary Magistrate and a Municipal Commissioner, and died respected by his countrymen and regretted by those British officials who had known his worth and his goodness. No more trustworthy or loyal native servant has the British Government ever had, and no more trustworthy or reliable source of information could be obtained than the record he has left behind of the Summer of 1857. On the occasion of the Imperial Assemblage at Delhi, he gave me the original diary he had kept, and he procured also for me the official Court Diary, kept by the Moulvi or Royal Chaplain, of the King's private mosque in the Palace.[1]

A long-standing family connection, since 1767, with India, and since 1803 with Delhi, brought me, in addition to acquaintance with Munshi Jíwan Lall, some connection with one Mainodin Hassan Khan, previously referred to. This man, styled by courtesy Nawab Mainodin Hassan Khan, was descended from a noble family, who came as freebooters from Samarkand to try their fortunes in Hindustan. As a boy he was taken some notice of by the then Resident of Delhi, Sir Thomas Metcalfe, and was, later in life, together with his younger brother, appointed to an Inspectorship of Police. He held a like appointment in May, 1857, at the outbreak of the Mutiny. Well known to

[1] The practice of keeping diaries is common throughout the East: every law-court, police-station, and temple of note has its authentic record of daily events. The priests of Juggernauth boast that they have a diary of a thousand years.

the King, to the courtiers and intriguers about the Palace, he, by his imprudent conduct at the very first outbreak, became identified with the King's party—first, as the City Kotwál, or Police Officer, charged with the police administration under the rebellious King; next, as a Colonel, commanding one of the rebel regiments, which was formed by him out of the mutinous soldiery. Flying, after the capture of the city by the British, with a price on his head, he made his way to Bombay, as the nearest port from which he could escape to the deserts of Arabia. There he lived for some years, in company with many others of the rebel leaders, who had also managed to escape from India. In the meantime, his brother Mahommed Hassan, who, during the siege had attached himself to Sir John Metcalfe, and had subsequently travelled with that officer in Kullu and Thibet, urged him to return. He ventured as far as Bombay, and there stayed for some time, until the longing for home became too strong to be resisted.

He yearned to see the few surviving members of his family. Under advice, he surrendered to the authorities at Delhi. Sir John Metcalfe, then in England, telegraphed out that the best Counsel available was to be retained for his defence. He was tried and acquitted of all complicity in the murder of Europeans, and was pardoned for his share in the fighting at Delhi. At the time of the Imperial Assemblage in that city his case was represented to the Government of India, which granted to his family a small donation, in consideration of his services to Sir John Metcalfe, whose life he had saved at Delhi during the Mutiny. After his acquittal, Mainodin from time to time visited me in the various districts in which I was stationed, and later he busied himself in writing, from materials in his possession, the narrative which I have translated and placed first in order in this book. The part which he played he has described, with characteristic honesty. He undoubtedly threw himself into the rebellion with all the zest of a Mahommedan, eager to see the re-establishment of the Mogul Dynasty. His conduct, I have no doubt, was moderated by the recollection of kindnesses received from the Englishmen whom he had served, and from the knowledge that the master whose life he had so recently saved was watching his career beyond the ridge at Delhi.

From the foregoing remarks it will be seen that the great value attaching to these records lies in the fact that they are from purely native sources, and are, so far as I know, the first trustworthy contribution, from the native side, to the history of the Indian Mutiny. To prepare the English reader for these narratives, I propose to enumerate briefly (1) the causes which led to the mutiny of the native army; (2) the position of the titular King of Delhi at the time of the rebellion; and lastly the weakness of the British position in India, which made the temporary success of the mutineers possible, and comparatively easy of achievement.

The Causes which led to the Mutiny.

Many opinions have been expressed as to the causes which led the Bengal Army to mutiny. Some have contended that it was the revolt of a class, which had long been injudiciously pampered and petted into insubordination. Some have declared it to be the result of a national movement, to free the country from foreign government and to re-establish a Mahommedan rule. The Annexation Policy of Lord Dalhousie has been assigned by others as the primary cause. Sir John Kaye quotes a statement of Sir James Outram that the rebellion was set on foot by Mahommedans long before we took Oude from its rulers. An impression has been created by some writers, that the native army was corrupted by agents of the old princely houses, which English power had from time to time destroyed, and that these agents had wandered from city to city, sowing the seeds of sedition. Another writer believes the Mutiny to have been the result of fanaticism, created by a Royal Proclamation, emanating from the Court of Persia, copies of which had undoubtedly been circulated throughout India. Some have contended it was a purely Mahommedan rebellion, others a joint Hindu and Mahommedan revolt; and that in order to create a sympathetic movement of both Hindu and Mahommedan in a joint resistance to the British power, the cartridge grievance was created. Possibly the publication hereafter of Lord Canning's papers may throw some light on this much debated question. In the meantime the opinion of a native, himself an actor in the rebellion, and in close communication with more than one of the rebel leaders, when refugees together in Arabia, is of extreme interest. No positive evidence has been published since the rebellion, to throw much new light on the subject, although I have personally inquired from many distinguished natives. No new facts have ever been elicited beyond that, for years before the outbreak, there had been a growing disaffection towards the British rule. Gradually we had spread from South to North, and from West to East, enforcing British authority with a cold, unyielding hand; controlling the predatory habits of the lawless and fighting classes, checking the unlawful practices of the landed classes and wealthy Rajahs. Every class found itself curbed and subjected to law, with curtailed privileges. The professional thieves, robbers and dakoits, of whom whole villages existed, found their occupation becoming more and more hazardous.

Thugs and poisoners, smugglers and distillers of illicit spirits, slave-dealers, forgerers and perjurers, coiners and cattle-lifters, all had for years felt the strength of the new Administration. Under Mahommedan and Mahratta rule there had been some repression of crime, but an infinitesimal amount as compared with that under the English police. Bribery might still deliver some evildoers from the penalties of crime; but as years went on, money failed more and more to provide an avenue of escape. From one end of the peninsula to the other, the silent power of the English administration was creeping over the land, and using natives for its agents. For generations past, village had hated village, State had been jealous of State, the sword and club had been the arbiters when men's passions were loosed. It had become an hereditary instinct to decide every dispute by an appeal to force. That practice was being gradually repressed.

The landholders, who, from the days of their ancestors, had tortured recalcitrant tenants to extort rent, found they could no longer do so with impunity. There was repression and control over every class of society, in every grade of the population. The very law-courts, more particularly the lowest Civil Courts, constituted a grievance, although the Judges were native, for they undoubtedly were often used as a means by the rich to oppress the poor. The leaders of the Hindu race, the Brahminical class, found their influence fading, their priestly dignity lowered, privileges which they had enjoyed under native dynasties curtailed, their sacred language learned by the detested foreigner, their creed controverted by strange missionaries. Discontent reigned everywhere; Hindus were disaffected; Mahommedans, mindful of their warlike traditions, were dreaming of the past glories of their Emperors, and were daily praying for the restoration of their power; Mahrattas were still mourning over the conquests of Lake and Wellesley. Hatred of the British amongst the higher classes, ignorance and fanaticism amongst the lower, intrigue everywhere, a partial rebellion here and there, now amongst the Coles, again amongst the Sonthals and Khonds. A handful of Englishmen holding a continent, not by overwhelming forces, but mainly by the impression on the native mind that they were invincible. As years went on, familiarity with our system of government and resources opened the eyes of many to the belief that our numbers were insignificant. "What number of fighting men could a wretched little island (Japu) ever so far away in the Northern Seas produce?" and "Who was this John Company (Ján Compani) Bahadur who ruled so vast a territory as Hindustan? Was he an individual?" Opinions differed as to who or what he was. It was clear that "he" or "it" held India by a native army. If that could desert his cause, what could the few Feringhis scattered here and there do, cut off from all co-operation and assistance? It needed no teaching to instil this idea into the native mind. The truism was patent to everyone who devoted a moment's thought to the matter.

Whether, then, this idea first suggested a plan to tamper with the native army, or whether the tampering was attempted on the discovery that there was serious disaffection in the ranks, has never been, and probably never will be, satisfactorily ascertained. The general impression is that the Mahommedans were the instigators, and induced the Hindus to join them. But Mahommedans are bad conspirators: their methods are too clumsy, they are too ready to break into violence; they are wanting in many essentials to work out a successful conspiracy. On the other hand, the Hindus have a genius for conspiracy: they possess a power of patience, of foreseeing results, of carefully weighing chances, of choosing time and weapon, of profiting by circumstances, never losing sight of the object desired, taking advantage of every turn of fortune—all qualities invaluable for success in intrigue. The circulation of the chupattis before the outbreak was an exact repetition of what happened before the Mahrattas invaded Northern India, only in place of goat's flesh a sprig of millet had accompanied the bread. Before the Sonthal rebellion, a branch of the sál-tree (*Shorea robusta*) had been sent from village to village. Hindus being vegetarians, it seems probable that a bit of raw flesh had a Mahommedan origin; or, as has been suggested, it might have signified extermination. I am inclined to think that this was its real meaning. A Mahommedan Jehád would have been proclaimed by preaching, and raising the standard of the Prophet. The probability is that it was a joint proclamation, the work of Hindus as well as of Mahommedan conspirators. It may be accepted as a historical fact that the annexation of Oude intensified the prevailing disaffection and hastened the Rebellion. That act would have affected both sets of religionists, as the Hindu population is largely in excess of Mahommedans in Oude. Other instances, as that of the mutiny of the cavalry at Segowlie, which was brought about by Mahommedan emissaries from Lucknow, and the rebellion of Koer Sing, a Hindu of Shahabad, show clearly that both religions were at work against British authority. Koer Sing was no doubt influenced by that arch-fiend, the Nana, from Bithur, with whom he had been in constant correspondence. Koer Sing, in his turn, attempted to influence the Rajahs of Behar; but in the cases of the Maharajahs of Dumraon and Dev, and the old Maharaní of Tikhari, the English found loyal friends, for they turned a deaf ear to both threats and promises. It has always been a matter of surprise to me that the histories of the Indian Mutiny have taken so little notice of the part played by the Nana of Bithur, whose rôle it was to stir up the Hindu population.

The Position of the titular King of Delhi at the time of the Rebellion.

In 1737 the great paramount power over the Continent of India was the Mahratta. A confederacy of Mahratta States under a Minister of ability and tact, with Scindia and Holka as Generals, held the country under subjection. Bundelkund, Agra, and Delhi all at one time acknowledged Mahratta rule. The Mahommedan power, which had so long prevailed, was dead and gone. When Lord Lake crossed the Jumna on September 15, 1803, and entered the city of Delhi, he found the Mogul Emperor virtually a prisoner, blind and helpless, emaciated and infirm, his face marked with extreme old age and the settled melancholy of a broken-hearted man. The British found him a puppet without a Court or a Treasury, and as such they retained him. The sequel has shown it was a fatal error, though under the circumstances, at the time, it seemed the safest policy. The Mahommedans attached to the dynasty accepted our rule in a certain fashion, as an improvement on Mahratta severity. A considerable portion of the conquered territory was set aside to meet the stipends of the pensioned King and his family. The old Mogul was allowed to appoint his own agents for the management of the estates assigned to him, as well as the city police. So delicately did the British deal with the King, that the Resident was debarred from all interference with the executive control of the city. On municipal matters, and on the revenue administration of the assigned territories, the Resident might advise the King; but he was to exercise no executive authority. The King was to be absolute, within his own palace grounds and in the city. He was to be surrounded with all the dignity of a monarch; he was to live in luxury and pomp, with a remnant of fiscal power over a limited territory. "He was to be the mere shadow of an Eastern potentate; he was to be preserved, not because he was wanted, but because his existence would gratify the Mahommedan Princes of India, and make English rule more acceptable to a conquered people." The policy was fatal, and the evils of such an arrangement soon became manifest. The Emperor Shah Alum, old and blind as he was, wasted his money, and encumbered the estates set apart for his maintenance by reckless gifts of land to favourites. Surrounded by avaricious dependants, his money thrown about with lavish hand, there soon gathered in and about the palace a band of dissolute and desperate men. The palace stood, as it now stands, immediately on the banks of the Jumna. It was built about 1631–2 by the Emperor Shah Jehan, and in the early part of this century covered a space of a mile in circumference. The actual palace was about 3,000 feet long and 1,800 broad. It contained the beautiful Dewan-i-Am, or Public Hall of Audience, and the Dewan-i-Khas, or Hall of Private Audience; the latter built of white marble, beautifully ornamented, the roofs supported on colonnades of marble pillars. In the centre of the Hall stood the famous Peacock Throne, which was ascended by steps, covered by a canopy with four artificial peacocks at the four corners. Around the exterior of the Dewan-i-Khas was the well-known inscription: "If there be a paradise on earth, it is this, it is this, it is this!" The terrace of the building is composed of large slabs of white marble, and the building itself is crowned with four pavilions or cupolas of the same material. To the north of the Dewan-i-Khas were situated the palace baths, surmounted with domes of white marble. Adjoining the baths was a large mosque. The palace gardens occupied the river frontage, its walls looking down upon the sands of the river. Adjoining, but connected with the palace by a bridge, was the Fort of Selimghur. On the river-side, the palace was protected by a solid masonry wall of red sandstone, loopholed; and on the city side by a substantial wall of brick. Inside these walls was a maze of houses, some of masonry, some of mats, some of mud. The larger houses contained underground rooms, intricate passages, enclosed courtyards, dark and mysterious holes and corners, secret doors and outlets, which communicated from house to house. Dirt and filth were everywhere, inside and outside. Rich carpets and dirty mats were side by side on the floors; ivory and silver chairs were covered with filthy rags. The English mind of the well-to-do classes, trained in the domestic life of an English home, and to a great extent guarded from contact with evil, has no conception of the life within an Eastern palace, such as existed at Delhi. Hundreds of young men and women living without occupation and with little to amuse them; hundreds of worn-out old men and women, with nothing to look forward to but the grave were—the young, given over to lust—the old to intrigue. Conceive a life where human passions were inflamed by every possible indulgence, and stimulated by devices unheard of even in the lowest haunts of vice in Europe; every natural law violated. Where there is no restraint there can be no morality. Incest, murderings, poisonings, torturings, were daily occurrences. A school of professors of the art of crime flourished in the purlieus of the King's Palace. Men and women skilled in the preparation of poisons, of drugs to cause unconsciousness, so as to facilitate robbery and incest, throve within the palace walls. Wrestlers, jesters, dancing-girls who danced naked to inflame the passions of old age, musicians, forgers, swindlers, thieves, receivers of stolen property, distillers of spirits, compounders of sweetmeats and opium, all formed a part of the palace community. Criminals, to escape punishment, sought refuge there. Political intrigue was as rife as sensual. Wives intrigued against wives, harlots against wives, mothers against sons; men and women scoured the country far and wide for beautiful girls to sell as slaves within the palace. In such a hotbed of villany, any conspiracy was possible. Assassinations were frequent, and the silent river was close at hand to bear away all traces of the victim.

Such is a true picture of the palace life shortly after the British occupancy of the Delhi province. But while inside the palace, debauchery and villany ran riot, the estates assigned to the King for his sustenance, had so far benefited from the peace and order consequent upon English administration that the revenue collections, which in 1803 were some £41,058, in 1804 had increased to £145,754. A very short experience of the arrangements made for the King's stipends showed that whilst the outside of the platter was getting cleaner, there were serious apprehensions of danger from the internal intrigues of the Mogul's retainers. The folly of the whole arrangement was noted and commented on by General Ochterlony as "more injurious than beneficial." In 1807 his successor, Sir Charles Metcalfe, wrote as follows:—"I do not conform to the policy of Seton's mode of managing the Royal Family. It is by a submission of manner and conduct, carried on, in my opinion, far beyond the respect and attention which can be either prescribed by forms, or dictated by a humane consideration for the fallen fortunes of a once illustrious family. It destroys entirely the dignity which ought to be attached to him who represents the British Government, and who, in reality, is to govern Delhi, and it raises, I have perceived, ideas of imperial power and sway, which ought to be put to sleep for ever. As it is evident we do not mean to restore imperial power to the King, we ought not to pursue a conduct calculated to make him aspire to it. Let us treat him with the respect due to his rank and situation; let us make him comfortable in respect of circumstances, and give him all the means, as far as possible, of being happy. But, unless we mean to re-establish his power, let us not encourage him to dream of it. Let us meet his first attempts to display imperial authority with immediate check, and let him see the mark beyond which our respect and obedience to the shadow of a king will not proceed." Mr. Archibald Seton, who was at the time Resident at Delhi, did not sympathize with these views. He held that the British could not do too much to soothe the feelings of a family so situated. He thought that the most obsequious attentions on the part of the Governor-General's Agent did not hurt the Resident, but that in yielding in small things, he could, with a better grace, assert his authority on great occasions. There has been a traditional tendency on the part of the Government of India always to adopt a middle course. Take, for example, the two recent cases of the Manipur State and the Age of Consent Bill. Any course which does not push matters to a conclusion has always commended itself, generally with evil results. It was deemed a better policy to tolerate a double executive authority in the city, to retain the shadow of a Mogul dynasty, lest the King's deposition should alarm the whole Mahommedan race in India. Yet it was patent to the dullest comprehension that, although the new power which possessed Delhi might for the time being, in the estimation of the natives, be the virtual ruler of Hindustan, still, so long as the shadow of the old dynasty remained, it would be regarded as the one and only fountain of honour, the one authority to be reverenced. Princes still bore the titles conferred by the King. The current coin of every kind still continued to be struck in the name of the existing monarch; applications for confirmation of successors to the chieftainship of petty States, still were made to him; and when from time to time these applications were refused, appeals were lodged with the Resident to use his influence with the Mogul to grant the prayers of his petitioners. When serious riots occurred, as they frequently did, the people looked to the King for protection from the British authorities. "I am convinced," wrote the Assistant Resident, on the occasion of one of these riots, "that it would never have taken place" if the "people had not expected that the King would (as he did) protect them. It had its origin in the palace, and if traced to its primary cause would be found to have arisen from the effect of the Resident's too delicate and submissive conduct. Ideas of the exercise of sovereign right ought, I think, to be checked in the bud. It may be difficult to destroy them when they have been suffered to grow for some time—at least, greater difficulty than there would have been in suppressing them altogether." By-and-by, under pressure from the British Resident, the Court of Directors consented to modify the system: while the actual administration over Revenue and Customs was vested in the Resident, every honour was to be continued to be paid to the puppet king. He was to be treated as a mighty potentate, and particular attention was to be paid to the feelings of His Majesty. The result was again that, while these modifications in the Delhi administration resulted in failure, the real political danger was tolerated—the existence of the Emperor in the very heart of the city, in a palace capable of being converted into a formidable fortress. In 1806 died the blind old Emperor Shah Alum, for 45 years the nominal Emperor of Hindustan. He was succeeded, November, 1806, by Shah Akbar II. In 1809 increased allowances were demanded by the Shah, and sanctioned by the Court of Directors. Not satisfied with this increase, there was shortly another demand for a larger stipend, and the aid of the Nawab Wazir of Oude was sought to further these claims. The more the Governor-General yielded, the more was asked. Intrigue followed upon intrigue, pretension upon pretension, until in 1814 the Mogul claimed precedence of the Governor-General himself.

In September, 1837, died Shah Akbar II, leaving issue eleven sons and six daughters. He was succeeded by his eldest son, Shah Mahommed Abu Zuphur Saraz-o-dain Mahommed Bahadur, titular King and Emperor. He was the pensioned representative of the Mogul Dynasty when the rebellion of 1857 occurred. The internal condition of the palace had in no way improved since the days of Shah Alum. The "dalals" of India are a professional class—solicitors, who live by the results of intrigue. It is their business to stir up litigation, to find out the heartburnings in every family circle, and convert them to their own purposes by framing them into plaints at law. They hang about every law-court, every royal court, and every family of wealth and position. They gamble and speculate in law-courts, ever ready to suggest or frame demands in the hopes of sharing the pickings. This class was not wanting around the King. Under their advice the feeble old Mogul made demands which had to be resisted. Ever in debt, the greed of his family for money was unlimited. He was a burden on the administration, but it was rightly deemed impolitic to wound the feelings of the whole Mahommedan race in Hindustan by his removal from Delhi. No inducement could make him leave his palace; not so much a fear of a revival of the Mahommedan power was entertained, as that the King might become the rallying-point of a confederacy of native states. From time to time the English newspapers pressed the necessity of removing the King. On January 13, 1849, the *Delhi Gazette*, then the leading paper of the North-West Provinces, wrote as follows:—"On Thursday morning departed this life Prince Dara Bukht, heir-apparent to the throne of Delhi, leaving Shahzada Fakir-u-dín as heir, and with him we have some reason to believe that all the right of the Royal House to the succession dies out, such having been guaranteed to him individually and to no other member of the family. We sincerely trust that such is really the case, and that our Government will now be in a position to adopt steps for making efficient arrangements for the dispersion, with a suitable provision, of the family on the death of the King." "It is a curious fact," writes the author of "The Wanderings of a Pilgrim," "that nearly all the native papers have long since omitted the designation of 'Padshah' when alluding to the King, styling him merely 'Shah.'" For six centuries Delhi had been the seat of the imperial power in India, and the opinion had long existed among the better informed class of natives—an opinion which had leaked out of the earlier dispatches of Lord Wellesley—that the British had contemplated the extinction of the Mogul Dynasty; that their intention had been to rescue their former Emperor, Shah Alum, from the dominion of the Mahrattas, and to retain possession of his person in safe custody as a guarantee; to protect him and his successors from the oppression of the Mahrattas. The capture of Delhi by Lord Lake was, at the time, hailed with genuine delight by the Mahommedans of the Western Provinces.

That their great city should be captured and plundered, and its inhabitants massacred, was familiar history to the natives of Delhi, but each conqueror had respected, though he had humiliated, their king. Timour, in 1398, although he pillaged the city and for five days gave up its inhabitants to the sword, constructing a pyramid of human skulls to mark his departure, left Nazir-u-dín on the throne. Again, when in March, 1739, Nadir Shah captured the city, he massacred, so native historians say, 100,000 of its inhabitants, yet he spared and left Mohammed Shah on the throne. After each humiliation the Sovereign continued, and gradually regained his ascendancy. Therefore, whilst the natives accepted the position of a humiliated monarch for their Emperor, there was always the possibility of his once again regaining power, and they were content to wait. But when it was known that the British intended to close the succession and disperse the family, the deepest feelings of both Hindus and Mahommedans were roused. When Bahadur Shah succeeded to Shah Akbar in 1837, an attempt was made, under instructions from the Governor-General, to obtain a formal renunciation of all claims upon the East India Company. The King, who was an old man when he succeeded, refused to comply. Another proposal to remove the King to the Kutub, was also indignantly rejected. A little later, a Board was appointed to discuss and report on the course to be followed with regard to the retention of the Royal Family at Delhi. To this Committee were nominated Shahzada Fakir-u-dín, heir-apparent to the King and the eldest of nine princes, of whom the next in succession was Mirza Kobash. Sir Henry Elliot, Mr. Thomason, and

Sir Thomas Metcalfe (Resident at Delhi) were the other members. The Committee submitted their report, and the whole subject was still under consideration, when Lord Dalhousie's tenure of office expired in 1856. It is a painful and yet noteworthy fact that of the persons who composed that Committee, Shahzada Fakir-u-dín died of poison 10th July, 1856; Sir Thomas Metcalfe, Bart., of symptoms believed to have been the result of vegetable poison, November 1.

Lord Canning, who entirely concurred in Lord Dalhousie's views of the danger arising from the position of the strong fortress at Delhi, in the very heart of the principal city of the Empire, recognized Mirza Mahommed Kobash as the heir-apparent on the death of Fakir-u-dín.

The Weakness of the British Position in India at the Time of the Mutiny.

The English were living over a volcano ready to burst into deadly violence at any moment, but they could not, or would not, apprehend their danger. Of warnings there were plenty; but they made little impression, for reasons which are not difficult to understand. In the first place, the distances in India are so great and the circumstances of each district so varied, that rumours reaching a central authority in a far-off capital appear too contradictory and uncertain to be entitled to credit. In the second place, the natives have an unfortunate habit of sending anonymous information to the authorities with the view of injuring some personal enemy. All such communications are generally disregarded and consigned to the waste-paper basket. Every civil and military officer, with district experience, has felt the difficulty at some time or other of making those above him see with his eyes, and hear with his ears, what is going on around him.

He finds he is misunderstood, and often discredited. Another distinctive feature of Indian official life is, that the higher the grade of an officer the less he is likely to hear of what is going on around him. Members of Council and Lieutenant-Governors derive *direct* information only from the higher class of natives, of whom a few pay them visits of courtesy, or from their Secretaries. Such information then as reaches these high State officials comes through the medium of reports and minutes carefully conveyed in locked boxes. Secretaries are not always free from a tinge of contempt for the reports of subordinate officers, the more particularly if they express opinions different from the Secretary's own experience of ten years before. Excellent as secretarial work has always been, it has invariably adopted a traditionally cynical tone in its relations with its subordinates on all occasions of alarmist reports, whether they contain the first whisperings of a coming famine, or hints at a local outbreak, or the ravages of an epidemic that may, if unchecked, sweep away thousands of lives. And so it was in 1856-7. From both civil and military subordinate officers warnings were repeatedly given that some portentous event was brooding. Little credit was attached to them, except by Sir John Lawrence. But even if the readiest credit had been given to every rumour, the Government of India was helpless to act. Its chief armour, offensive and defensive, was the Indian Army, and that in Bengal was more or less disaffected. How far the Bombay and Madras Armies were faithful was a matter of conjecture. The European soldiers were few and isolated. There were no railways and no ready means of communication. There was no possible move but to summon such native allies as the Government could trust, and to summon large drafts from England. What steps the East India Company may have taken to move the Ministry at home to increase the European Army and send out regiments, can only be ascertained from unpublished records. The only course open to the Indian Government was to put a calm and bold face on the dangers which threatened its existence, and await the course of events. When the warnings were fulfilled in fact, it was found that the conspirators had chosen well their time and place. The *season* was the most deadly and trying to the European constitution, when the annual drafts of European troops had ceased, the time-expired men gone, and the small force left still more depleted by the exodus of the sick and delicate to the hills. The *place* selected for the outbreak was Meerut, some forty miles only from the residence of the titular King of Delhi, and the first move was on to a fortified city with its magazines of powder and stands of arms and ammunition held by a native force only. There was, however, one calculation which had never entered into the plans of the conspirators, viz. that England would declare war against China, and that a considerable European force should be sailing through the Indian Ocean within hailing distance of Calcutta. To this fortuitous circumstance, under God's providence, was due the early re-establishment of British authority in North-Western India.

A Description of Delhi.

It may not be out of place here to give the reader a description of the city of Delhi, in which so much interest was centred from May to December, 1857. Delhi is situated on the western bank of the river Jamna. The present city is about ten miles in circumference, surrounded on three sides by a high wall of brick and stone. It has seven gates, viz.: the Lahore, Delhi, Ajmere, Turkoman, Moorgate, Cabul, and Cashmere. These are all built of stone, and have handsome arched entrances, with quarters for the city guards. The Cashmere Gate had been renewed not many years before the outbreak by Colonel Edward Smith of the Engineers. The present city is the work of Mahommedans, having been laid out and constructed by the Emperor Shah Jehan A.D. 1631–2. The more ancient city lies further inland back from the river, outside the walls. When Richard, King of England, was leading the Crusaders against Saladin and the Saracens, a Hindu Raja "Prithvi" was King of Delhi. Under the Hindu Dynasty the city was called Indrapesta, or the abode of the God Indra. It is identified as the modern Marowli, the site of the famous wells and the burial-place of the three Emperors Bahadur Shah, Shah Alum, and Akbar Shah. The tombs and ruins which on every side surround the modern city for a circumference of twenty miles, are evidence of the sites occupied by the city during different periods of its history, for with a Hindu it is a duty never to repair the works of his ancestors, but to build on a fresh spot. The country is, on all sides, much cut up by ravines and broken ground. The north and west of the city are occupied by the remains of spacious gardens and the country-houses of the nobility. About a mile and a half away stands an observatory erected by Jey Sinha, of Ambhere, about 1693, called by the natives the Jantr Mantr. This great astronomer also prepared a set of tables, which are to this day used by the natives in their preparation of almanacks. The buildings consist of a large equatorial dial built of stone, with the edges of gnomon, and the arches where the gradation was, of white marble. There is also a second equatorial dial—a graduated semicircle for taking altitudes of bodies that lie due east or due west from the eye of the observer. A double quadrant is for observing the altitudes of bodies passing the meridian either to the north or south of the Zenith. Two other buildings stand near designed for the same purpose, so that two persons may make observations at the same time. There is also a concave hemispherical piece of masonry to represent the inferior hemisphere of the heavens. The buildings are a copy in masonry of the brass instruments used in the observatory at Samarcand. To the north of the city lie the Shalimer Gardens, from which a wide expanse of the suburbs of Delhi may be seen, covered with the ruins of many a mosque, mausoleum, and garden-house. Within the city are many beautiful palaces, large, substantial, stone-built structures, with baths of white marble, and underground rooms for use in the hot weather, with many a safe corner in which to hide a fugitive, if only the house-owner were so minded. Alas! the only use made in 1857 of these palaces was to gather the fugitive Europeans, in order to deliver them over *en masse* to their murderers.

In the centre of the city stood the beautiful Jumma Musjid or principal mosque, on an elevation named Jujula Pahar, which had been scarped on purpose. It is ascended by a flight of stone steps, with an entrance through a gateway of red stone. The courtyard or the body of the mosque is an open space, 1,400 feet of red stone. In the centre is a fountain in which the faithful perform their ablutions, previous to prayer. It was on the walls of this mosque that, after the capture of the city, some discontented versifier chalked the lines of which the following is a rough translation :—

> "When war is nigh, and battle sighted,
> 'God and the soldier is all the cry!'
> When battle ends in victory,
> God is forgotten, and the soldier slighted."

An arched colonnade of red sandstone surrounds the whole of the terrace, which is adorned with octagonal pavilions for sitting in. The mosque is of an oblong form, 261 feet in length, surmounted by three magnificent domes of white marble, interspersed with black stripes, and flanked by two minarets, of alternate black marble and red sandstone, rising to the height of 130 feet. Each of these minarets has three projecting galleries of white marble, their summits crowned with light octagonal pavilions of the same. The whole front of the building is faced with large slabs of beautiful white marble, and along the cornice are ten compartments, four feet long and two and a half broad, which are inlaid with inscriptions in black marble in the Nishki character,[1] and are said to contain the greater part, if not the whole, of the Koran. The outside of the mosque is paved throughout with large slabs of white marble, decorated with a black border, and wonderfully beautiful and delicate. The slabs are about three feet in length by one and a half broad. The walls and the roof are lined with plain white marble, and near the "Kibla" is a handsome niche, looking towards Mecca, adorned with a profusion of frieze-work. Close to this is the pulpit (*mimbar*) of marble, with an ascent of four steps balustraded. It would be interesting, could we know, what counsel was given from this pulpit during those eventful months in 1857. The ascent to the minarets is by a winding staircase of a hundred and thirty steps of red sandstone, and from the top a lovely view of the city and palace is obtained. The domes are crowned with cullises of copper, richly gilt, and present a glittering appearance from afar.

This mosque, begun by the Emperor Shahjehan in the fourth year of his reign, was completed in the tenth. It cost

[1] "Wanderings of a Pilgrim," by Mrs. F. Parke.

ten lakhs of rupees. The musjid stands so far from the outer fortifications as to have escaped injury from the shells fired from the ridge by the English; but one shell did reach the mosque, and exploded within the courtyard. The city possessed about forty other mosques besides Hindu temples—amongst them the Kala Musjid or Black Mosque, built 450 years before the building of the modern city of Delhi, i.e. about 1181 A.D. No religious service is ever performed here, and none but the lowest dregs of the populace ever go near it. The place is regarded as unholy. Then we must mention the English church built by Colonel Skinner, an ugly building with a dome, inside the Cashmere Gate. The mutineers attempted to destroy the gilt cross which surmounts the dome, but failed to do so. The Tomb of Humaon is a building rendered doubly interesting since the Mutiny as being that to which the Emperor fled when the city was attacked. The mausoleum stands on a terrace of red sandstone, which measures 2,000 feet in circumference: it is circular, and surmounted by a stupendous dome of white marble, so shaped that a man can walk up the slope, which from below looks too steep for such a possibility. For miles around the mausoleum can be seen. Minarets at the four corners, of red and white marble, mark the extremities of the terrace. These are crowned with octagonal pavilions of red stone, having marble cupolas. Franklin (to whom I am indebted for the above details) judges the height to be 120 feet. A staircase leads from the ground to the terrace below, which consists of a series of arched rooms. The principal room is paved with large slabs of white marble; it contains the tomb of Humaon, elegantly decorated with chisel-work. In adjoining chambers are interred several princesses of the House of Timour. The terrace is occupied by the graves of various princes who were from time to time assassinated: the Emperor Alumgir is buried here, assassinated at the instigation of the Vizier Gazi-ud-dín Khan. The Zínut-al-Musjid, another beautiful mosque on the river bank, with inlayings of marble, and a spacious terrace in front, and the Musjid of Roshan-ul-Dowlah, at one end of the Chandni Chauk—from which the King of Persia witnessed the slaughter of men, women, and children, without distinction of age, sex, or condition—are also marked features of the city. In the suburbs are the remains of many splendid palaces: among others of "Metcalfe House," built by my father, Sir Thomas Metcalfe, when Resident at Delhi. Having elected to make India his home, he stripped his family seat in England of all his books and family treasures, little apprehending the fate in store for them, all being destroyed in one morning by the villagers of Chundrowli. The house stood in a large garden of about 1,000 acres, planted with orange-trees, which were all cut down during the siege. Besides the injury caused by fire, the house was considerably knocked about by shot and shell during the siege, so that little remained but its walls. The only relic found amongst the ruins was a lady's glove, which a falling roof had guarded, while the lady to whom it belonged had been providentially saved from the horrors of a terrible death.

> "There all the silence, here love,
> In the slow long Summer months when
> There are none to break the stillness.
> The stillness cannot be so still, but that for my sake
> The memory-haunted, lonely rooms will take
> Some echo of my vanished voice."
>
> ALICE ROLLINS.

NARRATIVE OF MAINODIN.

In the name of the most merciful God.

Praise to the Almighty Creator of earth and Heaven, who at His first command created the heavens, and the tablets on which the decrees of mortals' fates are written, who brought into existence the universe, and invested it with divers forms of man and animal, with objects animate and inanimate, and devised means for their support.

And among these He gave excellence to mankind, and endowed him with wisdom and intelligence.

Man's very language in His glory fails.

Wisdom fails in proving His unity.

His Benevolence defies all description.

Praise to Mahommed Mustapha, the most excellent and chosen of mankind. Blessings on him, his friends and his children, him of whom God had said: "I would not have created the world but for you."

And now it is necessary that I should relate my story, and the reasons which have led me to write this narrative.

I, the writer, am the descendant of Mu-in-uddin Hassan Khan, son of Nawab Ashruf-ulla Dowlah Kudmit-ulla-beg-Khan Bahadur, son of Nawab Shurruf-ul-Dowlah Cossim Khan Bahadur, a general, and sometime Kotwál of the province of Delhi, during the Mahommedan Dynasty. The real birthplace of my ancestors was Samarcand and Bokhara. My ancestor Nawab Shurruf-ul-Dowlah, together with his two brothers, Kochuh Mirza and Arif Khan, died, and Aruni Beg Khan made his home in the Punjab in the time of

Shah Ahmed Allum Padshah, Emperor of Hindustan. After the decease of my ancestors, when English sovereignty was established and the Mahratta rule was declining, I took service under the English Government.

In the year 1848 I took up my residence in the province of Delhi, in Perghunah Hill, and was appointed a police-officer, carrying out loyally all the orders that I received, and receiving kindness and encouragement at the hands of those in power, above all, from Sir Thomas Metcalfe, then Commissioner and Agent at the Court of Delhi. He was well acquainted with the nobility of my ancestors, and showed me great kindness, as also did his son, Sir Theophilus Metcalfe, at the time Joint Magistrate at Delhi; and after the events to which this history belongs, I received much kindness and protection from his younger brother, Mr. Charles Theophilus Metcalfe, of the Bengal Civil Service, at a time when I was helpless and friendless. And here I may say that I have always received much kindness at the hands of European gentlemen.

Of the mutiny of the Native Army in 1857 I was more than a witness, and by the force of circumstances I became acquainted with all that passed at the outbreak of the rebellion. I was in charge of the police division of Pahargunge, and it is through loyalty and faithfulness to Sir Theophilus Metcalfe that I am about to record the real circumstances of the mutiny as they came to my knowledge.

It has been said that I was an active participator in the mutiny. It is true that, after the capture of Delhi, through the evil machinations and falsehoods of a Chuprassie, by name Chuneri, and on account of my own evil fate, I dared not present myself before Sir Theophilus Metcalfe. After the assault, my house and all my goods were plundered.

I was dejected and in terror of my life. It seemed to me that I had neither bravery nor sense left. I believed at the time that my younger brother had gone, with all the members of his family, to Bombay, and thither I made my way in disguise.

There I lived as a merchant as best I could, and there I was joined by my younger brother. From Bombay we wrote to Sir Theophilus, asking him for certificates of character, and proofs of my loyalty and devotedness to him.

Sir Theophilus had gone to England, but from him I received both money and the proofs I wanted. But I was in such a distressed state of mind at all that had occurred, that I could determine on no course for the future.

Ever haunted by the fear of the extreme penalty of the law, I fled to Arabia, and there I remained for more than three years, sending my younger brother back to Delhi to ascertain all that was happening, as he was guiltless of any participation in the mutiny.

A weary time passed, during which I was separated from all dear to me. In 1863 I heard from my brother that he was then on a journey with Sir Theophilus Metcalfe through Kohistan. In 1864 I returned from Arabia, but still remained in concealment at Bombay. At this time Sir Edward Bayley[1] had been appointed Secretary to the Government of India, and knowing his generosity and nobleness, I determined to give myself up through him to the British Government. I presented myself before him, and under his instructions I gave myself up to Colonel McNeil, then Commissioner of the Delhi Division. I found, to my sorrow, that I was regarded with suspicion by the Commissioner, to whom I was personally unknown. He looked upon me as an

[1] Brother-in-law to Sir Theophilus Metcalfe.

enemy to the British Government. I was put on my trial, and through the justice of the English, and on the proofs I was able to produce of my devotedness to Sir Theophilus Metcalfe, I was acquitted.

I remained three days in Delhi, and then returned to Bombay, and thence went to Hyderabad, whence, being attacked by severe illness, I returned to Delhi, a restless wanderer. After remaining a few days in Delhi, I desired to return to Bombay, but, penniless and ruined, I threw myself on the generosity of the Nawab of Rampur, who with noble liberality gave me a home and an income. On the 1st of January, 1877, when the great assemblage of the Kings of Hindustan was held at Delhi, by order of H.E. Lord Lytton, Governor-General of India, my poor circumstances (through the disinterested kindness of Sir Edward Bayley) were pointed out to his Lordship, who was pleased in the generosity of his heart to confer on me a sum of money to be settled upon me and my heirs. During the time that the deeds connected with this money were being drawn up I was constantly in communication with Mr. Charles Metcalfe, then Commissioner of Police in Calcutta. Mr. Metcalfe one day asked me if I had any papers in my possession connected with the occurrences at Delhi in 1857. I replied that as police-officer I had been accustomed to keep a "Roznamcha," or diary of daily occurrences, and so through the troublous time I had kept a record of daily events, but as the hand of destiny had been against me, it would be better to leave unwritten this page of my own life-history.

I was assured there were no grounds for further proceedings being taken against me, and I was encouraged to write of events in which I had been personally concerned, or which had come under my immediate knowledge.

My answer was that I would comply with whatsoever Mr. Metcalfe might desire, but that I was afraid to write of the events with which I was acquainted, for fear I might commit some blunder. I said it is a general defect with writers that instead of putting down the true and actual occurrences they may have witnessed, they fill their books with false statements and high compliments, colouring them as real facts. How could I write of the true events without implicating myself? for I had been an actor myself in these great occurrences as well as an eye-witness.

My patron comforted me, saying that time had smoothed away many obstacles to writing a true history, and that I need no longer fear personal consequences. Paying my respects, I promised to write of every true occurrence of which I had been an eye-witness, and of every fact with which I was acquainted. Sir Edward Bayley, too, gave me encouragement in this.

Now the duty devolves upon me to write in detail. Though many have written about the Mutiny of 1857 in forms of memoranda, histories, and diaries, yet I consider all of them mere hearsay. I will not write of rumours and of unauthenticated stories, but of such events as have happened in my presence, and that which has been reported to me by reliable persons.

I will commence my narrative with the statement that, however the English may regard themselves, they are regarded by the natives as trespassers, and this feeling was intensified on the annexation of the province of Oude. Thence first arose dissatisfaction among the native troops, most of whom were natives of that province. Then followed the events of the mutiny and the arrangements made for its suppression, the calamities of the Ryots, the destruction of many native estates, the final ruin of several noted families and large cities; the penalties inflicted on rebels and "Budmashes," who received the proper punishment for their misdeeds, and in consequence of whose acts many innocent persons were hanged and disaster hurled down upon the country. Their behaviour, instead of bearing any fruit, ended in the destruction of their own families. Now after a great revolution and fatal agitation, peace has been restored, and the former state of public tranquillity again enjoyed by every subject. I call this book the "Khodang godur." May God bring prosperity and long life to those through whose accomplishment of purpose and effort the compiler of this book has come among the list of authors! It is my earnest request to my readers that if they come across any mistakes in the language or in the usage of idioms, that they will pass them over indulgently, because man is born to err; besides, I am not a man of letters, but a soldier by profession, therefore it is absolutely necessary to overlook my shortcomings.

The English are familiar with the views of English writers on the causes of the mutiny of the Indian Army. These views differ in some respects from those held by natives, who trace the outbreak to a different source.

When Amjad Ali Shah Padshah, King of Lucknow, died in 1847, he was succeeded by Shah Wajid Ali, who devoted himself to the organization of the Army. Orders were issued that after morning prayer all the regiments in Lucknow were to parade daily at 5 a.m. The King was in the habit of taking command at the parade, dressed in the uniform of a general; he used to drill the troops for four or five hours daily. Furthermore, he issued an order that if he were absent from parade, except through necessities of the State, he was to be fined 2,000 rupees, to be distributed among the regiments in garrison. An equivalent fine was to be levied if any of the regiments were late on parade, and as a further punishment two regiments of infantry and a *resalah* of cavalry were to remain under arms the whole day.

This activity of the King created suspicion. The British Resident inquired the cause of his exertions in creating an army, and suggested to him that if he required forces for the protection of his province he should employ British troops, to be paid out of the revenues of Oude. The courtiers of his Court also advised him not to raise suspicion by his personal activity. The King, discouraged by these remonstrances, replied that he would employ himself in future with some other occupation, as his interest in his army was not approved of. Henceforward he began to neglect the affairs of the State, and took pleasure in debauchery. The former Minister, Findad Hossim Khan, was removed from his post, and Ali Tukí Khan, a man of good family, was appointed to succeed him. The King married the niece of his new Minister, and then his daughter. He left the management of all the affairs of State to Ali Tukí Khan.

From the neglect of his kingdom there arose results which man's wisdom could not foresee. There was a Rajah, Dursham Sing by name, a nobleman of old family, the son of a Brahmin, Mahender Sing, a soldier by profession. This Dursham Sing had three sons—Buktour Sing, Durshin Sing, and Cholauka Sing. The eldest obtained the King's favour and a title of nobility, as did also Durshin Sing. They also obtained appointments as "Chakladars."

Durshin Sing next proceeded to force defaulting zemindars to draw out bills of sale of their property in his name. Thus he gradually formed for himself a large estate. His *talook* (property) adjoined a place called Hanumanjari, in the vicinity of Fyzabad, where there was a Mahommedan mosque which Durshin Sing annexed, together with its endowment.

Durshin had two sons, Hanuman Dull and Man Sing. These two men refused to allow the "Arjan" (call to prayer) to be sounded from the mosque. A few days later a travelling Moulvie, Fakir Hossein Shah, came to the mosque to pray, and not knowing of the prohibition, sounded the Arjan. The Brahmins of a neighbouring temple, hearing this, came to the mosque, assaulted the Moulvie, and taking from him the Koran which he held in his hands, threw it into a fire and burned it, and then drove the Moulvie out of the mosque.

The traveller went on his way to Lucknow, and told in the bazaars what had happened. It so happened that in the Hyderabad Mehalla ward of the city, the story interested a man called Hyder Khan, who lived there with his four brothers. All were soldiers in the service of the King. On hearing of the outrage, the two younger brothers offered to assist the Moulvie to obtain retribution for the insult to the Prophet. The three, in pursuance of their plan, returned to Hanumanjari, and the next day at the usual hour of prayer, they sounded the Arjan loudly and repeatedly. Brahmins came running to the mosque; an altercation followed; then a fight, in which the two soldiers were killed; Hossein escaped, and returning to Lucknow, laid a complaint before the criminal court. The native judge, seeing that the case was likely to prove troublesome, put it aside. The Moulvie then appealed to one Syud Amir-Ali, Resident of Kasbeh Intaband, who bore a great reputation in the city as a holy and just man, and who had lived for many years as a recluse in a corner of the mosque at Kusbeh Amaitie. On hearing the story, he took up the Moulvie's cause. He first called a public meeting at the mosque, and issued a Futwa (law decision) on the consequences of burning the Koran, and the murder of two zealous Mahommedans, who had fallen in defence of their religion. He then began to preach a *jehad* (holy war) in the streets of Lucknow, and in the adjoining country. He pointed out that there was a danger to the Mahommedan religion, and this excited and inflamed the public mind. Eventually he started for Hanumanjari with a large following of persons burning to revenge the insult offered to their religion. The matter came to the ears of the British Resident, who hastened to the King, and urged him to take immediate measures to allay the excitement. The King sent for Kadum Hossein, and urged him to use his influence to settle the matter amicably.

Hossein Bux and Mahommed Tyer Khan were deputed to bring back the Moulvie, who, however, refused to return. Nawab Ali Tuk Khan then suggested to the King that Bashir-ul-Dowlah should be sent to bring back the Moulvie. He agreed to go if justice were done, and threatened if it were not that he would join the Moulvie. The British Resident again urged the King to prevent widespread bloodshed, and impressed on him his responsibility.

Both the King and his Minister for the time forgot their anger with the Resident for his interference with the King's military ardour, and consulted upon the measures necessary to suppress the impending trouble. They sent for Moulvie Kadim Hossein, a resident of Feringhee Mehal in Lucknow, a man of ability and position, and asked him to publish a contradictory Futwa, so as to cut away the ground from beneath the feet of those who desired war. The King also summoned Shah Hossein Bux and Mahommed Fakir Khan, and urged them to do all in their power to quiet the Moulvie; but their efforts were fruitless. The Moulvie would listen to no terms other than that the Brahmins should be expelled from the Hanumanjari mosque, and the Mahommedans protected in the exercise of their ceremonials and prayers, and offenders punished in accordance with the laws of the Koran. Promises were made, but no steps were taken to fulfil them. The Moulvie remained at Lucknow for eight or ten days as the guest of Bashir-ul-Dowlah, who repeatedly urged upon the Vizier the fulfilment of his promise. The Moulvie then sent a message to the King that he would take the enforcement of justice into his own hands, and he returned to Hanumanjari after quarrelling with Bashir-ul-Dowlah for non-fulfilment of his promises. On this, the King ordered Colonel Barlow, who commanded the King's troops, to take a regiment of Hindus only, and to stop the Moulvie by force, and if necessary he was to blow the Moulvie from a gun in case resistance was offered. The King's soldiers were encamped four miles from the Moulvie's camp. When the Moulvie attempted to march from Radli Maidan, Colonel Barton forbad his doing so and surrounded his camp.

Attacked by the Moulvie's followers, the guns opened fire, and killed 111 of the assailants, many of the King's troops falling also. The news of this engagement spread throughout Hindustan and was the forerunner of still greater events. Little by little evil thoughts were generated. The British Resident, impressed by numerous petitions against the grave oppressions to which the people were subjected, and convinced of the inability of the King to rule the province in the interests of his people, recommended annexation. It is singular to record that under a Mahommedan sovereign injustice should have been perpetrated in the matter of a mosque, and that the people should subsequently have arisen in rebellion against the British, to whom they appealed for justice and protection. On the 17th of February, 1856, the British annexed Oude. They little anticipated the result. Thousands of men in the service of the King were thereby thrown out of employment, and were deprived of the means of livelihood. The worse the administration had been, the greater was the multitude of soldiers, courtiers, police, and landholders, who had fattened on it.

Those who had petitioned the English for redress were the poor and the oppressed. But the oppressors saw in British rule their own suppression. Oude was the birthplace of the Purbeah race, and these feelings of dissatisfaction affected the whole Purbeah race in the service of the British Government. To the native mind the act of annexation was one of gross injustice, and provoked a universal desire for resistance.

The King, and all those connected with him, although bowing to the hand of fate, became henceforward the bitter enemies of the English. At this time there were stationed at Lucknow two regiments, the 19th and the 34th, which were in the pay of the English Government. They had frequent consultations together on the injustice of the step which had been taken, and on the resistance which should be offered, and the attempts which should be made to create a rebellion for the purpose of overthrowing the British authority. It so happened that at the time of the annual change of regiments in 1857 one of these two regiments was sent to Berampur, the other to Barrackpur. Both these regiments were full of bitterness towards the English Government, and from them letters were written to other Purbeah regiments. The 34th took the lead. These letters reminded every regiment of the ancient dynasties of Hindustan; pointed out that the annexation of Oude had been followed by the disbandonment of the Oude army, for the second time since the connection of the English with Oude; and showed that their place was being filled by the enlistment of

Punjabís and Sikhs, and the formation of a Punjab army. The very bread had been torn out of the mouths of men who knew no other profession than that of the sword. The letters went on to say that further annexations might be expected, with little or no use for the native army. Thus was it pressed upon the Sepoys that they must rebel to reseat the ancient kings on their thrones, and drive the trespassers away. The welfare of the soldier caste required this; the honour of their chiefs was at stake.

The proximity of these two regiments to each other enabled the conspirators to carry on a constant correspondence (the circulation of these letters being conducted with great secrecy), and frequent consultations ensued. By degrees it became known in native society which regiments were disaffected, and it began to be inculcated as a creed that every Purbeah must withdraw his friendship from the foreigner; must ignore his authority, and overthrow his rule. Although these sentiments had become national, the methods to be employed in carrying them into action were but indistinctly known when the actual outbreak occurred. When the rebellion had begun, the full force and significance of all that had preceded it became apparent, and men understood what it meant.

* * * * *

In the month of January, 1857, the house of a European gentleman and the Telegraph Office at Ranigunge were burned down. This was a concerted signal; it was calculated that the burning of a telegraph office would immediately be communicated along the line from Calcutta to the Punjab, and that those in the secret would understand on hearing of it that they too must fire houses. Information of these incendiaries was widely circulated in all directions, and it is said that letters were sent from regiment to regiment inciting them to commit similar acts.

In the following month, February, another signal was given by the widespread distribution of chupattis (flat unleavened cakes), an ominous sign. At the time I was "Thanadar" (Head Police Officer) of the Pahargunge Police Station just outside the city of Delhi. Early one morning the village watchman of Indraput came and reported that the watchman of Seraie Faruck Khan had brought him a chupatti (which he showed me) and had instructed him to cook five similar chupattis, and send them to the five nearest villages of the neighbourhood, with orders that each village *chowkider* was to make five similar ones for distribution. Each chupatti was to be made of barley and wheat flour, about the size of the palm of a man's hand, and was to weigh two *tolahs*. I was astonished, yet I felt that the statement of the watchman was true, and that there was importance in an event which undoubtedly created a feeling of great alarm in the native mind throughout Hindustan. No extraordinary incident occurred until it was rumoured that on February 26 the 19th Regiment of Foot at Berampur had refused to take[1] cartridges served out to them, and that the 34th Regiment had behaved in a similar manner, and that seven companies of that regiment had been dismissed. When I heard this I suspected it was the beginning of a time of trouble. Information of the behaviour of the different

[1] There were two men of the British Army cashiered from their regiments at Meerut (see p. 1 of Narrative). One of these became a Mahommedan and took the name of Abdulla Beg. From Meerut he visited Umballa, Ludiana, and Ferozepur, and, again returning to Meerut, took up his quarters near the Cantonments, daily receiving visits from men of the native regiments, and gradually ingratiating himself. Consultations were daily held on the burning question of the greased cartridges. On one occasion, addressing a number of the Sepoys, he said : "I know these cartridges are smeared with the fat of pigs and cows, and the Government intends to take your caste. Even if you smear them with ghee and oil, as soon as you use them your example will be cited, and other regiments will use them."

regiments was widely circulated by the Press, in a native newspaper published at Umballa. Suspecting some significance in all this I deputed men at once to visit the whole of my police jurisdiction, and, after ascertaining whether chupattis had already reached other villages, to forbid their circulation.

My younger brother, Mirza Mahommed Hossein Khan, was Thanadar of the police jurisdiction of Buddapur, about sixteen miles from Delhi. The same day that I received information about the circulation of chupattis in Pahargunge I heard from my brother, by a mounted messenger, that chupattis were passing from village to village throughout his jurisdiction; that pieces of goat's flesh were also being distributed; and he asked me what was to be done. I wrote to him at once to use all his influence to prevent the circulation, and immediately sent word to the authorities.

For some days I received no orders: subsequently an order came to inquire and report what was intended by this circulation. Other letters now came to me from Thanadars of Alipur and Shepur, who asked for advice what to do.

I then received orders to stop the circulation. In the meantime my brother was deputed to go both to Allyghur and Muttra and inquire whether this circulation was general throughout the country. From him I learned that he had travelled over a large part of the Delhi division, and wherever he had gone he found the chupatti had been received from some place still further east. He was beset with questions, but whence the sign had come no one could tell; neither its origin, nor its intention, were known.

My brother suggested that letters should be sent to the civil authorities of other districts to trace this matter, or else that he should be allowed to trace it to its very source; but no permission was given. Next, I received an order from Sir Theophilus Metcalfe, then Joint Magistrate at Delhi, to report privately what I believed to be the origin of the matter. I wrote that I had heard from my father how, in the downfall of the Mahratta power, a sprig of china (or millet),[1] and a morsel of bread, had passed from village to village, and that it was more than probable that the distribution of this bread was significant of some great disturbance, which would follow immediately. I had no further official communications or orders on this matter.

Following on this circumstance, there arose a hue and cry that the English were plotting to destroy the "caste" of the native Sepoys, by causing them to use a cartridge dipped in the fat of cows and pigs. The officers of the Government seemed to attach no importance to the matter, and paid no heed to what we regarded as significant warnings of a serious spirit of disaffection, which was spreading far and wide over the country.

On the morning of the 11th May I was engaged in a case in the Criminal Court of the Magistrate and Collector, Mr. Hutchinson. Shortly afterwards Buldeo Sing, Darogah in charge of the Jumna Bridge, came and said that he had just received information that there had been a fight between the European and native troops in Meerut, and that the latter were marching straight upon Delhi, burning all the bungalows, and killing all the Europeans and Christians along their route. The mutineers were reported to be close to Delhi. The Collector at once ordered Buldeo Sing to hasten to his post and make arrangements for closing at once the city gate leading to the bridge. The Collector then drove off in his buggy in the direction of the Commissioner's house. Mr. Fraser, being asleep, was aroused and informed

[1] The Sonthals send round a sprig of the sál-tree (*Shorea robusta*) if they desire to attract public attention.

of all that was happening. Among the natives it is said that late the night before a sowar had arrived from Meerut with a letter for Mr. Simon Fraser, the Commissioner, which the Jemadar took to him; he was sitting in his chair asleep after dinner, and the Jemadar had to call several times to his master before he awoke. The Jemadar then told him that a sowar had brought an urgent letter from Meerut. The Commissioner, however, rebuffed him, and taking the letter from the servant's hands mechanically put it into his pocket, falling asleep again afterwards. The servants were afraid to awaken the Commissioner again, and all that they gathered from the sowar was that he had learned from the patrol who had given him the letter that there was a great *goolmal* (confusion) at Meerut, and he had been urged to gallop at speed with the letter. I learned all this from the chuprassis while awaiting Mr. Hutchinson's return to the Cutcherry. While I was thus speculating on what had happened at Meerut, Mr. Hutchinson arrived. Seeing me, he ordered me to go off at once to the city and warn the Kotwál (or chief police-officer); then I was to return to my station in Pahargunge, and do my utmost to preserve order. Leaving him I rode through the city, and on my way met the Kotwál and gave him the magistrate's orders. He rode with me part of the way. According to him the city was quite quiet. While we were riding along a watchman from the Rajghaut city gate ran up, and reported that a number of native cavalry had reached the city walls from Meerut, and he had seen a still larger body approaching in the distance.

He said, in reply to a question, that the gates had been closed, but that when he left there was a great disturbance outside to have the gates opened. Leaving the Kotwál, to go to the city gate, I galloped back to report to Mr. Hutchinson that the mutineers were already at the Rajghaut Gate. He quietly told me to go off to my own post. He asked a chuprassi if anyone had seen Mr. Le Bas, and then drove off as if in search of him.[1] I mounted my horse and galloped off to Pahargunge, through the Ajmere Gate of the city. Arriving there I turned out all the police "Burkundazies" and ordered them to look to their arms.

Whilst I was talking to my Burkundazies I suddenly saw a horse ridden by a European galloping towards the police station. As soon as I saw the rider I recognized him as the Joint Magistrate, Sir Theophilus Metcalfe. I rose from my seat, and coming forward to meet him, called out the guard, and gave him a salute. At this time he was without any clothes save his shirt and underdrawers. I asked him what had happened. He replied: "The mutineers have got into the city and are killing all the Europeans. I have escaped by seizing this horse and have been pursued through the city." He then said to me, "Are you willing to do me a service?" I replied: "All that I have is yours: what service can I perform?" He then dismounted from his horse, and asked me for some clothes to put on. I took him to the police station and opened my box. He selected a suit of native dress and a good sword of the kind known as Jari Ghaut. He then ordered his horse with the view of returning to his own house. I begged of him not to go. He then said: "I have left in my bedroom, in my house, a box containing 13,000 rupees in notes and some gold in

[1] From inquiry, I afterwards learned that Mr. Hutchinson had driven round to see that all his orders had been carried out, and had driven to the Kotwáli, with Mr. Le Bas, the Judge. From Mr Fraser's chuprassi I also learned that when he had carefully read the letter, which he had received the night before, he sent orders to secure the safety of his office, and ordered his carriage and gun to be sent after him into the city. Then taking with him Karim Buxt Khan, the Jujjur Rajah's Resaldar, he went towards the city. He does not appear to have issued any orders to employ his Bodyguard.

coins." He desired me to send two trustworthy persons to bring the box. I at once deputed Kaluja Sing Mohurur and Omrao Mirza for this purpose.

I then questioned Sir Theophilus as to how he had escaped, for it seemed to me an all but impossible feat. I learned from him that he had arrived rather late at the Court House. He had found the Courts all empty, and only the Assistant Magistrate present, who was waiting, not knowing what to do. Nazir Rani Chand Dass then reported to him that the Treasury Guard had been overheard the night before saying that the Government was tampering with their religion, and "What would be, would be." This report was followed by one from the Darogah of the Jumna Bridge, that the mutineers were hastening towards the city; he was warned that they were already under the city wall. He then drove with the Assistant Magistrate to the Magazine, where he turned out the guard of twenty-four Nujíbs, and sent them to guard the city gates. The men pointed out that they had no cartridges. They were sent off, and Sir Theophilus then drove by himself towards the Calcutta Gate. He was met by a crowd hurrying towards him; from them he learned that the mutineers had already entered the city. Sending the Kotwál[1] who was with him to guard the Kotwáli, he drove on. On reaching Dariagunge he was met by three sowars, who, pulling out their pistols, fired at him. As each man met the buggy, and raised his pistol, Sir Theophilus lashed him across the face with the buggy whip. Flinching from the lash, each sowar missed him. He galloped on until he became separated by a crowd from his assailants, but another crowd ahead barred his progress. Jumping out of the buggy,

[1] I was informed afterwards that this "Kotwál," Buldeo Dass by name, on arriving at the Kotwáli, learned that Mr. Hutchinson had been already murdered. He galloped back to warn Sir Theophilus, but met his buggy, with the horse galloping, without a driver, or a "syce" (groom).

he threw off his coat, pulled off his trousers, and ran down one of the many lanes of the city towards the garden house of Madub Dass. On his way he had suddenly come across the Resaldar of the Rajah of Jujjur's Cavalry, Mahommed Khan by name. He called on this man to give up his horse, but he refused. On this Sir Theophilus suddenly seized him by the leg, tilted him out of the saddle, wrenched the reins from his hands, and jumping on the horse rode hard for the Choree Bazaar. Again he was headed by sowars. He turned, and was pursued by them in the direction of the Ajmere Gate, through which he passed and reached Pahargunge.

Whilst he was relating these adventures, two policemen came and reported that the road to Sir Theophilus's house was completely blocked by bodies of mutinous soldiers and ruffians, who were past all control and bent on murder and rapine. The men betrayed by their faces the fear they felt, but Sir Theophilus was not to be scared by such a tale, and he still declared he would ride back to cantonments where the troops were quartered. I warned him of the danger of such a step. How would he escape if the native troops at Delhi mutinied also? I begged him to go and take refuge in my family house in the city, where my eldest brother, Amír-u-dín Khan and his tribesmen would answer for his life. I offered to conduct him myself to the house, suggesting also that his presence in the city might possibly benefit the English Government. But he replied: "My duty is with the troops. It may be that by this time I am the only civil officer alive; it is not fitting that I should think of personal safety, while there is a military force near at hand to restore order." He then mounted, and we rode towards the Farashkhana Bridge. On our way we saw a large body of mutineers marching out from the Lahore Gate, and coming towards us. We met Kallian Mohurur and Omrao Mirza, who had been sent to try and save the money-chest from Sir Theophilus Metcalfe's house. They had been terrified by what they had seen. They reported the whole road as occupied by Bazís and Budmashes. They were so frightened that they returned with their mission unaccomplished. We consulted, and it was thought madness to proceed by the straight road. We determined to go back and ascertain what the troops at the cantonments were doing. I again proposed that Sir Theophilus should go to my house. He refused, on the ground that his presence would become known and lead to the destruction of my family and all my property. We cautioned our companions against revealing Sir Theophilus's presence, and we rode off to the Durza of Kadím Shuríf; passing it, we went through Molea Khand, Múllam Dhanda, Buki Sahian, until we reached Bagh Kutapi in the surburbs, some three miles from the city. Stopping our horses before the house of Bhúra Khan Mewattí, we dismounted. The man was not known to me personally, but he bore the character of being a fearless, upright man. He held the position of a "Lumberdar." On inquiry, I learned he was absent; but his son came out to inquire what we wanted. I sent him to look for his father, and we waited quietly near the house. In a short time Bhúra Khan came, and, after salutations, I said: "Do you know who this is?" pointing to my companion. He looked earnestly at him; recognizing him he said: "It is *Mutculub*[1] Saheb." I related to him the occurrences of the morning. He recognized my companion's danger, and of his own accord offered his services. Sir Theophilus Metcalfe was anxious to learn the

[1] Corruption of "Metcalfe." Illiterate natives of India have a ready aptitude for corrupting Saxon names: thus "Abercromby" becomes "Bikrom"; "Alexander," "Secunder"; "Hastings," "Istink."

fate of the other European officers, and bade me go into the city and try to save any European lives I could. But it was too late to avert evil. It is probable if earlier steps had been taken to rouse the leading men of the city, many human lives might have been saved. When as yet comparatively few mutineers had entered the city, the personal retainers of the nobles might have been sufficient to deal with the handful of marauders. The Rajah of Bulubghur was, at the time, in the city with his followers. He, together with Nawab Amír-u-dín Khan and Zia-u-dín Khan, who were men of great influence and loyal to the British — these, I say, could easily have raised a sufficient force, on the spur of the moment, to attack the Meerut sowars. The sowars were mounted on horses, and they would have been helpless in the narrow lanes of the city, crowded as it was with people. Alas! the suddenness of the inroad of a handful of men created a panic. Ignorance of the strength of the mutineers, and exaggerated reports of their number, quite paralyzed the better disposed part of the inhabitants.

In the mind of the natives, blame is attributed to the unfortunate inaction of the Commissioner, due to his neglect of the very important information which reached him the day before. By nine o'clock of that fatal morning the principal executive officers of the Government were dead. Then there ensued a panic. Every man thought of his own safety and that of his family and property.

But to get back to my narrative. I returned first to Pahargunge police station. I was questioned where the magistrate had gone. I replied that he had outpaced me, and had ridden I knew not where. Changing my costume, and adopting the habit generally worn by natives, I rode towards the city. I found the gate open and unguarded. I rode to my family house, where the terrified inmates were closing the doors. I rode on to the fort, finding all the shops on the road closed, both those of artizans and those of the Bunyahs or provision merchants. On every side the scum of the population was hurrying to and fro, laden with the plunder of European houses. Arriving at the central police station I found it plundered even to the doors, which had been carried off. The place was apparently deserted. Calling aloud I was answered by two policemen; from them I learned that the convicts who had been working on the roads had been taken to the station-house that morning for custody as soon as the disturbance had commenced. Shortly afterwards two Mahommedan sowars had ridden up, and called out, "Are you all here for your religion or against it?" The Kotwál had replied, "We are all for our religion." The convicts then made a rush for a blacksmith's shop, and assisted each other to cut off their irons. After this, two men mounted on camels and dressed in green with red turbans rode by at a trot, calling out, "Hear, ye people, the drum of religion has sounded." Whence they had come or whither they went, my informant knew not, but the excited and terrified crowds in the streets believed they were heavenly messengers. The convicts, freed from their fetters, returned and stormed the police station. The doors had been closed, but they forced them open with the assistance of some Sepoys. The Kotwál saved his life by jumping down at the back of the premises from the roof, and escaped in the direction of Roson-ud-Dowlah. The Naib Kotwál similarly got away. Foiled of their victims, the convicts plundered the house and destroyed all they could lay their hands on. My informants, who were natives of Lower Hindustan, not knowing what to do or where to go, still hung about the premises for shelter.

I learned that the mutineers had all gone in the direction of the Cashmere Gate to plunder, and to kill the Europeans who lived there. Still hoping to prevent some butchery, I ordered the two policemen to go and collect as many of the police as they could find. I told them to say I had been appointed City Kotwál by the King. To reassure them I gave them five rupees to purchase sugar, and instructed them if any mutineers came to the place to mention my name as having been appointed Kotwál. If any Sepoys came there, they were to be welcomed and offered sugar to mix with water. I then rode on to the Palace to ask for an interview with the King, in hopes that I might get some appointment to give me influence to stop the butchery of Europeans, and ensure the protection of my own family.

As I passed the Lahore Gate of the city I found the Volunteer Company of Native Infantry standing in line, ready for action. They, however, took no notice of me. Leaving my horse outside the "Red Purdah," I entered the Palace on foot. The place was untenanted and deserted. On reaching the Taswir Khana I found four head servants and two eunuchs in attendance. One of the servants, whom I knew, asked me why I had come. I replied, "I must see the King," and inquired where he was; I induced him to seek the King. I was summoned, and, prostrating myself, replied to his questions that my object in seeking an audience was, that plunder and butchery were going on; and all the bad characters were searching for European and Christian women and children to destroy them. I begged the King to stop this, and to arrange for the restoration of order. The King replied: "I am helpless; all my attendants have lost their heads or fled. I remain here alone. I have no force to obey my orders: what can I do?" I replied: "If your Majesty will tell me the desire of your heart, possibly I may be able to carry out your commands." I described my proposed line of action. The King replied: "My son, this duty will I expect from you; you have come to me in a moment of difficulty and danger; do whatever seemeth good to you: I command you." I then said to the King: "If anyone should speak evil of me, charging me with occupying myself in suppressing disorders, be pleased to say, 'He is acting under my orders.' If your Majesty will give me the services of one or two of your Chobdars,[1] and let them come with me to the scene of the massacre and butchery, giving them orders to support me with your authority, the slaughter of the helpless ones may be stayed. They could be brought here in custody to await your Majesty's pleasure. If their lives are saved, such an act of benevolence will benefit your Majesty above everything, if it be possible to carry out this scheme." I asked also that one of the Royal Princes should be sent to ride through the city and order the shops to be opened. The King approved of this proposal, and sent for Hakim Ahsanullah Khan. He came, and was ordered to listen to my proposals. He replied: "What necessity is there for Chobdars to accompany you? The *bagheelog* (runaways) will never abandon the slaughter of Christians. If they are interfered with, yet worse things may happen. When satiated with the blood of Christians, they will direct their attention to us and to our property. Let us take care of ourselves." I replied: "Hakimjee, your judgment is not good. The massacre of innocent women and children is not a good work in the eyes of the Most High God. When this insurrection is suppressed, and the English power re-established, the saving of these lives will stand you in good stead. Even if you incline to the opinion that the

[1] Bearers of the Mace.

English power is gone for ever, these lives you have saved will redound to your glory and honour." I told him it was my opinion that the insurrection would continue only a short while, and besought him to act on my advice. Hakim Ahsanullah remained silent as if lost in deep thought.

The King, inclining to my advice, ordered the Chobdars to accompany me. I hurried with them to Dariagunge, where the greater number of Europeans lived. Here was a sad scene, for the wicked and miserable murderers were employed in burning bungalows and killing the women and children. May God be merciful, and not lay to my charge the terrible sights I witnessed! I and the Chobdars loudly proclaimed the orders of the King. Our interference was so far effectual, that the lives of some dozen persons were spared. They were sent to the Palace, and confined in the *chota kasa* apartments, and orders were given to feed them. Until late in the afternoon I laboured, going from bungalow to bungalow, hoping to find some one still living whom I might rescue. A few Christians only were found alive and taken to the Palace.

Later on I met a large number of Christians, men, women, and children, closely guarded. Using my authority I ordered them to be sent to the Palace or to the Kotwáli for trial, to prove if they were or were not Christians. I said: "If they be found hereafter to be Christians let them be slaughtered; but if they are falsely accused, the King's orders are, they must be set free. These are not Europeans, but men of the country." I said all this to save their lives. Nineteen of them were given up to me and sent to the Kotwáli. About four o'clock I was startled by the report as of a hundred cannon fired together. Astonished, I went towards the Cashmere Gate, and learned from some persons running towards me that the Magazine had been blown up.

I then went on to the Magazine. The wall facing the river was blown down, and some of the inmates escaped that way. When the smoke had blown away, I entered the place; six wounded Europeans were found after the explosion. I had them sent away to the Palace, saving them from immediate slaughter. It was now towards evening. The Treasury was still untouched, and the guard on duty present as usual. I learned that early that morning, when the mutineers entered the city, the officers in charge of the Magazine had closed the gates. They pointed the cannon at the gates and surrounded the place with prickly shrubs. Several Europeans from Dariagunge had taken refuge there. Working hard, they heaped up bundles of cartridges and barrels of powder in such a position, that on a match being applied the whole place could be blown to pieces. All natives were turned out of the place. When the mutineers attempted the assault, they were driven back by the guns being fired at them. They reassembled, this time with scaling-ladders. The Magazine was then fired. Only twenty-five Sepoys were killed by the explosion, but a mob of 400 onlookers perished. Indeed, many of the bodies were blown far into the city. After sending away the six wounded Europeans, I went towards the Kotwáli. On my way I saw the bodies of many Europeans lying about the roads, some near the Church, and many in front of the Assistant-Magistrate's Cutcherry. I passed the bodies of Kalla Saheb, Deputy-Collector in charge of the Treasury, and of his son. I saw sights that unmanned me. I dared not look. As I passed the Treasury the sentinel was still pacing on his accustomed beat.

On reaching the Kotwáli I assumed great severity of manner, and ordered the native Christians sent there to be carefully guarded. I found the two policemen had carried out my orders, and in the course of the day had collected the main body of the police, who were again in attendance at the Kotwáli. As soon as it was night, the native Christians were passed out of the city, and thus escaped. I did not reach my home until about midnight, when I heard the firing of heavy guns. Mounting my horse, I rode towards one of the bastions. There I learned that another regiment from Meerut had arrived to join the mutineers, and a salute had been fired.

On the morning of May 12th I rode up to the cantonments, and found the whole place in disorder; ruins of burning bungalows, and remains of property scattered here and there. The three regiments stationed here, the 38th, 54th, and 74th, had all moved off into the city, together with a battery of artillery. I learned that on the previous morning, about nine o'clock, information had reached the cantonment that a body of mutineers had arrived in Delhi from Meerut. The Brigadier at once ordered off two guns and a force of infantry to protect the city. The force detached joined the mutineers. As soon as the news of this fact reached the cantonment, and it became known that the officers had been killed, the 38th broke out in a body, killing their officers and such Europeans as they came across. The men of the 54th behaved better; a few joined the mutineers, but the greater part refrained from joining the insurrection. The 74th assisted their officers to escape, and committed no murders. The men of the 38th fired the cantonment bungalows, and did as much mischief as they could.

Many ladies in the cantonments made their way to the Flag Staff Bastion, and were there joined by a number of Christians and half-castes of both sexes. The 54th and 74th had refused to attack the mutineers of the 38th, and had refused to help their officers to drag guns to the bastion to defend it. All the murders were committed by the 38th, and that regiment was answerable for the trouble and terror to which the ladies and children had been subjected.

All the officers who escaped assembled with their wives and children at the Flag Staff Bastion. About five o'clock in the afternoon, when it became evident that no help was at hand, they began to make arrangements for flight. In this they were assisted by the servants, as well as by the Sepoys of the regiments. Some in carriages, some in buggies, they started for Kurnoul. By that time, the city and cantonments being without officers, they were given over to lawlessness, and were beyond control. The battery of artillery did not leave the cantonments until after the Europeans had left, and so it was night before they marched into the city, and encamped at the Dewan Kam. The infantry did not march into the city until the next morning.

The Gujurs (a tribe of robbers) had not been slow to appear. Bands from Wuzirabad and Chandraul were plundering right and left. Metcalfe House was plundered by the Zemindar of Chandraul, and then burned. Every house belonging to a European or a Christian had been first plundered, then burned. After seeing the condition of Metcalfe House and the cantonments, I returned to the city. I appointed Mahommed Khan "burkundaz" and Gopal "chowkidar," and sent them to convey to Sir Theophilus Metcalfe information of all that had occurred. I despatched them on this errand, for though I wished to go myself there was no opportunity, since my duties occupied every minute of the day. Outrage and murder were of hourly occurrence. Thirty Europeans, of both sexes, who had taken refuge in the Rajah of Kishenghur's house, had been attacked and butchered in cold blood. On the third day I was warned that I was thought to have concealed some Europeans.

I felt that the mutineers suspected me, and regarded me with hostility.

On the fourth day I determined, at all hazards, to visit Sir Theophilus Metcalfe. Taking a brave and trustworthy man, by name Imam Khan, with me, I started. I had already passed out of the city, by the Ajmere Gate, when he drew my attention to two men who seemed to be following us. They had water-vessels in their hands, and were pretending that they were going out into the country to answer a call of nature. Believing that I was the object of their suspicions, I stopped at the rest-house used by travellers in Pahargunge. I rested there some time as if wearied, and then went on to the shop of a man who sold lime. I entered into a conversation with him for a supply of lime for the repairs of the Kotwáli. To lead them off the scent I leisurely returned to the city by the Delhi Gate, *via* Kundrat. The two spies entered the city with me, and I then watched them until they joined their comrades. This occurrence determined my plan of action. I felt I had incurred suspicion, that my life and my family were in danger. It was necessary to take some decided measure. In all hours of difficulty and danger, action is better than inaction—a golden rule. It struck me that if I were to maintain my influence and position in the city, I too must become a mutineer, and checkmate the designs of those who would destroy me. When two men are contending, the one who is the less energetic must be worsted. I determined to go at once to the Palace, and offer my services to the King. At the gate I found a company of the Volunteer Regiment of Native Infantry. I called for the Subahdar, and speaking as if I had some authority, I inquired if they had received their pay. A knot of non-commissioned officers surrounded me, and began most eagerly to discuss their difficulties. No officer had been appointed to command them, and they were without pay. I suggested to them that they should ask the King to appoint me. I told them my name, and offered to get them their pay. They readily assented. I then wrote a petition on their behalf, which they were to present to the King. In an interview with Prince Mirza Mogul I proposed to him that he should take this regiment as a bodyguard, and be appointed their Colonel, as his brothers had been appointed to the commands of other regiments. He accepted the proposal, and at an interview with the King obtained the issue of the necessary orders. These steps, no doubt, implicated me in the rebellion; but I was actuated by no feeling of opposition to the English, against whom I knew the struggle was hopeless.

If I had remained a passive spectator of this rebellion my life would certainly have been taken, while if I had left the city, and joined the English, the honour of my family would have been destroyed, and the rebels would have wreaked their vengeance upon them, for I was not an obscure man. I knew the position of the English, and how it would be, before the English Government could again reassert its authority and sovereignty; so in my inmost heart I thought I was doing the best I could during this interval. To procure influence over the men of the regiment I advanced 5,000 rupees out of my own purse and personally distributed the money. That night I took up my quarters with the regiment. Next morning (May 15th) I was informed that the Sepoys who held the Ajmere Gate of the city, had come to search for me. I took my sword and went down among my men, who were falling in for morning parade. I recognized the two men who had followed me the day before. As the men did not salute me, I turned to the men of my company and pointed out to them the disrespect shown me by these two. An altercation ensued; the Ajmere Gate Sepoys then openly charged me with concealing some Europeans. My men retorted with abuse, on which my two accusers retired. On this day I again communicated with Sir Theophilus, informing him that matters were not mending, and that I saw no hopes of speedy succour; but, "Whatever must be, would be." After despatching my messenger, I was filled with the greatest anxiety for the safety of Sir Theophilus, the King having issued a proclamation offering a reward of 10,000 rupees for his capture. While debating with myself how to act, I received a verbal message from Sir Theophilus, asking for assistance to travel to Jujjur. The same evening I sent him a good horse, and some money, to Bura Khan's house, with advice how to travel. I felt I was in great difficulty, for if I myself went, and if my purpose became known, all my labour would be lost. It was arranged that Sir Theophilus should be dressed as a native soldier, and should be called Shere Khan,[1] by which name henceforward he passed in all our communications. Next day I received a formal receipt for the money from Jujjur. My anxiety was much lessened by learning that Sir Theophilus had safely reached Jujjur, in company with Bura Khan and two of his brothers.

I placed myself from that day on the sick list, and remained at home, at the same time confining my military duties to attendance on the King. This line of conduct satisfied the men, for the Subahdars retained command without interference, while my position as Colonel protected me from immediate danger from my foes.

A man called Mir Nawab had taken charge of the Kotwáli with my consent and my connivance. Subsequently,

[1] *Shere* means "Lion."

one Farg-ulla Khan was appointed Kotwál, and Abdul Hakim was appointed his assistant. My position was better than that of the Kotwál, for the city was in the hands of the Sepoys, and these recognized no authority that was not military. The following Princes were appointed as Colonels to Regiments: Mirza Jewan Bukt, Mirza Mogul, Mirza Kider Sultan, Mirza Surub Hindi, Mirza Sidu Beg, Mirza Buktour Shah, Mirza Abdulla, son of Mirza Shali Ruk, Mirza Abu Bakr.

One of the first native houses plundered was that of Mohun Lall, who was said to be a Christian. I was informed that he had been arrested and placed in confinement, and was awaiting sentence of death. Now, Munshi Mohun Lall had during the Cabul War done good service to the English. He fell into the hands of the Afghans, and to save his life had passed himself off as a Mahommedan, under the name of Aza Khan. He was a man of good family, and was thoroughly loyal to the English. . . . . Learning that he was to be executed, I went to the house where he was confined, and using my authority ordered his release. I took him, after some difficulty, to my own house, and then sent him off to Ballaghur, under the protection of Nawab Wali Dad Khan, Talukdar, who was related to the King's family, and had been in Delhi for some days. The King had[1] appointed him to be a Subahdar of the Province of the Punjab, giving him a retinue of fifty Sepoys. Mohun Lall, in company with Mirza Agham Hossein Khan and Wali Dad Khan, reached Ballaghur in safety, and thence escaped to Meerut.

The houses of the following men were plundered, as they were reported to be friendly to the English, viz., Munshi Rudur Mull, Golam Mirza, Juli Begum, all situated in

[1] The appointment was somewhat premature, as John Lawrence still held that Province.

Mehalla Buri, Baran. The house of Hamid Ali was next plundered on the accusation, that he had given shelter to Europeans. To put a stop to this wholesale destruction of property a meeting was held of the better-disposed classes. It was agreed to buy up a regiment by a monthly payment, to protect their lives and property. The plan succeeded, and for a time at least they lived in security. Soon, however, the Princes, who had been placed in command of the different regiments, resented this arrangement, and calling together the Committee who had hired the regiment, fined and imprisoned them, appropriating the fines to their own purposes.

Even the leaders of the rebellion were not safe, for some enemy, in order to get Mahbúb Ali Khan and Hakim Ahsanullah Khan into trouble, wrote a letter in their names, addressed to the Lieutenant-Governor at Agra, which was allowed to fall into the hands of the mutineers who guarded the gates. The letter was taken to the King, and the immediate execution of the writers demanded. Mahbúb Ali Khan was very ill at home, and was taken in his *palki* to the Dewan-i-Khas. He fell into the hands of the mutineers. Hakim Ahsanullah managed to escape from his house and take refuge in the Palace. The King saw through the treachery and acquitted Mahbúb Ali Khan. Nevertheless, the mutineers, in anger, plundered his house. Frightened at the turn affairs had taken, Hakim Ahsanullah treacherously gave up a number of European women and children, whom he had placed in security. The unfortunates were taken to the Dewan Ám and seated in the reservoir. A sowar first fired a carbine, then all were mercilessly massacred, to the horror of the whole city. In other parts of the city, fugitives were found and massacred at the order of native officers in command of detached parties.

Day by day *perwanahs* were extorted from the King, addressed to particular regiments of the British Indian Army, promising monthly salaries of thirty rupees to infantry soldiers and fifty to cavalry, if they would join the King's Army. In every instance the King's *perwanah* had the effect of causing the soldiers to mutiny and make their way to Delhi. At the sight of the King's *perwanah* the men who had fought for the English forgot the past, in the desire to be re-established under a native Sovereign; thus, daily, the city became more and more the centre of the rebellion. The English never thought of the truism expressed in these lines:

"Dushman natawan, hakfr bechara shamurd."
("You should consider a weak man a despicable enemy.")

In the false security of their position, the English had long lived. As in nature, so in politics, a cloud the size of a man's hand often passes into a hurricane. It is quite true that the rebellion actually broke out on the excitement caused by the use of the new cartridges; but the real cause of the rebellion was an old enemy who, long vanquished, still existed.

But the enemies were not all natives: one of the most active of the mutineers was a European—a discharged soldier of the 17th Foot—who had resided at Meerut. This man turned Mahommedan, and assumed the name of Abdulla Beg. He became a resident at Delhi on the arrival of the mutineers, and immediately identified himself with them, and became virtually a leader and adviser. It was under his advice that the King issued *perwanahs* calling on regiments to join the King's forces. Since the 12th May the mutineers had taken possession of the King's private office, and had placed a guard over the Dewan Khan. They also insisted on the King holding a *durbar* daily, at which they could be present, and ensure a hearing. In place of the usual staff in attendance on the King's person, the mutineers substituted their own men, who were most violent, and quite wanting in ordinary respect to the King.

The force of mutineers in the city on the 12th May was as follows:—

5 Regiments Native Infantry	...	...		2,000
1 " Cavalry	...	...	...	350
1 Battery Artillery ...	...	...	...	180
Total ...	...	...	...	2,530

Of these, two Infantry and one Cavalry regiment were from Meerut, and three Infantry regiments and one battery of Artillery from Delhi. They were stationed thus:—one Infantry regiment to each of the following posts: Selimghur, Lahore Gate (Fort), Lahore Gate (City), and Ajmere Gate (City), and Delhi Gate. The battery of Artillery remained at the Dewan Ḱam. The Cavalry encamped at Mahatub Bagh.

The period between the 11th and the 25th was occupied in restoring order and discipline in the city. An attack from the English was expected, and there was great want of powder. The powder magazine was situated outside the city at Wuzirabad, which had been plundered of its contents by the zemindars who had made away with the powder. Upwards of one lakh of rupees' worth of arms had been found in the magazine, which had fallen into the King's possession, but there was no powder. Orders were early issued for its manufacture, and towards the end of May a supply was ready. The King repeatedly urged an attack upon Meerut, but the mutineers delayed, first on one pretext, then upon another. At last, under pressure from the King, Mirza Abu Bakr, as Commander-in-Chief, started with a force on the 25th of May to attack the English at the Hindun River. The force consisted of Cavalry and of Field and Horse Artillery. The battle began with artillery fire. The Commander-in-Chief mounted on to the roof of a house near the River Hindun close to a bridge across the river and watched the battle. From time to time he sent messages to his Artillery to tell them of the havoc their fire was creating in the English ranks. Near the bridge he placed a battery with which he carried on an exchange of fire with the English, which became like a conversation of question and answer. Presently a shell burst near the battery, covering the gunner with dust. The Commander-in-Chief, experiencing for the first time in his life the effects of a bursting shell, hastily descended from the roof of the house, mounted his horse, and galloped off with his escort of sowars far into the rear of the position, not heeding the cries of his troops. A general stampede then took place. When the news reached Delhi that the troops had been defeated, orders were issued to close the gates and exclude the Sepoys. When these arrived they found the Jumna Bridge had been broken down. In a hurried attempt to cross it the bridge gave way, and about 200 were drowned. The English did not follow up the victory; they were not to be seen, and gradually the Sepoys forgot their fright.

The next morning (May 26) the English army crossed the Hindun and took the guns which the mutineers abandoned; then they returned to Meerut. The Sepoys had now contended with the English on the open field. They had felt certain of success, but they had been worsted, and were filled with grave apprehensions for the future.

In the city there was rest for a time. News came of the assembling of the troops in the Punjab, and of their march upon Delhi. Four days before the arrival of the English, Ahmed Khan, Resaldar of the 4th Cavalry, made his way into the city. He sought an interview with the King, expressed his loyalty, and said his regiment was prepared to join the mutineers. He stated that the day the forces would meet, he would lead his men away to the right and join the mutineers. Ahmed Khan was received and treated with great courtesy. On the third day he took leave of the King, and returned to the English force. This man proved to be no rebel, but loyal to the English! On the same day the whole of the rebel force was paraded, under the command of Mirza Kizr Sultan, and marched to Alipur, where they entrenched themselves and rested.

On Monday, June 9th, the English arrived at Alipur. A regiment dressed in the uniform of the 4th Bengal Cavalry led the way on the right flank. The mutineers, seeing the advance-guard approaching, naturally believed them to be the regiment of Ahmed Khan coming to join the rebel army. A cry of "Deen Deen!" was raised, to welcome this addition to their forces. When the cavalry had approached near to the native army their squadrons suddenly wheeled, and immediately their front was cleared a battery opened fire from the centre of the column. The shells tearing through the ranks of the mutineers created great havoc, and immediately the Sepoys fled. The first to run was the Commander-in-Chief. He was met by Nawab Mahbúb Ali Khan near the garden house of Mehaldar Khan. Explaining that he was hurrying back to the city for more artillery and ammunition, Mirza Kizr Sultan, in spite of all remonstrances, galloped away. The Nawab used every effort to stop the retreat, but nothing could stay the Sepoys as they hurried towards the city, into which they poured through the Cashmere, Lahore, and Cabul Gates, leaving these gates open behind them.

The English halted at Subzi Mundi, and then marched towards the Rajpur Cantonments. If they had instantly marched on the city, the place would have fallen easily into their power. On reaching the cantonments, the English force proceeded to take up position. Many of the guns which had been loaded to stop the English advance, were abandoned and taken by the English. The hesitation on the part of the English inspired the Sepoys with confidence, and, arming the city walls with guns, they soon began to fire shots in the direction of the cantonments. The English advanced to Mr. Fraser's house, where they erected a battery, as also at the place known as Futtehghur, and replied to the rebel fire. The din of the artillery fire lasted night and day. The rebels had four batteries at work—one at Selimghur, two at the Cashmere Gates, and the fourth at the bastion at the Cabul Gate. The English replied from only two batteries. Very little was done by the English fire, the shot falling on unoccupied land and hurting no one.

The rebels were daily receiving additions to their ranks. The manufacture of gunpowder was begun in the house of Begum Simurd, being removed from the Dewan-Kam for fear of an explosion. In this some two hundred to two hundred and fifty men were daily employed. News was received of the death of Nasir-ul-Dowlah, Nizam of Hyderabad, and that he had been succeeded by Afzul-ul-Dowlah. The King ordered a *killut* and honorary titles to be sent to the Nizam. Every morning a *durbar* was held, the King seated on his throne.

The rebel forces assembled daily on parade early in the morning, and marched to Mithar Bridge, where they halted, and, spreading into skirmishing parties, fired at random (*bad-hawai*), till 4 p.m., when they were withdrawn into their own lines. The casualties were about four killed and half a dozen wounded. The new arrivals were the most energetic and anxious to fight, but gradually their energy and bravery wavered, and they became more ready for retreat than for advance. The Sepoys were laden with rupees ; they thought more of their plunder than of fighting.

Omrao Bahadur, a Talukdar of Alighur, with fifty stalwart sowars, and Umur Shobab, presented themselves before the King. Their names were entered as sirdars in the King's Army.

The rebels were becoming clamorous for pay. They were really laden with money, but they wished to extort as much more as they could. They threatened to leave the King's service unless paid, and they proposed that the wealthy men of the city should be ordered to subscribe for their maintenance. A Committee was formed of Nawab Hamud Ali Khan, Ruja Deby Sing Saligram, Nawab Músa Khan, Nawab Ahmed Mirza Khan, and Hakim Abdul Hug. Some money was extorted, but too little to satisfy the rebels. Another device was then attempted: Nawab Amin-u-din Ahmed Khan and Nawab Zia-u-din Ahmed Khan were deemed wealthy men, and pressure was brought to bear upon the King to extort money from them. Gangs of armed men were collected in Rasim Khan's *mohilla*, to stop Sepoys from plundering. Orders, sealed with the King's seal, were then sent to these two men commanding their attendance at the Palace. Collecting their relatives and retainers, they consulted on the best means of escaping from this extortion. After putting their houses in a state of defence, they rode to the Palace, with a retinue of a few armed men. On reaching the Lal Purdah Gate, they were stopped by the sentries, as no armed men were allowed to enter the interior of the Palace. Nawab Amin-u-din at once knocked the sentries over, and pushing through the gate, passed into the Palace. On this occasion I was present. An audience was demanded of the King, who was at that time surrounded by the rebel Subahdars. Elbowing his way through the crowd of rebels, Amin-u-din Ahmed Khan presented himself before the King, together with his relatives. The King seemed pleased to see them, but the rebels seemed to be nonplussed, and scowled at them. A further attempt was thereupon made to extort money from Amin-u-din. By the advice of one of the rebels it was suggested to Mirza Mogul to feign pleasure at seeing Amin-u-din, and to invite him to his house ; the others would take care to go there at the same time, to extort money from him. Accordingly, Mirza Mogul begged the King to request Amin-u-din to go to Mirza Mogul's house, as Mirza Mogul wished to consult him on an important matter. The King conveyed this invitation to Amin-u-din, and Mirza Mogul repeated it himself. Being pressed by the King to accept, Amin-u-din rode with his relatives to the Mirza's house. There he found large numbers of the rebels, and with difficulty obtained a seat. The rebels were ordered to be seated, but excused themselves. In the course of the conversation one of the rebels taunted Amin-u-din with living at his ease and in safety, while they were starving for want of food. This was followed by abuse. At once those who had accompanied Amin-u-din raised their carbines, and, covering the spokesman, challenged him at the peril of his life to repeat what he had said. The rebels were for the moment awed. Information of what was going on was carried to the King, who at once hurried to Mirza Mogul's house with his attendants, to prevent bloodshed. Bukt Khan, who had been appointed Commander-in-Chief, rode to the place, taking an escort of fifty soldiers with him, and severely reprimanded the rebels. Under the care of Bukt Khan and the soldiers who were with him, Amin-u-din Khan left the Prince's house, and reached his own in safety. He determined to leave the city : of course he was at once suspected of deserting to the English. On reaching the Cashmere Gate he was stopped by the rebel guard, threatened with immediate death, and detained. Unable to get out of the city, he returned to his own house.

A rebel regiment from Nusserabad arrived this day, and importuned the King for money. After taking up their quarters in Mobarah Bagh, they marched out at once to fight the English. The fighting commenced at three o'clock, and "tutors" and "pupils" met face to face. From firing the troops came to close quarters and crossed bayonets. The fight lasted for three hours; the ammunition was entirely expended. Towards sunset the Nusserabad regiment was withdrawn. In the morning the English took possession of the battlefield.

Buldeo Sing, the Darogah of the Jumna Bridge, was secretly conveying provisions this day to Sir Theophilus Metcalfe, when an informer pointed him out to the mutineers at the gate. He was stopped and searched; attempting to run away, he was caught and taken to the Kotwáli; there he was killed, and his body suspended by the leg to a Neem-tree.

A force arrived that day consisting of part of the Rajah of Ulwar's troops, and a regiment from Nímuch, after a fight at Akbarabad, under the command of Herra Sing. Immediately after arrival they too proposed to go out and fight the English. The bridge over the Canal had been destroyed by the English, so it was planned they should march *viâ* Nazufghur and engage the English from that side, while a counter attack was made from the city. The force therefore marched to Nazufghur. The English were aware of the movement, and arranged an ambuscade on the road, where the rebels, falling under a heavy artillery fire, fled, abandoning their guns. The force never again attempted an offensive movement.

The butchers accused of supplying the English with meat were decapitated. There were daily accessions to the ranks of the rebels, and daily attacks on the English position; daily the rebels were driven back until this became the recognized rule. The gunpowder manufactory was blown up, whether by accident or design it was not known; two hundred artificers were blown up with it.[1]

An attempt was made to plunder the house of the Kazi. The inmates defended the house, and killed several of the assailants with arrows. Mirza Mogul ordered a general review of the troops outside the Delhi Gate; they were extended to the Cashmere Gate. Seventeen regiments of foot, twenty-two regiments of cavalry, in all about 9,000 men, appeared at this parade. A quarrel between the sixth regiment and a regiment of infantry was excited by jealousy. The sixth, leaving their horses, issued by the Cashmere Gate, and attacking one of the English batteries, took the guns, and began to plunder the camp. When the infantry regiment arrived they found the plundering going on, and set to plunder too. Reserves coming up, the English attacked the mutineers and killed some two hundred of them, whereupon the force fled back to the city.

The mutineers represented to the King that the Sepoys were reluctant to attack the English, and demanded his presence in the field. This he promised to give. A large force was ordered to assemble in the evening. The King headed the force and passed by the Delhi Gate, and showed himself to the assembled troops. Passing by the Lal Dighi Tank he went on towards the Lahore Gate. One of the

[1] Hudson, who commanded the guides, used to send his spies daily into Delhi. They reported to him that the manufacture of powder was going on, and eventually on their saying that the factory could be blown up, he promised the men 1,000 rupees reward if they could succeed in doing it. It was blown up as stated in this diary, but the reward was never claimed, nor did the men ever return. No doubt they were blown up.

Palace dependants was substituted for the King, who secretly retired to the city by a back way. This show of force ended in nothing. The troops gradually moved back to their own quarters, and the threatened attack ended in smoke.

Three months had now passed, and the whole city had become accustomed to the sound of cannon being fired at all hours. A *nuzzar* was received from Bareilly from Khan Bahadur Khan. From Lucknow a *nuzzar* was brought from Mirza Abbas, consisting of gold mohurs of Badshah which bore the inscription—

> " Ba-zar-zad-sicca-éh-nasrut-tarazi
> Suraj-u-din Bahadur Shah gazi."

The bearer of this *nuzzar* was lodged at the house of Mozuffer-ul-dowlah. The *nuzzar* was presented to the King.

A letter was written to Hakim Ahsanullah Khan by Rajub Ali Khan Mohussim, asking why the Standard of the Prophet had been erected in the city, since there were no English left in the city. He had forbidden its remaining there, and he had directed Mufti Mahommed Sadan-u-dín Bahadur, Judge of the City, to instruct the people and explain to them that it was folly to raise the Standard. Soon afterwards a warning proclamation was issued that the city was about to be attacked, and that the batteries of the English were ready to fire upon the town. They commenced a cannonade upon the Cashmere Bastion. For eight days such a fire was kept up that the walls began to crumble away, and the shot began to fall inside the city. All the inhabitants of the quarter near the Cashmere Gate abandoned their houses and took refuge in more sheltered parts. Before the 14th of September the bastions upon which the English concentrated their fire, had become dust.

On this day, Monday, September 14th, the English made

the attack on the Cashmere Gates, by which they entered and took possession of the city. The mutineers, abandoning the guns on the bastions, fled in every direction. The English penetrated as far as the Kotwâli and Jumma Musjid in their assault. At the Kotwâli a gun had been planted and was fired by some sowars and bad characters. This fire fell in the midst of the English advancing column, killing and wounding upwards of fifty of them. The mutineers defended the Jumma Musjid and checked the English advance. The English fell back on the Cashmere Gate. A further stand was made by the mutineers at Pulbin Bund and at the Calcutta Gate. The fighting continued for five days through the city. The Princes fled to the Tomb of Humaon at four o'clock in the morning—a bad omen. The mutineers then began to leave the city in every direction, as did also the inhabitants. The fugitives were attacked by the Gujurs (robber tribes), who plundered them of their arms and money. Nawab Yakub Khan, who had lived shut up in his house in the city throughout the siege, left the city secretly with his family. He was attacked by Gujurs, plundered, and killed.

General Mahommed Bukt Khan, collecting a force, went to the King, and begged him to fly to Lucknow with him. He also offered to collect the scattered rebel forces outside the city and again fight the English. But the old King refused his help. Bukt Khan then marched for Lucknow with all the forces he could collect.

Mirza Abbas Khan, the *vakîl* of the King of Oude, who had arrived four days before the assault with the *nuzzar*, now fled with his escort in the direction of Rajputana. The King fled to the old fort Killa Kahoma. The whole city once more came under the dominion of the English. When the English learned where the King had fled they sent orders to Mirza Elahi Bux and Hakim Ahsanullah to prevent the King from leaving the city, and directed them to bring him to the English camp. A force was sent with them of 100 cavalry, with the complement of officers, and proceeded to the old fort.

Mirza Elahi Bux and Hakim Ahsanullah went to the King, who was in great terror, but was reassured by those about him, who told him that a dish of *pillau* alone was in store for him. Four of the Princes were in company with the King, viz., Mirza Mogul, Mirza Abu Bakr, Mirza Kizr Sultan, Mirza Meddu. The party, on leaving the fort, was surrounded by the English escort. The King was placed in a *palki*, the Princes in a bullock-cart, and taken towards the Palace. When the Princes reached the place in front of the Dewan-i-Ám, where the English women and children had been butchered, they were shot. The city was plundered from the Lahore to the Cashmere Gate. Mirza Buktour Shah, who was subsequently caught, was also executed. The King was placed in custody. Shah Samund Khan, the commander of the King's Bodyguard, was caught leaving the city by the Cashmere Gate. He was identified as General of the Rajah of Jujjur's forces, and was summarily shot. In the city no one's life was safe. All able-bodied men who were seen were taken for rebels and shot.

Mahommed Ali, son of Nawab Jung Khan, nephew of the Rajah of Dadra, had closed his doors for safety. Some Gurkhas and Europeans who were plundering the city tried to force the doors. Baffled in the attempt, they mounted the wall. A wet-nurse seeing them was so terrified that she threw herself and the child she was carrying into a well; the other ladies of the house, panic-struck, followed her example, and threw themselves into the same well and perished.

Mahommed Ali from the centre of the house fired his gun and killed three Europeans. The house was immediately attacked by a large force and the inmates killed, Mahommed Ali among the number, fighting to the last. Some sixty men found with weapons were killed, including Sheik Imam Bux and his son, masters of the Mahommedan College, who were mistaken for mutineers. Among those slain was Falla-ulla Khan, a well-known native physician, and others who were innocent of all participation in the mutiny. In Bhojla Pahari, Meah Amin Saheb, a well-known scribe, foolishly interposed to prevent soldiers from entering his house. He killed the first English soldier who entered, but was himself immediately bayoneted; still, he died taking his murderer with him.

Moulvie Furíd-u-dín was on his way from his morning prayers, when he was met by the advancing column of English and fell in the rush, with which the English burst like a pent-up river through the city. Hakim Ahmed Hossein Khan and Hakim Razi-u-din Khan fell in the same way. Mirza Eusuf Khan, brother of Mirza Asadúlla Khan, who had long been out of his mind, attracted by the noise of the firing, wandered out into the street to see what was going on; he was killed. Many other well-known men of the city were killed, being mistaken for rebels. In this way God showed His anger: the green as well as the dry trees were consumed; the guiltless shared the same fate as the guilty. As innocent Christians fell victims on the 11th of May, so the same evil fate befel Mahommedans on the 20th September, 1857. The gallows slew those who had escaped the sword. Among them were Nawab Mozuffer-ul-dowlah, Mahommed Hossein Khan, Mirza Ahmed Khan, Mir Mahommed Hossein Khan, Akbar Khan, Mir Khan, Nowshir Khan, Hakim Abdul Hug, Kalifa Ismail, Mahommed Khan,

Resaldar Safdar Beg Khan, Asjur Yar Khan, besides Princes of the King's family. Many died in jail. Numbers perished, until Sir John Lawrence re-established order, and Courts were once more opened for the trial of the guilty; every man who had an enemy declared against him. False witnesses abounded on every side. On one side a man feared the rebels; on the other he dreaded the false accusations of relatives and compatriots. The slaughter of innocent, helpless women and children was revenged in a manner that no one ever anticipated.

There were several ancient and noble families in the vicinity of Delhi: Jujjur, with a revenue of fourteen lakhs, Dadra, Patuli, Bulubghur, with two lakhs subsidy from Government, Dogana, Faraknujjur, Loharu. Mention has already been made of Jujjur and the part he played. Dadra became disloyal to the English. Patuli opposed the rebellion; he was attacked by the mutineers, defeated, and his palace looted. The Rajah, however, joined the English. Dogana remained loyal to the English throughout. Bulubghur was virtually Governor of the city during the siege. He, together with Jujjur and Faraknujjur, were hanged for rebellion. The death of Mr. Munder was brought home to the Rajah of Bulubghur. Loharu was virtually a prisoner in Delhi during the siege. His house and property at Loharu were plundered by the neighbouring zemindars. The bodies of the three Rajahs were buried in the same grave with the Delhi Princes, in the Durga of Kazi Bakibulla. Their estates were also attached. Perghanah Narnal, which yielded a revenue of 200,000 rupees, was given to Puttiala. Perghanah Karonda was sold by public auction, and was allowed to be purchased by the Rajah of Puttiala, on account of his steadfast loyalty. Perghanah Kauli was given to the Rajah of Nabha. As a reward for his disloyalty Dadra was confiscated and made over to the Maharajah of Jeend. The Rajah of Dadra was banished to Lahore. The officers of the Rajah of Jujjur were banished to Ludiana. No action was taken by the English Government against the properties of Dogana, Patuli, and Loharu. The King, with his Begums, and Joan Bukt and his wife, with certain Princes, were banished to Rangoon, and sent there under a European guard. A suitable allowance for their maintenance was sanctioned by the English Government, and the King was allowed to take with him four of his old retainers as servants.

NARRATIVE OF MUNSHI JEEWAN LÁL.

On the morning of the 11th May, between eight and nine o'clock, a wonderful report reached me as it spread through the city, that some cavalry and foot-soldiers had arrived from Meerut, and were in the bazaar plundering and killing the people. Whereas by the mercy of God the English rule was established in the country, the rumour was disbelieved, and it was stated that some ignorant people had escaped from Meerut, and were misconducting themselves. It was affirmed that English troops from Meerut had been sent in pursuit of them, and would immediately arrive and severely deal with the plunderers and those persons who were spreading false alarms. I had been that morning to Captain Douglas, the Assistant Resident, who was in charge of the Palace Guard, and I had returned home about eight o'clock. It was the practice for the Assistant Resident to make a copy of my diary for his own information, and that of the Resident, as to all matters connected with the Court. After returning home I was preparing to go to Court at ten o'clock, and had ordered my *palki* to be ready, when some of the Moharers (clerks) of the Court came to my house and begged me not to leave the building, as it was no longer possible to go through the streets in safety. They told me that strife and bloodshed were rife in the city, and it was rumoured that some of the authorities had been murdered, but that the Commissioner and Magistrates had escaped. One of my informants stated that he had met the officers hurrying to the entrenchments. It was reported, too, that the city gates had been closed, and there was no way of getting out; also that the Hospital

Assistants had all been murdered, and that the city Budmashes had begun to plunder. I despatched one of my servants, Sakun, to go to Captain Douglas in the Fort and to ascertain if any orders had been issued for me to obey, and also to inquire what the officers in cantonments were doing. After a time he returned and reported that the road to the Palace was blocked; that groups of soldiery were standing about in front of the King's Palace, the door of which was closed; that crowds of Budmashes were pointing out to the soldiers the residences of the Europeans and wealthier natives. Europeans were being killed in every direction, and their property plundered. The Bank had been broken into and robbed; Mr. Bensford, the Manager, and Mr. O'Hara murdered; others had hid themselves. Mr. Nixon, Head Clerk of the Commissioner's Office, had been killed, and his body was lying on the road; Mr. Neil, the Second Clerk, together with Mr. Peppe and the children, had concealed themselves, but the soldiers had managed to find out their hiding-place, and had killed them all. Sakun further told me that he had been to the Commissioner's Cutcherry, and had seen Mr. Nixon's body, lying, with a bullet wound, on the road. He had heard such dreadful screaming and wailing that he had lost all courage and had fled. The man wept as he spoke; I, too, was terrified, and my heart almost ceased to beat. I wept to feel how utterly powerless I was. Next came news that Mr. Simon Fraser, the Commissioner, and Mr. Henderson had escaped; and that Sir John Metcalfe, the Joint Magistrate, and Mr. Le Bas, the Judge, had also got away, no one could tell where. Sir John was thought to have gone to the Kutub. As he knew the environs of the city well, we guessed that he might possibly have taken refuge in the Dilkusha at Merowbe in the tomb of Rahun Alla-u-dín, which his father, the former Resident, had converted into a residence. Then came a man and reported that the Budmashes were naming me as being the Mir-Munshi[1] to the Agent of the Governor-General, and as one worthy of death, and offering to point out my house, which I was advised to fortify. Terrified and horror-stricken, I ordered the gates to be locked. The house had been built in the days of the Emperor Ferozeshah, and was of solid stone, and as strong as a fort. The doors and windows were all closed. There were underground apartments, into which my family entered, and there remained concealed. I arranged all the servants for watch and ward, both in front and behind, with orders to admit no one, and to give me information if any persons came. I was moved by the thoughts that for many years I had eaten the salt of the English Government and wished it well, and now was an opportunity to do all that was possible with heart and soul for those I had served. So I sent Sakun with instructions to ascertain if I could be of any service to Sir John Metcalfe and my other patrons, as well as to my friends, and to inquire about several Englishmen, in the same office as myself, who lived in the city, in houses in Dariaganj, and about the Cashmere Gate. Chief of these were Mr. Davis, his brother Tommy, and Mr. Maley. He was to urge them, if they had no place of concealment, to come to my house, where, with the help of God, I would guard them like the apple of my eye, or the soul in my body. I would personally attend to them; Sakun should conduct them through by-lanes to my house, and, please God, they should suffer no hardships.

With a view to obtaining news of the rebels' doings, I engaged the services of two Brahmins, Girdhari Misser and Heera Sing Misser, and of two játs, who were deputed to bring me information, from time to time, of all that happened

[1] Chief writer.

at the city gates and inside the Palace by night as well as by day, in order that I might keep a true and faithful account of all that passed for the information of the high officers of the State. About twelve o'clock came Jubmul, the Court newswriter, and Makun, Chowkidar, to Captain Douglas. They reported the city panic-struck—all houses and shops closed, the inmates concealed inside sitting silent in terror, or praying to God for His mercy and protection. Next came news about Mr. Simon Fraser, Agent and Commissioner of Delhi. Early in the morning, on rising, he was informed that a number of cavalry and soldiers of different regiments from Meerut had arrived at Delhi, and more were coming. They had burned down the toll-collector's bungalow, had shot the European officer on duty, and left his body lying on the sand. The men, it was said, had expressed their intention of coming and taking possession of the city. At that moment, Mr. Henderson, the Magistrate, rode up, made a report to the Commissioner and immediately drove off towards Cantonments—at Rajpur—probably for the purpose of summoning troops and artillery. Mr. Fraser at the same time ordered his carriage to be got ready, and drove off, taking with him the troopers of the bodyguard belonging to the Nawáb of Jajjar's cavalry, who were always told off with a Resaldár for duty with the Commissioner. He told his servant to follow at once with his pistols and sword. He drove first by the Calcutta Gate to the river-side bastion. He met there Mr. Le Bas, the Sessions Judge, Captain Douglas,[1] Mr. Nixon, and others, and carefully examined

[1] It is said that Captain Douglas gave a letter to Mr. Fraser, and it is believed that this letter contained information of the mutiny of troops at Meerut, of the murder of their officers, and of the intention of the men to march to Delhi. Some said at the time that the letter was written by the wife of the bridge toll-collector, and that she asked for assistance to bury the dead body of her husband, for a message was sent to her saying that under the circumstances no help could be sent.

the river-course and bridge with a telescope. The burning bungalow was seen in flames. A consultation took place, when Mr. Henderson, the magistrate, rode up. The group conversed eagerly for some minutes, looking towards the river as if expecting every moment to see a European force pushing forward from one side, and troops from the Rajpur Cantonments from the other; but no help came from either side. Some men then hurried up from the bastion, calling out that the rebel troopers had entered the city by the Rajghát Water Gate, and had killed the surgeon, Dr. Chuman Lál, who had been as usual attending his patients in the Dariaganj Hospital. The staff had all fled, it was said, and the place had been plundered. Suddenly five troopers came galloping up and fired a volley at the group of officers. A bullet struck Captain Douglas on the foot. Mr. Henderson, Mr. Le Bas, and the others fled in the direction of the courts. Mr. Fraser took refuge inside a sentry-box on the bastion, in which a sentry was posted.[1] In the confusion he was not seen, and snatching up the Chowkidar's musket, which he had left standing in his sentry-box, he shot one of the sowars, who fell together with his horse, and the life imprisoned in his body escaped like a bird out of its cage, far above all reach. The troopers seemed frightened by this sudden apparition and by the death of one of their comrades. They fled. Possibly they may have thought there were more Europeans concealed. Mr. Fraser ordered one of his orderlies to gallop as hard as he could go to the house of Durga Pashad, agent of the Nawáb of Jajjar (Abdur Rahman), and direct him to send to Jajjar at once and tell the Nawáb of the outbreak, and request him

[1] The bodyguard all this time seem to have been looking on, unconcerned spectators. Another account says that some of the Jajjar Cavalry, riding up, caused the sowars to gallop away.

to send two regiments with cavalry to Delhi without delay. Mr. Fraser, mounting his buggy, then drove off in the direction of the Palace. On the way he was attacked by several sowars, who fired pistol shots at him. He ordered the Jajjar orderlies to cut them down, but they made no attempt. The Commissioner swore at them in English, and putting his horse to a gallop he reached the Lahore Gate entrance to the Palace and ordered the agent and the "*mooktear*" of the King to be sent for. On the King's vakíl appearing, Mr. Fraser desired him to go at once to the King and require all his armed men to turn out as well as the two guns. Mr. Fraser also asked for two *palkis* to convey the ladies who were in Captain Douglas's quarters, viz., Miss Jennings, daughter of the chaplain, and another young lady, Miss Clifford, to the Begum's palace for protection. The message was conveyed to the King, who immediately gave the necessary orders, but such was his confusion that neither the guards, nor the cushions for the *palkis*, nor the bearers to carry the *palkis*, were forthcoming. No heed was paid to the orders given. The will to obey was wanting; the King's household had become rebellious, refusing to obey all orders. The Commissioner remained for some time awaiting the *palkis*. Seeing that no attention was likely to be paid to his orders, he turned away as if to enter Captain Douglas's house. Pressed by the crowd, he ordered them to stand off. The gateway was guarded by a company of native infantry, whom he ordered to load and close the gate; but they refused to obey the order. Mr Fraser then remonstrated with the men on their behaviour. They remained silent. Mr. Fraser then turned to mount the steps leading to Captain Douglas's rooms. As he placed his foot on the first step, two Budmashes, by name Karlik Beg and Mogul Beg, rushed forward with drawn swords and cut him down. It has been stated how Captain Douglas received a wound at the bastion. As soon as he fell, he was assisted by his two orderlies into a buggy and driven to his quarters. On arrival there, they carried him upstairs in a fainting condition. Revived after drinking a glass of water, he gave orders to close all the doors and windows. Almost immediately he was joined by Mr. Jennings, the chaplain, and a friend, two married ladies, and the two girls, Miss Jennings and Miss Clifford. The ladies employed themselves in dressing Captain Douglas's wound, the pain of which caused him repeatedly to faint. Remembering that he had dropped his sword, he told his orderly to return to the bastion and recover it. Loud cries were now heard outside of "Allah-dád, Allah-dád!" followed by the breaking open of the doors, and a crowd of rebels came rushing into the house. Mr. Jennings tried to get out of the door, but was immediately cut to pieces by the blood-thirsty ruffians, who in their fury spared none of the Europeans, not even the helpless women.

[Here the diary breaks off to give some further incidents connected with the movements of Captain Douglas, Mr. Henderson, and Mr. Davis, and the escape of Sir John Metcalfe, These are given separately.]

About nine o'clock a frightful explosion was heard, accompanied by a sound like roll of thunder, with an earthquake, causing the ground to tremble. The sound came from the direction of the Fort. The whole city was panic-struck and terrified. It soon became known that the Magazine had been attacked by the mutineers, assisted by the bad characters in the city. The officer in charge had then set fire to the gunpowder and blown it up. A great number of rebels and faithless men, lookers-on, and city residents were thus released from attendance in this world. There was both rejoicing and sorrow in the city at this occurrence; rejoicing that so many murderous and faithless men had been blown up, and sorrow that the English soldiers, who had all day been anxiously expected, had failed to appear, and the Government had failed to re-establish its supremacy. As night drew near, the inhabitants of each "*Mohalla*" were occupied in arranging for the watch and ward. The night passed, everyone being on the alert. Suddenly the sound of heavy guns was heard, and the watchers counted twenty-one reports. The first impression was that the English force had arrived and had defeated the rebels, and in order to notify this to the dwellers in the city, had fired this salute. The majority of the citizens were delighted. In the morning I ascertained that the four regiments stationed at Rajpur had joined the mutineers, and the guns had been fired to express joy that the mutineers had gained them over to their cause. I learned, on inquiry, that, as soon as the Brigadier commanding had issued orders for his troops in cantonments to be put under arms, the Sepoys showed by their conduct that, while some were still loyal, the greater number were insubordinate and quite prepared to disobey orders. After some delay and entreaty on the part of their officers, a detachment of troops was induced to march towards the city; at the word of command the men loaded and shouldered their arms, but as they marched away it was evident that no dependence could be placed upon them, for their march was purposely slow, the men not even keeping step. On approaching the Cashmere Gate the Sepoys met the mutineers. They were ordered to fire, but not a shot was fired; Sepoys and rebels interchanged compliments. The European officers collected into a group, whereupon they were charged by the troopers. The officers ran in different directions. One or two were cut down, but the others went off together, and after waiting a little in perplexity, eventually reached cantonments, one or two of them being wounded. In the meantime the Sepoys fraternized with the rebels.

Later on in this day, the two Subahdars who had been admitted to an audience with the King in the presence of Captain Douglas, were again admitted to a private audience as the representatives of the crowds of soldiery that thronged the neighbourhood of the Palace. They formally tendered the services of the troops of the King. They were directed to take their orders from Hakim Ahsanullah Khán. They sought him out and gave their message. It is said that Ahsanullah looked much perplexed what reply to give. He looked upon the outbreak as a passing thunder-cloud, too black to last long. His reply was: " You have been long accustomed under the English rule to regular pay. The King has no treasury. How can he pay you?" The officers replied: "We will bring the revenue of the whole Empire to your treasury." Hakim Ahsanullah then called for a return of the troops who had mutinied. The officer in charge of the King's Palace was sent for. News of the death of some of the officers killed next reached the Palace, followed by the arrival of a regiment of cavalry, who took up a position in the courtyard of the Dewán-i-Khás. Many of the men forcibly intruded into the presence of the King, who was seated in the Dewán-i-Khás. Ahsanullah sought a private audience of the King, and on his advice a camel sowar was sent off with a letter to the Lieutenant-Governor at Agra. From time to time more troops arrived. The court of the Palace became a scene of the wildest confusion, quarrellings, and disputes. With a view to introduce discipline among the troops orders were issued by Ahsanullah Khán directing the different Princes to assume command of the several regiments.

Early this morning (May 12th) I learned the occurrences at the jail. It became known to the prisoners about midday (on the 11th) that there was a great uproar in the city, and that the English had been overpowered. The prisoners received this astonishing news with loud cries, and a scene of great excitement ensued. The Jailor, Lalla Tokúr Dass, a man of great bravery and loyalty, nevertheless maintained discipline until about five o'clock in the afternoon, when the men who guarded the jail gave signs that they too had become affected with the spirit of the mutiny. They complained bitterly that by remaining at their post they were prevented from sharing in the plunder which was going on. They then began to show themselves in their true colours and to reveal the villany which actuated them. The Jailor was patient and calm, awaiting orders and aid; but, alas! there was no one to give an order, or to send succour. Helpless, he waited until the evening, when he quietly went to his own house. The citizens in Delhi applaud his conduct and behaviour. They owe him a deep debt of gratitude for not adding to the horrors of that eventful day by withholding the unrestrained action of desperate men. It is related how, when the prisoners first showed symptoms of attempting to break from the jail, a trooper having ridden up to the jail inciting the guard to open the prison gates, Tokúr Lál, taking a musket from the sentry, shot him dead. Throughout the day he restrained all by his presence.

On this morning (12th) the whole body of native officers of the regiments that had arrived yesterday, concerted together and demanded an audience of the King. It was granted; the native officers presented *nazzars* (tribute money) and described themselves as faithful soldiers awaiting his orders. Hákim Ahsanullah Khán secretly warned the King that no dependence could be placed on them, and expressed the fear that as soon as a sufficient number had been gathered together there would be a general plunder of the city. Later in the day Hákim Ahsanullah took counsel with some of the leading men of the city. He summoned for consultation Amin-u-dín Khán, Mirza Zera-u-dín Khán, Hassan Ali Khán, uncle of Jajjar. Their former connection with the Mahommedan power was appealed to, and they were desired to form an executive council for the purpose of maintaining order in the city and providing food for the soldiery. Hassan Ali absolutely refused, on the grounds of his unsuitability for any executive duty. The council broke up without any definite decision, beyond arranging for supplies of food for the soldiers to prevent their plundering. This work was entrusted to Mahbúb Ali Khán. Mahommed Mir Nawáb, son of Tafagúl Hossein, pleader of the Civil Court, was appointed Governor of the City. All trade in the city ceased entirely, for every shop that was opened was cleared of its contents. Nawáb Hamud Ali Khán was this day accused of concealing Europeans, and their persons were demanded from him. The Nawáb was then dragged to the Palace, and only released under orders from the King's Wazir; the soldiery only consenting to his release on the condition that his house should be thoroughly searched, and that he should be dealt with as they pleased, should a single European be found concealed there. Letters were despatched to the Rájas of Patiála, Jajjar, Bulubgarh, Bahadurgarh, and Ellore to march at once upon Delhi with all their forces to join the King's army, and to repel any attack on the city by the English. All this afternoon the Palace was thronged by a turbulent mob of soldiers, calling out that all the grain-shops were closed and the King's loyal servants were starving. The soldiers demanded of the King that he should pass through the city accompanied by his Army, and personally allay the fears of the citizens and order the people to resume their ordinary occupations. The King yielded, and, mounted on an elephant, passed in procession through the streets. He did personally order the shops to be reopened, and some were opened and again closed; but the shopkeepers generally were deaf to his orders. When the King returned to the Palace, he found the courtyard of the Dewán-i-Khás crowded with troopers and their horses. They assailed him with loud cries, complaining that the men of the regiment which had mutinied at Delhi had possessed themselves of the treasure from the Delhi collectorate, intending to keep it, and had refused to share it with the Meerut mutineers. The King, utterly distracted and bewildered in the conflicting counsels, ordered the Princes, who had been appointed to the command of the troops, to send every mutineer out of the city, locating regiments in separate places, and leaving only one regiment in the Palace for the defence of the city, and another on the sands in front of the Palace, between the fort and the river. The King pointed out to some of the Subahdars present that the Dewán-i-Khás had hitherto been an enclosure sacred to Royalty alone, and had never before been forcibly entered by armed men. Another regiment was ordered to hold the Ajmere Gate of the city, a fourth the Delhi Gate, a fifth the Cashmere Gate. These orders were partially carried out. From house to house the unwilling King was distracted by cries and petitions—now from the servants of Europeans who had been murdered, now from the shopkeepers whose shops had been plundered, now from the higher classes whose houses had been broken into—all looked to the King for immediate redress. Appeals were made to him to repress the plunder and rapine now common throughout the city.

The King, in a Persian *rubakari*, beautiful with flowing language, called on all the Subahdars to remember that such a state of things was most unbecoming in the reign of a Mahommedan king who was a bright light in the histories of the world, and at whose feet all other kings and monarchs waited with bended knee; and that it must be suppressed. Towards evening a number of his native regimental officers came and again represented the difficulty they experienced in getting rations. Forgetful of the lofty tone of the morning's order, and of the high-toned phraseology expressive of the King's dignity, they addressed him with such disrespectful terms as, "I say, you King! I say, you old fellow!" ("Ari,[1] Bádshah! Ari, Búddha!") "Listen," cried one, catching him by the hand. "Listen to me," said another, touching the old King's beard. Angered at their behaviour, yet unable to prevent their insolence, he found relief alone in bewailing before his servants his misfortunes and his fate. Again summoned by loud cries from outside the Palace gates, he passed a second time in procession through the city, calling on the shopkeepers to open their shops and resume trade. Throughout this eventful day he was distraught, perplexed, and cowed at finding himself in a position which made him the mere puppet of those who had formerly been only too glad humbly to obey his orders, but who now, taking advantage of the spirit of insubordination which was rife in all classes of the city in this day of ruin and riot, were not ashamed to mock and humiliate him.

May 13.—Information reached the Palace that the house of the Rajah of Kishengarh was surrounded by Sepoys, who had detected Europeans there. Hearing this, I sent my servants to see quickly if any assistance could be given,

[1] "Ari" is a slang expression used by the common people to attract attention, but a most insolent form of address to use to a monarch or any superior.

but they found the place so guarded as to be unapproachable. It appears that a party of thirty persons, Europeans and East Indians, had taken refuge in the underground apartments of the Rajah's house. For two days the refugees had remained concealed there, suffering intensely from hunger and thirst. On the third day a water-carrier passing by was asked by one of the refugees to give him a drink of water. He gave the water, but on leaving the place and meeting some Sepoys, he told them where the Europeans were concealed. The house was strongly constructed, and the refugees, who were armed, opened fire at the Sepoys who attempted to approach. Finding it impossible to get at the Europeans by force, the Sepoys opened negotiations, offering to conduct them to the King if they would leave the house. In the meantime, Syed Gholám Abbás, otherwise known as Saif-ul-Dowlah, hearing the news, at once informed the King that Mr. Davis, Mr. Bailey, and other clerks of the Agent's office, were in great danger of their lives. Gholám Abbás pointed out to the King that if he should succeed in saving their lives, that act would place him in a favourable light before the English. The King at once became interested in their fate, and inquired where they were. Orders were then issued that they were to be saved, and a messenger was sent to bring the refugees into the King's presence. The messenger selected was his eldest son, Mirza Kobash. It is said he used his best endeavours to save the refugees from the hand of the mutineers. The King had a great personal regard for Mr. Davis, who had been for years in charge of the monthly payments to the King of the pension given him by the East India Company. Mr. Davis was paid out of the King's allowances, and had been in constant communication with regard to all monetary transactions between the King and the British Agent. Alas! before

Mirza Kobash arrived at the Maharajah's house, the refugees, worn out with anxiety and want of food, yielded to the assurances that they would be taken to the King. On emerging from their place of refuge, they had seated themselves in the courtyard. A Sepoy, addressing one of the defenceless women, began to use revolting abuse. In reply to a question as to what she would give to save her life, Mr. Davis's sister retorted: "Has such a one as you the power of life and death? It is God only who can give and take life." Angered by the reply, the Sepoy raised his sword. Cowering beneath the expected blow, the lady turned to shield the infant she bore in her arms—what necessity is there to relate what then took place![1] "These tears cannot be restrained: they overflow all bounds." A few only were saved and taken to the Palace.[2]

Mirza Mai-u-dín Hassan Khán was this day appointed Kotwál and head of the Commissariat in the city, with orders to make immediate arrangements for the supplies to the soldiery. Mirza Mai-u-dín, Mirza Kizr Sultán, and Mirza Abdullah were appointed Colonels of Infantry. It was reported that a son of Mr. Joseph Skinner was detected dressed in native costume: he was seized by the ruffians and taken to the police station, where he was murdered. Orders were issued to Mai-u-dín Khán to notify in the city that whoever wished to serve the King was to present himself. Nawáb Wallidád Khán and Nawáb Hamid Ali Khán presented themselves and gave nazzars, and were ordered to be present every day at the audience to carry out commands. Information reached me that the remaining

[1] An alternative account of this massacre is given in the Appendix.

[2] In the diary of Mainodin Khán it is stated that *all* were massacred and none escaped. It is also stated that the King's messenger arrived *before* the massacre took place, and demanded that the captives should be sent to the Palace, but his orders were treated with contempt.

European ladies and gentlemen who had been concealed in the underground cellars of the Kishengarh House, and had been confined there, were taken by the mutineers and murdered in cold blood. Upwards of 200 rebel soldiers and bad characters of the city attacked the house of a canal-water Revenue officer, Narain Dáss, and plundered it. One European, an Englishman, who was found in concealment there, was murdered. To-day, orders were issued by the King to write at once to Jeypur, summoning the forces of the Rájah to his aid.

May 14.—The King, distracted and perplexed, shut himself up, refusing audience to all. Both Amin-u-dín Khán and Ja-u-dín Khán sought to see the King on pressing business, but were refused. Later on, in the course of the day, the King sent for Moulvie Suden-u-dín Khán Bahádur, and appointed him City Magistrate, to try all cases, and decide them with impartiality and justice. The Moulvie excused himself on the plea of bad health. The Treasurer of the Collectorate was next summoned, and questioned as to the cash balance in the Treasury on the 11th May. The man either could not or would not give any information. Others among the Mahommedan nobility were sent for. Orders were issued to the Rajahs of Jeypur, Jodhpur, and Bikanír personally to attend, or to send soldiers to rally round the King. Mirza Amin-u-dín Khán was ordered to proceed to Ferozepur, to arrange for a Mahommedan Administration, and to raise a force of Mewattís. Mirza asked for orders to allow him free egress and ingress to and from the city, which orders were accordingly issued. News came that the Gujars of Chundrowlí had risen in great numbers under the orders of one Damar Ram, and were plundering the country as far as Sundeir Mundai. A force was sent out under the orders of Mirza Abu Baksh to repress the rising; a Gujar village was fired. Two persons, a man and a woman, of European extraction, were found and brought in; orders were issued to detain them in safety in the fort. Much excitement was caused throughout the city by information received that a European force had marched from Meerut; the messengers who brought the information were declared to be spies sent by the English, and were ordered to be imprisoned. The officer in charge of the city reported that many European corpses were lying about. The King ordered a search to be made for the bodies of Mr. Simon Fraser (the Commissioner) and Captain Douglas, in order that if found they might be buried in the Christian burial-ground; but all other bodies were to be thrown into the river. The native officers again assembled to demand food for the troops, who could no longer be prevented from plundering. Hákim Ahsanullah Khán and Nawáb Mahabúb Ali Khán were ordered to arrange for a supply of grain at once to save the city from plunder. Two men, Kami Khán and Sarifaraz Khán, were apprehended as bad characters and confined.

May 15.—Orders were issued to appoint a police force of 100 men for the "safety" of the city. Abdul Kadir obtained an audience, to present a list of executive officers for the new Administration. Mahabúb Ali Khán gave Abdul Kadir the command of two regiments of cavalry. Gholam Khán, Agent for the Nawab of Jajjar, accompanied by Akbar Ali, a sowar, arrived, and represented that the Jajjar forces had all mutinied, and that Jajjar was engaged in reducing them to order, but that fifty sowars had been sent as an addition to the King's Army. Moulvie Ahmed Ali attended on the part of the Rájah of Bulubgarh to represent that he was employed in quelling a rising. That finished, he would attend on the King with his horses. Orders were issued to hasten his arrival. News was received that the magistrate and collector had reached Rohtak with a force of one regiment of foot and one of cavalry to save the treasure. Orders were issued to Abdul Karim Khán to raise a force of 400 infantry and 1,000 cavalry on salaries of Rs. 5 and Rs. 30 respectively. Orders were also issued to remove Abu Baksh from the command of his regiment, and no orders were to be carried out unless issued by the King. Kázi Mahommed Farzulia was appointed City Kotwál, after presenting a nazzar of 5 rupees. Abdul Hákim was appointed Naib Kázi for the administration of justice. News was received that the mutineers were intimidating the city people, and that 200 troopers, having plundered a quantity of money, had deserted and gone off to their homes, and had in turn been attacked by the Gujars and plundered. The Sepoys resented the authority of Hákim Ahsanullah Khán and Mahabúb Ali Khán, on the grounds that they were in correspondence with the English, and sending letters from the King to the English. They denied all such transactions, and swore to hold no further communication with the English. News was received that Sir John Metcalfe and Mr. Ford had been seen at Jajjar and had been denied shelter and hospitality by the Nawáb. A threatening letter had been sent to the Nawáb with orders that unless he at once joined the cause of the King he would be attacked. The Sepoys were much disheartened by the news that the Gurkhas had all elected to side with the English, and that a mixed force of Gurkhas and English was marching from Simla. The house of Girdhari Lál, son of Sukíchund, was this day surrounded. The Sepoys were bought off by a payment of sixteen rupees. The city bankers were this day called upon to provide supplies for the Sepoys. Several respectable men were seized and made to carry burdens to intimidate them and extort money. Such were their sufferings that the better class of city people offered prayers this day for the speedy advent of the English and for the defeat of the rebels. All valuable property had by this time been buried, and a private police force had been raised by the better class of citizens to protect themselves and their property from plunder and violence.

May 16.—The Sepoys assembled early this morning before the Palace, threatening the King and his officers, accusing them of saving the lives of European ladies and gentlemen and concealing them in the Fort, and through them communicating with the Europeans at Meerut. The following are the names of the King's officers appointed to assist in the administration of affairs: Mufti Usuf Ali Khán, Mir Adul Bahádur, Captain Ali Dildar Khán, Mahommed Hyder Hossein Khán, Syed Shuruf Ali Khán Fozdár, Nizarul Khán Bahádur.

I learned to-day that nearly forty Europeans were concealed in the King's Palace. The Sepoys went to the Palace in great anger, as they said they had seized a messenger with a letter cursing the mutineers. The Sepoys threatened to kill Ahsanullah Khán and Nawáb Mahabúb Ali Khán, and also threatened to take away Zínat Mehal Begum Sahiba and keep her as a hostage for the king's loyalty. There was a great uproar in the Palace, the Sepoys on the one hand, and the King's household on the other, contending with violent language and harsh vociferations. To appease the mutineers, Mahabúb Ali Khán took an oath that he was not the author of that letter, nor had it been written with his knowledge. (It was on this date that the Europeans in the Palace were butchered in a manner that defies description. May God preserve them in the next world! All good men, when they think of that day, exclaim, "May God, who is our Protector, Preserver, and Guardian from all fear, protect us through this life and in the life to come!") The King and his assembled councillors stood like dumb puppets. The King ordered the Sepoys to separate themselves into two parties, Mahommedans and Hindus, and he appealed to each to consult their religious advisers to see if there were any authority for the slaughter of helpless men, women, and children. But "Khúni janini kiske súnti hai?"—"Whose word will a frenzied murderer obey?" Let it suffice to pass over that awful day in silence. In the afternoon a man was apprehended in the garb of a cavalry trooper, who had been taken whilst plundering. He was brought before the King, who ordered the property he had stolen to be taken from him, and that he should be released with a warning. Daily it was coming to pass that the dead by means of the living were bringing sorrow on the King, for the mutineers would neither leave the city nor protect it. They remained only for plunder and violence. This day the King gave audience to Moulvie Mahommed Bakr and Moulvie Abdul Kádir, who had greatly commended themselves for the intelligence and bravery with which they had performed their respective duties. The latter reported that he was making such arrangements that the Sepoys would willingly leave the city. The King gave a *khillat* to Moulvie Mahommed Bakr, and with great pomp sent Moulvie Abdul Kádir, seated in a royal *howdah*, to his house. A body of mutineers this day visited the house of Munshi Mohun, with the intention of killing him, but he was saved by Hazrut Nizam-u-dín, the son of a holy and influential man, who interceded for him as being a Mahommedan. Many of the neighbours also bore testimony to his being a Mahommedan and not a Christian. The shopkeepers at the Lahore Gate complained this day to the King that Kashi Nalei Thanadár was troubling them to give him a bribe of 1,000 rupees. The King ordered the Thanadár to be sent to jail. The King this day ordered a special inquiry to be made into the fate of Sir John Metcalfe. Under his directions the bodies of the murdered were carefully examined to see if his body were among the dead. Friends too, anxious for his safety, inquired in vain for him. Anxious to learn the fate of the civil officers, I had early deputed Girdhari Misser and Heera Sing, two trustworthy Brahmins, to go out and ascertain all that had happened. I charged them specially to bring me news of Sir John; but they could learn nothing. It was reported later in the day to the King that Sir John Metcalfe had not been identified among the killed.

May 17.—Some troopers to-day brought in some supplies which they had plundered from Shahdara. News received by the King that Sir John Metcalfe was still at Jajjar, claiming protection from the Nawáb. Mr. Hatharlet, who was under the Nawáb's protection, had also asked permission to be allowed to go to Kalera for safety. The Nawáb allowed him to depart. The mutineers this day elected Abu Bakr as their King in place of the old King, whom they declared to be too old and infirm. Hakimulla had an audience and represented that the mutineers were a treacherous, bloodthirsty class, on whom no dependence could be placed. The King summoned many of the Sepoys to his presence and spoke to them very severely. The Vakíl of Rawalyi presented a bottle of Kewara water from Jeypur, which was accepted. A trooper arrived and reported that as several lakhs of treasure were coming in from Gurjawan to Delhi under charge of one company of foot and several cavalry, it had been attacked by a body of Mewattís, and he had left them, still fighting, to ask for aid. Moulvie Bakr ordered two companies of foot and one troop of cavalry to rescue the treasure.

May 18.—The following Princes were appointed to the chief command of the mutineers: (1) Mirza Mogul; (2) Mirza Kizr Sultán; (3) Mirza Abu Bakr; (4) Mirza Abdullah. A message arrived from the Ráni of Ujjain; she was told in reply that it was optional with her to attend the King's Durbár. Two companies of sappers and miners arrived at the bank of the Jumna, and there halted. Orders were given to send sweetmeats to welcome them. Ali Khán received orders to recruit for the King's Army, but he excused himself on the plea of ignorance of his duties. Two sowars, sent with dispatches, returned stating that they had been attacked by the Gujars, who had taken their horses and torn the dispatches in pieces. A camel sowar sent on a like errand, returned having been waylaid and maltreated.

The Subahdar in command of the sappers and miners presented himself at the audience and complained that his English officer at Meerut had ordered his men to remain there; on their refusing to do so they had been fired at, and upwards of 200 of their number had been shot down. He reported that the survivors had arrived under his command. They were ordered to take up their quarters in the Selimgarh Fort. Several bankers went to Mahabúb Ali Khán and reported their inability to provide funds for the troops, as they were beggared. They were warned that unless they found funds for the use of the soldiers, these latter would without doubt plunder and take the money by force.

May 19.—The King held an audience. Moulvie Jajjar Ali Thanadar attended and presented a sicca of gold mohurs as tribute money. On the coins was inscribed the following: "Sicca zad bar simú zar dar Hind, Sháh wa dín panáh Zil-i-subháni Suráj-u-dín bahádur Bádshah," and on the reverse: "Sicca Sáhibi Koráni zad ba táyíd. Allah Sáya i yazdán

Suráj-u-dín bahádur Bádshah."[1] The King presented Mirza Jawan Bakht with a *khillat* and appointed him his minister. The King gave an audience to the native officers of the mutineers, who related to him the particulars of the fight between the English and the Sepoys at Meerut, and stated that the force at Allahabad had turned away from the English. In consequence of this the Lieutenant-Governor had ordered the gates of the fort at Allahabad to be closed, and no one was allowed to pass without permission. Several thousand rupees of the Gurgaon treasure was reported to have been received from the Mewattís and was on its way to Delhi. The King was much pleased, and ordered the money to be put into his private treasury. Information received that the Maharajah of Patiála had joined the English with his army, and that the mutineer Sepoys coming from Umballa had been attacked by the Patiála troops, their weapons taken from them and the men despoiled. The mutineers, in revenge for this, attacked the house of Kumar Újít Sing, brother of the Maharajah of Patiála, and seized him. Being unable to walk, he was carried by his servants to the King's Palace. The King, hearing of his arrival, went out to meet him, and was presented with a nazzar of gold mohurs. The King received him with great courtesy and kindness, and remonstrated with the Sepoys, pointing out that the Kumar was on bad terms with his brother, so that in punishing him they would in no way be punishing Patiála. The King set apart quarters for the Kumar. A petition was received from Nawáb Akbar Ali Khán, of Patudiwalah, excusing his absence. He was ordered to appear as early as possible. Two European men, one child,

[1] Translation.—"Silver and gold coin struck by the King of India, the protector of religion. The sovereign Suráj-u-dín the brave." Reverse: "Coins struck by the Lord of the Faith with the help of God. The shadow of God, the sovereign Suráj-u-dín, the brave."

and three ladies were this day found concealed in the house of a tailor. They were seized by the mutineers, and the house was destroyed. This day the standard of the Holy War was raised by the Mahommedans in the Jumma Masjid. The people of Dharampur and the low characters of the city were concerned in this act. The King was angry and remonstrated, because such a display of fanaticism would only tend to exasperate the Hindus.

May 20.—Information received that an English force was approaching. On hearing this news the cavalry and infantry were dismayed; men began to run about taking advice from one another. In a short time it was rumoured that this information was bare of the garment of truthfulness. Scouts who had been sent out returned stark naked, having been plundered by the Gujars and stripped even of their clothing. Moulvie Mahommed Said demanded an audience, and represented to the King that the standard of Holy War had been erected for the purpose of inflaming the minds of the Mahommedans against the Hindus. The King answered that such a *jehád* was quite impossible, and such an idea an act of extreme folly, for the majority of the Purbeah soldiers were Hindus. Moreover, such an act would create internecine war, and the result would be deplorable. It was fitting that sympathy should exist among all classes. It was pointed out that the Hindus were leaning towards an alliance with the English and had no sympathy with the Mahommedans, and were already holding themselves apart. A deputation of Hindu officers arrived to complain of the war against Hindus being preached. The King replied: "The Holy War is against the English; I have forbidden it against the Hindus." The King gave Mirza Amin-u-dín Ahmed Khán and Hossein Ali Khán a dact with steel point. Certain men attempted this day to steal a brass fieldpiece:

they were caught and ordered to be blown away from a gun. At three o'clock Hákim Ahsanullah Khán represented that the soldiers were looting in the city, and requested that they should be expelled. To get rid of them, orders were this day issued to Mirza Mogul to proceed with a strong force towards Meerut to attack any English force assembled there. Two Europeans were this day discovered and murdered by the mutineers. Mahbúb Ali Khán reported that a European lady had been found and was in the hands of the mutineers, who had intended to kill her, but that he had prevented this under the authority of the Mahommedan law. The King approved of what he had done. It became known that the dispatch of troops to Meerut to fight the English was a device of Hákim Ahsanullah Khán to rid the city of the mutineers and soldiers, who were beyond all discipline.

May 21.—Under great pressure from the King, the newly appointed officers and city bankers raised one lakh of rupees for the payment of the troops. The Punjábis and merchants, who were Mahommedans and not permitted to take interest, could not be called upon to supply funds. Three sowars went into the city: a Sepoy asked one of them for his sword; words ensued, and the sowars attacked and killed the man. His comrades went to the King, who ordered the sowar to be arrested. He was tied to a gun to be blown away, but was pardoned. News was received that the Maharájah of Patiála had contrived to gain over to his cause two regiments of Purbeahs, who had also promised to extinguish the fire of mutiny amongst their relatives serving in the regiments which had mutinied at Meerut. News received that both Jeypur and Patiála were taking precautions to prevent the mutineers from remaining in their territories. Certain sowars and Telingas were this day reported as having been killed at Gurgaon. The King ordered Gholám Nabbi Khán, Agent to the Rajah of Jajjar, to proceed at once, and bring his master to Delhi. The Palace was this day crowded by a howling mob of men demanding pay. Representations were made to the King that to-morrow being the 22nd May, the last day of the Ramzán, he should issue orders for a *jehád* against the Hindus. The King, together with the members of the Royal Council, replied very angrily that the greater part of the mutineers were Hindus and well armed, and that they would easily destroy all the *jehádls*. Information was received that Rajah Nahen Sing of Bulubgarh had made himself master of the country as far as Palwab. All the Europeans had fled, and Muha Kivani had arrived at Bulubgarh. The King issued a proclamation by beat of drum that Hindus and Mahommedans must not quarrel. The Hindus had closed all their houses for fear of their lives. Large bodies of mutineers from Jullundur arrived this day, telling of their bravery, and how they had killed their officers ; but this information was not believed, the statements made by different men differing in many respects. The King went out in state to say his prayers publicly, accompanied by Mirza Mogul Bahádur and Mirza Abu Bakr, who were in attendance. The house of Sobha Chand Kaest was this day plundered on the charge that he was in league with the English and supplying them with news. It was reported to the King that the mutineers had possessed themselves of much money and were buying gold mohurs at 32 rupees apiece, and that many mutineers who had left the city with money had been plundered of everything and had returned to the city with only their lives. At the evening parade 200 men were found missing. The demand for gold increasing, many of the soldiers were duped by the city Budmashes, who, leading them to one of the Mohallas, invited them to sit down while they brought them the coveted gold mohurs. Then taking the money to buy the gold, they decamped by another way and left the soldiers to deplore their loss. The soldiers revenged themselves upon the innocent people of the Mohalla. About three o'clock this day Abdul Samad Khán, the father-in-law of the Nawáb of Jajjar, arrived with a following of 100 sowars. A body of troops was sent to Rohtak to bring in treasure.

May 23.—Seeing the atrocities the mutineers were committing in the city, Hákim Ahsanullah Khán induced the King to issue an order commanding the troops to leave the city, on the ground that they would only plunder and cause blood to be shed. The Jullundur troops, who had brought treasure with them, divided some of the money this day amongst themselves, and paid the balance of 80,000 rupees into the Imperial Treasury. Mirza Abu Baksh went to the Kotwáli and decided on the fate of the Jews and Christians in confinement. Imperial orders were issued that, in accordance with the advice of one Runjít, a jeweller, the old coins should be withdrawn from circulation, and a new coinage introduced. The soldiers plundered the house of Kanheyal Lál, of Hyderabad, a severe fight having first taken place between the retainers of Kanheyal and the mutineers. Eventually, Mirza Kizr Sultán was induced by the offer of a bribe to go to his assistance, and thereby saved his life. One Kami Khán, a notorious Budmásh, was ordered to be blown from a gun this day, but he, too, saved his life by a bribe. Nawáb Mir Ahmed Ali Khán, under instructions from the King, issued orders to seize all the bankers and wealthy men of the city—particularly those favourable to the English—and to extort money from them for the pay of the mutineers. Mirza Mahommed Ali Bey was appointed tehsildar of the Mehrowli. Jewan Lál's garden and house were this day plundered by the soldiers, of property to the value of 2,000 rupees, on suspicion of his being in communication with the English.

May 24.—Some flatterers attended the King's audience to-day and informed him that all the English had fled the country, and that there were no English at Meerut except a few sick persons. Orders were again issued to General Abdul Samad to cause the attendance of the Nawáb of Jajjar. Most of the Princes attended the audience, and presented nazzars to the King. In the evening, on the appearance of the new moon, this being the 29th of Ramzán, salutes were fired throughout the city. Some consternation was caused by the arrival of news that Sir John Metcalfe had escaped alive and had left Jajjar for Hansi Hirsar.

May 25.—The King left the Palace and attended service at the Jumma Masjid, this being the festival of the Íd. The Princes also attended. At the time of prayer a camel sowar arrived from the Rájah of Bulubgarh, to report that he had seen an English force advancing on the city. Great excitement prevailed, both the soldiery and the King's advisers going here and there, all uncertain what plan to follow, whether or not to leave the city. The native cavalry immediately began to saddle their horses, being chaffed by the city Budmáshes because their hands trembled in their haste to make ready. In the absence of the English, the mutineers were as lions, but on hearing of their approach, they sought places of refuge like rats in the presence of a cat. For about an hour there was great excitement in the city. Later on it was reported that the rumour of an English advance was false, and that the camel sowar had mistaken an Id procession for the advance-guard of an English army. When the excitement had subsided, the principal men of the city waited on the King, as was customary on the festival of the Íd. News reached the Palace that there had been a fight between the troops of the Rájah of Jajjur and some of the mutineers at Rohtak, in which the mutineers had been victorious and were returning with some of the treasure they had captured.

May 26.—A discovery was made that somebody had filled the guns on the Islamgarh bastion with "*kankar*" and stones. Suspicion fell upon Hákim Ahsanullah Khán, and he was charged before the King of collusion with the English. The mutineers threatened to kill the Hákim, together with Mahbúb Ali Khán. Swords were drawn. The two accused men swore that they were innocent, and asked how it was possible that they could have done this whilst the guns were guarded by sentries. The King shielded the accused and appeased the anger of the soldiery. About three o'clock in the afternoon, one of the Subahdars was suspected, arrested, and placed under guard. Several Gujars were apprehended for stealing gunpowder from the Magazine. Upwards of a lakh of rupees was brought in from the Government Treasury at Rohtak.

May 27.—Two regiments of Punjábis demanded an audience of the King to complain that the Sáhibs at Ferozepur had shot several men of the regiments to which they belonged, and requested that the King should take care that they should not be treated like their brethren at Ferozepur. They demanded guarantees from the King that he would protect them, otherwise they asked for permission to disband themselves. The King assured them that he was able and willing to protect them. Information was brought by the troops returning from Rohtak that the magistrate and collector had escaped by some means or other. This information excited much interest. It was discovered to-day that the guns on the bastions had been spiked, while others had been filled with stones, gravel, and ends of string. Great excitement prevailed, as it was clear that the English had some powerful friends in the city. About 200 armed men went to the Masjid and began to abuse the servants of the King, charging them with tampering with the guns. The King's friends retorted, denying the accusation and asking what kind of soldiers they were to allow such a thing to be done with guns under their charge. For two hours an uproar prevailed, before order could be restored. Abu Bakr was accused of disloyalty by Misr Mahommed Lál and charged with tampering with the guns. About three o'clock that afternoon it was reported that a Havildar was suspected of having filled the guns with gravel and iron nails. He was apprehended, tied to one of the guns, and there left. A body of Gujars attempted to carry off gunpowder and ammunition from one of the magazines, and were caught red-handed.

May 28.—At the audience it was stated to the King that the Gujars had arrived at Panipat. A statement of the military police raised for the protection of the city was handed to the King. The treasure, Rs. 175,000, brought from the Rohtak Treasury, was examined. Many of the bags were found to contain pice. The mutineers openly accused Hákim Ahsanullah Khán of intriguing with the English, and a guard was placed over him. He was told that he would no longer be permitted to hold any intercourse with the King, except in the presence of the guard. A guard was also placed at the house of Nawab Mahbúb Ali Khán. All night there was an uproar, and constant panics. The following men, Hákim Ahsanullah Khán and Mahbúb Ali Khán, were in attendance on the King all night. Order was issued to-day to pay the mutineers: this was done at the request of Mahbúb Ali Khán: deductions were ordered to be made on account of the sums already paid to them; nine for sowars and seven for infantry was fixed. A great uproar ensued. The cavalry demanded Rs. 30 for their pay, and no deduction for charges paid. The Subahdars of the Delhi Regiment accepted Rs. 7 as their pay. A violent, abusive altercation followed between the Meerut cavalry and the mutineers of the Delhi regiments. The Meerut sowars accused the Delhi regiments of having enriched themselves by plunder, whereas the Meerut men had by their good behaviour reaped nothing by plunder and robbery. They refused to receive Rs. 9. The foot Sepoys replied that the Meerut men were rebellious and utterly bad. Not only had they been the first to mutiny and kill their officers, whose salt they had eaten—and led others to do likewise—but they were desirous to quarrel and fight with their own countrymen. The Delhi Sepoys said they repented of their great fault—that they had not done their duty and blown them from their guns when they first reached Delhi. Fierce passions were so raised, that at one time there was every probability of a serious encounter. The King's servants rushed in between the parties, and with great efforts quieted both sides, Mahbúb Ali Khán promising the cavalry Rs. 20 pay per mensem. About 200 men arrived from Lahore and Ferozepur to join the mutineers. They came unarmed and many wounded. They were full of complaints that they had been attacked by the Maharájah of Patiála when they were sitting unarmed and unclothed on the ground, and had fled. They stated that others were in a worse plight than they were. They were slowly marching to Delhi also. A native contingent of 200 men from Gwalior arrived this day and asked to be enlisted. They boasted that they also had killed their officers. As they arrived with their uniform and accoutrements in good order, a story was spread that these men were an advance-guard of the British Army, sent to side deceitfully with the mutineers until the English should arrive, when they would join in attacking the mutineers inside the city. It was reported to the King that a number of Europeans were concealed in Mogulpura, one of the city wards. A body of soldiers was asked to find out and destroy them. The King ordered a few men to be sent, with orders to bring the Europeans, if found, to the Palace. Orders were issued accordingly. The Sepoys took the opportunity to plunder. About three o'clock a daily statement of the mutineer force was presented to the King. The following is the statement:—

Cavalry from Meerut;
Infantry from Meerut;
200 Volunteer Infantry;
200 Infantry from Ferozepur;
200 Umballa Regiment of Purbeahs;
240 Customs Pyádahs;
200 Gwalior Contingent;
100 Mutineers from Mutineer Regiments, not classified;
200 Mutineer Delhi Regiments.

Complaints were made to the King that some one was keeping up a correspondence with the English from inside the city. A request was made that the man should be found. It was also represented to the King that the Europeans at Meerut were hemmed in on all sides, unable to move, uncertain how to act, and were occupied in hanging such of the mutineers as fell into their power. Koer Wazir Ali Khán was reported to be daily in the habit of visiting the entrenchments. Report was received that a contingent from Gwalior and Akbarabád was approaching the city, also that certain

European troops had reached Karnaul. The General commanding the mutineer Sepoys stated that he had arranged to collect all his forces to attack the English the next day.

May 29.—Hákim Ahsanullah Khán and Mahabúb Ali Khán were assaulted to-day by native officers of the mutineer force, in consequence of the discovery of powder and shot in the Palace Granary, collected there, it was said, for the purpose of dispatch to the English. For a long time the mutineers continued violent; they contended that the King's Begum had arranged this in collusion with Mahommed Sadur Ali Khán. They were, however, subsequently appeased. A European was brought in to-day, having been found in Kudshiah Bagh. He was first of all declared to be John Lawrence. His captors said he had been identified by an old wound in his back. On his being stripped no wound was found on his person. From him, too, did these bloodthirsty wretches draw the clothing of life. He was dressed in the garb of a Hindu fortune-teller; he carried in his hand an almanack. It was suspected he was a spy. Inquiry was instituted by whose orders ammunition and powder, which had been found in carts containing grain, had been despatched the day previously. Suspicion fell on Abu Bakr. A nazzar of four gold mohurs was received from Bahádur Yung Khán, of Bahádurgarh. Two regiments of infantry and 200 cavalry encamped at Selimpur on their way to Meerut.

May 30.—The troops that had gone as far as Selimpur created a disturbance, and returned on the pretence that no arrangements had been made for *russad* (provisions) for them. Information also received that a small force of Europeans was encamped on the banks of the Hindun, intending to guard the bridge. A mounted scout, wounded by the Europeans, made his way into the city with this information, but he has since died. Troops were ordered out to engage the Europeans. At three o'clock to-day, at the Durbar, Mir Hassan Ali, Vakíl of the Maharájah of Patiála, was accused of being in correspondence with the English, and was taken under an armed guard with drawn swords to the Kotwáli. In revenge for the trouble caused by the Maharájah of Patiála to the mutineers, the tables were turned upon his agent. Towards evening news was received that there had been a fight with the English at the Hindun. It transpired that the artillery of the mutineers had been taken, and the gunners had fled. The firing of the English was so good that many of the rebels, covered with dust, had gone to hell; many, like birds borne on the wing, had fled back to the city. Report said that there had been a fight at close quarters with swords, in which the English were victorious. Many wounded men with sword and gun-shot wounds had been brought into the city in *doolies* (covered stretchers) during the night. The Delhi Hindus, who had suffered much at the hands of the mutineers since their arrival in the city, expressed their joy that these wicked men, like decapitated fowls, with bloody wounds, had now themselves been tossed hither and thither, and had lost all their manhood and bravery. The English were again coming in place of these men. The King ordered reserves to be sent to the assistance of the mutineers. Mirza Abu Bakr, who had commanded, arrived and boasted to the King of his bravery in the fight; the bystanders, however, understood that he gave himself unfounded praise. The King was much perplexed; all night he sat, surrounded by his advisers and those that adorned his court, taking counsel, and discussing the turn that affairs had taken.

May 31.—Bodies of cavalry arrived from the Hindun, and impressed every man, of every class, high and low, on whom they could lay hands, for transport service. The city was in great uproar. Many rose to resist such oppression by force of arms. Two or three European Christians or Jews were found to-day, taken to the Kotwáli, and killed in the customary manner. The Subahdars of the infantry came to the King and represented that a great many Mahommedans had fallen in yesterday's engagement, claiming that they had fallen in *jehád* (war for religion). Inquiries were made about the behaviour of the Sepoys. It was admitted, that as soon as the rebels received a volley from the English, they lost heart, and began to return to the city. Some one in attendance stated that three hundred English, and a native regiment from Umballa, had reached Nurella. A force of two thousand men was reported as being at Moal on their way to join the rebels. Some one also stated that this force had thirteen European artillerymen as prisoners with them, as the Sepoys had taken their guns. It was reported to the King that several wounded men had come in from the Hindun river, who were boasting of their capture. Later on it was reported that the English had encamped on this side of the Hindun river, and the Sepoys, unable to resist them, had retired into the city. It is said that between five hundred and one thousand Sepoys, throwing away their uniform, had left the city for their homes in the garb of fakirs (hermits). Very few artillerymen were left to work the guns on the bastions. The Sepoys set fire to-day to a village called Kukagadi, through which they passed, and destroyed it. The European force is to-day comfortably encamped. The rebels are reported as short of drinking water. The King is drawing on the Commissariat. The Sepoys returned to the city, hungry, thirsty, and vexed. It is reported that troops from Hansi and Karnaul are marching to the English camp.

June 1.—Orders issued to clear up the quarters at Jhumakpore, and turn out the Gujar (robber tribes) and Mewattís (predatory troops of cavalry), who had taken up their abode there, and to make room for Luchmun Sing, the Vakíl of the Maharájah of Jeypur. A quantity of sugar was also sent there for the use of the troops. A dispute followed. Certain Mahommedan soldiers had touched the dishes. In revenge the Hindu soldiers plundered the sweetmeat shops. This day Mir Chokali, the Vakíl of the Maharájah of Patiála, was roughly handled, and brought before the King; he was charged with being a correspondent of the English. The King's Vakíl told the soldiers they might dispose of the Vakíl as they pleased. A letter received from the Rajah of Bulubgarh, saying that he had imprisoned eleven soldiers found deserting to their homes, with gold mohurs to the value of 2,000 rupees. The orders for imprisonment were confirmed. A petition received from the prisoners, saying that five of their number had been plundered by Gujars at Kishen Dáss's tank, and one had been killed. They asked for justice. News reached the Palace from Bareilly that the English had been murdered at Meerut. Great complaints of the difficulty of getting provisions into the city, owing to the shops being closed: under the King's orders soldiers were stationed in the bazaar to keep the shops open. News came from Patiála that the two native regiments sent to assist the English had joined the mutineers, and had had a fight with the English. It was reported that the whole of the Patiála force was hostile to the English. The soldiers openly remonstrated with the Maharájah for sympathizing with the English, when the natives were fighting in defence of their religion. They reminded him that he had gained nothing by his behaviour during the Punjáb war, and his conduct had even been questioned by the English.

The King issued a proclamation that he would in future receive no more petitions in person. They must be sent to

Mahabúb Ali Khán and Nawáb Hákim Ahsanullah Khán. Orders were issued for the attendance of Girwar Sing and Girdhari Lál, bankers, who were directed to pay three lakhs of rupees to the King's treasury, under pain of punishment and the forfeiture of all their property. The bankers offered two lakhs and some thousands to buy off forfeiture of property. Fifty boatloads of salt and sugar, on their way from Agra, were reported as having been sunk in the river. News reached of the junction of four batteries of artillery (horse) from Kasauli and Umballa with the English troops at Karnaul. News came that the English had formally called upon Patiála to join his forces with theirs, and that he had agreed to do so, on condition of a remission of six *annas* in the rupee, i.e. three-eighths of his annual tribute. News came that the Patiála troops, with two English regiments, had reached Rohtak. Orders issued to the shopkeepers, that each man should keep a supply of *attah* (coarse flour), of *dal* (a kind of pea), twenty *seers* (measures), and salt, in his shop. Under a second order these supplies were to be sent to the Kotwáli. The King sent for Mirza Mogul Beg, Mirza Abu Bakr, and Mirza Abdullah, and expressed his anger at their sympathy with the Sepoys, warning them that one day they would be hanged, as soon as the English entered the city. "My fate," he said, "may be thus expressed :—

> " Kafan pahankar zindagi ki aiyyám,
> Kisi bág mén goozrán doonga."

(" For the rest of my life I shall live in the seclusion of some garden,
Clothed in my burial-sheet.")

The mutineers learned through their spies that the forces of the Rajah of Nabha and other chiefs had joined the English at Meerut. An advance was expected, and heavy guns were taken out of the Magazine and mounted on the walls, and their range tried with ball ammunition. At the sound of firing every shop was closed. The *gomashta* (business agent) of Seth Lachmi Chand (a famous banker of Muttra) reported at the Palace that the late Kotwál Sharaful Hak of the city had reached Agra, and had had an interview with the Lieutenant-Governor, and had given him a statement of what had occurred, of the murder of the Europeans, and other events. He had been assured by the Lieutenant-Governor that the English would speedily punish these evil-doers. The *gomashta* further reported that the Government had asked Seth Lachmi Chand for a loan of twenty-five lakhs of rupees for the current expenses of the war.

June 3.—All the nobles of the city attended the King's Levée. It was reported that nine regiments of British infantry, three regiments of cavalry, with field batteries and siege train, had arrived at Alipur. The mutineer chiefs declared their ability to defend the city. The King inquired at what points it was proposed to oppose the English. The places stated were at Dhiraj Ke Pahári Kenghur, Purtosa, near the garden of Mahaldar; also at Selimpur. The forces to be collected at each spot were to be specified, and an early attack on the city was anticipated. The conduct of two regiments at Lahore was discussed; they had secretly expressed their intention of joining the mutineers, but had been disarmed by Sir John Lawrence. It was reported that the Chief Commissioner of the Punjáb had visited the Maharájah of Patiála, and had returned to Lahore. In the Punjáb, it was stated, there was a feeling of peace and security, and little sympathy with the mutiny. The King issued orders that no one was to take or remove weapons out of the Magazine without orders from Mirza Amin-u-dín Khán. Certain Moguls presented themselves, and asked permission to raise the Flag of Jehád in order to arouse the inhabitants to oppose the English. The same evening all the remaining bungalows were destroyed and fired. Gazi-u-dín Nukur, the zemindár of Poonah, and Sátgáon issued notification that no supplies were to be given to the English; every straggler from the English Army was to be murdered, if caught; the village obeying these instructions to be held hereafter rent free. Other zemindárs took similar action, showing their hatred of the English and sympathy with the King. News received from Ferozepúr that the English had driven three native regiments out of the city.

June 4.—A meeting of the bankers was held under the orders of the King, and one lakh of rupees was subscribed, and a promise given of a second lakh, payable in four days. The King received information that the bridge over the Canal had been broken down, and a battery erected there. Amin-u-dín Khán returned from his walk. A *palki*-bearer returned from Hissár, and reported that five companies stationed there had mutinied, and three hundred Mewattís had joined them. They had murdered the collector, and after plundering the treasury were on their way to Delhi. Later on in the day this news was confirmed by two sowars; further, that the mutineers had reached Bouli Serái with the treasure. The King ordered a cavalry escort to be sent out immediately to bring in the treasure, which arrived the same evening. The mutineers were ordered to camp near the Jail. A Chobdár arrived from Muttra, and reported that one regiment had mutinied at that station, and was in a disordered condition, but was marching on to the city to join the mutineers. Six thousand rupees were paid out of the Treasury by Nawáb Mahabúb Ali Khán, as pay for the mutineers. The Agent for Rawulji presented the King with a basket of Jeypúr *keonas* (choice fruit), which was graciously accepted. A sowar arrived to report that a company of infantry, bringing treasure from Gúrgaon, had been attacked by Mewattís. Orders were issued to Moulvie Mahommed Bakr to proceed at once to rescue the treasure with two companies of infantry and one of cavalry.

June 5.—Provisions ordered to be sent to the Jail for the mutineers from Hissár. A guard was ordered to be placed over the house of Makhan Lál. A letter was ordered to be written to the Nawáb of Jajjar to come at once with all the troops he could gather and convey the King, in the garments of a Fakir, to the Kútub. A Brahmin from Delapur came and reported that when the Sepoys abandoned their guns, the Gújars carried off the artillery bullocks, and that the English had in their turn taken the bullocks from them, and had employed them in dragging the guns to Meerut. A Havildar deserted from the English force encamped at Alipúr. He wore a gold necklace round his neck; he addressed the mutineers, advising them to submit to the English. He was ill-treated, plundered of his ornaments, taken to the Lahore Gate, and there killed. It was reported that Lakú Sing, Thanadár of Alipúr, was providing *rassad* (supplies) for the English; his two brothers were seized in their house in Kuria Mohalla. They pleaded innocence, and said that they had long since separated from their brother, and had no connection with him. On the evidence of the neighbours the brothers were released.

June 6.—It was reported to the King that the salaries of all the servants had been paid. The King was pleased. A carter reported that the forces of the Maharájah of Patiála and of the Rájah of Jhínd, and the English, were to be seen between Umbálla and Delhi; also that heavy artillery was seen on the road drawn by elephants. The mutineers represented to the King that it was rumoured throughout the city that the English would enter the city that night, and requested orders that the city walls might be lined with soldiery. The King issued the necessary orders. Hakim Ahsanúllah Khán was ordered to serve out rations. One hundred *maunds* of *attah* and *dál* were taken from Dwalli, Baniyah. A letter was received from Lahore to the address of Gissarám and Tára Chand, intimating that all was peace and quiet there. The shopkeepers at the Delhi Gate of the city were turned out of their shops, which were taken possession of by the mutineers as barracks. The city Kotwál was ordered to have ample provisions ready. The officers in command of the mutineers reported to the King that twenty-four guns had been sent to the front to oppose the English advance. Reports were received that treasure was on its way from Hánsi, and that a force of three regiments, with some thousand irregular troops, comprised of Mewattís, were on the road to stop the English. Rumour had it that the English had taken three lakhs of rupees from the bankers at Paniput and Karnaul. A story was spread at Patiála, Umbálla, and Kaithal, that the mutineers were on their way to attack and plunder these places. All the approaches to the city, and the bridges, were destroyed by the mutineers.

June 7.—About 400 Moguls presented themselves before the King, and stated that they had raised the Flag of Jehád and were going to fight the English. They then went off in the direction of the artillery lines. About 450 mutineers arrived from Lucknow. The officers of two regiments of infantry and one of cavalry, which were stationed at Lucknow, presented themselves, and expressed their sympathy with His Majesty's cause. It was reported that they were marching on Delhi, having heard of the King's victorious reputation, and after having plundered and destroyed all the bazaar, magazine, and treasury. Seventy sowars arrived from Alipúr, and reported that they had defeated the English force, and pursued it for six miles. Orders were issued through the police that each sweetmeat-seller was instantly to prepare twelve rupees' worth of sweetmeats,[1] to be sent out to the victorious troops, to reward them for their bravery. A report was received that the English had attempted to destroy a native regiment at Agra, in consequence of which the Sepoys had mutinied, and, after killing all Europeans, were making their way to Delhi. News was received of villages burned by the English, and of the execution of four zemindárs, who were very popular, for insulting conduct to an English lady. News received that sixteen carts of provision for the English forces had been seized by the Gújars. The carts were taken to the King, and were plundered by city Musalmáns under the King's orders.

June 8.—Kazí Faiz-ullah Khán was ordered to collect all the bullocks, for the purpose of taking supplies to the troops. A sowar arrived, and reported that fifty Sepoys had been killed that day in a skirmish with the English. Forty camels were stolen from the English lines, and brought into the city this day. Dispatches came from Jajjar, intimating that a regiment at Jajjar had mutinied, and murdered Sawul Sing, and were intending to kill the Nawáb, who had concealed himself. The report was received of the murder of Mr. Mutton by mutineers from Bulubgarh. A statement came from the Kotwál of the city intimating that troops had started from the city. A letter was received from Lahore stating that a fight had taken place between the

[1] The giving of sweetmeats as a reward for services, or as a solace, or as a gift, is common throughout India. Even condemned criminals are allowed a feast of sweetmeats on the morning of their execution.

mutineers and the English, and that Máharájah Goláb Sing, of Cashmere, and his two sons, had arrived at Lahore, and joined the English. A newspaper from Peshawur was received which stated that Sardár Dost Mahommed Khán had returned to Cabul, and had placed one fort in a state of defence, in case of attack from the Persians. News received that the Maharájah of Patiála had undertaken the administration of the whole country from Umbálla to Karnaul. Fifty Sepoys went to the house of Pia Mull Maswarí, and charged him with supplying the English with supplies, threatening his life. They seized his son, and brought him before the King.

June 9.—A sowar arrived from Badli Sarái, to inform the King that the mutineers would engage the English that day at midday, and to tell the King that the English had sent spies into the camp of the mutineers in the disguise of the 4th Native Cavalry, who were acting as the King's body-guard. A fight had ensued, and the English had taken possession of the camp of the mutineers. The mutineers this day retired into the city, abandoning the country-side to the English. The mutineers reported a loss this day of 400 men. The English advanced as far as Mubárak Bágh, on the road to Sowári Mandái. Heavy firing continued all day till four p.m. Seventeen guns fell into the hands of the English during the day. Chia Mull presented himself before the King, and petitioned for the release of the son of Pia Mull, on the ground that his father had daily supplied rations to the mutineers, and had not in any way befriended the English. The bastions were fully manned, and the troops ready at their stations. The city people mounted on to the roofs of their houses, and watched with great fear the distant firing. Only Mahommedans were killed in this fight, and no Hindus. Ammunition and supplies were constantly despatched in the direction of the battlefield. The city people poured volleys of abuse upon the mutineers, who were seen returning to the city, accusing them of cowardice; while the troops at the city gates abused the native cavalry, which returned early in the day and took refuge in the city. Mirza Mogul issued orders to the troops to be on the alert. Owing to the result of the fight to-day, the soldiers seemed to lose all heart, although Mirza Mogul, in his general orders to the troops, stated that, as a castle in the game of chess, he was firmly seated beyond all fear of check being given. Yet the mutineers were panic-stricken. It is much to be regretted that the English did not advance this day. Had they done so, they would have taken the city, for the gates were open. The city people expressed their surprise at their holding back in the way they did.

June 10.—The King issued a proclamation for the forcible opening of all the shops in the city. A servant of Wali Mahommed arrived from Lahore, and narrated that there had been a fight between the English and the mutineers, and that the shops of Wali Mahommed, Hossein Baksh, and Kútub-u-dín had been plundered. News arrived of outbreaks at Rawal Pindi and Umritsar. All approaches to the city were reported to-day as dangerous. News received from Bombay that Sir John Lawrence had written to Bombay for assistance in troops, and that Bombay troops would arrive at Delhi towards the end of June. It was reported that the Bombay Government had advised that no attack should be made on the city until the arrival of the Bombay troops, and even if attacked the army should remain on the defensive. General Sammúd Khán attended in answer to a summons from the King. He agreed to attack the English if placed in command of the King's troops. The King ordered his appointment as Commander-in-Chief, with the presentation of the usual *khillat.* After repeated assurances of his loyalty, and having given the usual present of one gold mohur and five rupees cash, he retired. A proclamation was issued to the army to muster and advance under the generalship of Sammúd Khán, when victory would be their reward. About ten o'clock a force of 1,800 Sepoys and twelve-horse guns issued from the Lahore Gate and Cashmere Gate. On reaching the English position Sammúd Khán communicated with the English, to say that he had been sent by the Rájah of Jajjar to join the English force. This feint did not succeed, and an order was issued to attack. About 100 English were killed; the English then pushed forward their artillery. The General came under fire, and immediately retreated, leaving several fieldpieces behind him. The force retreated through the Cashmere Gate into the city. Artillery fire was then opened from the Cashmere Gate bastions. The whole force by the evening returned within the city walls. The heads of the Europeans killed in the fight were cut off, and paraded through the city. A shell from the English guns fell on the house of one Sádat Khán, destroying and killing many of the inmates. About fifty Sepoys went to the house of Rájah Ajit Sing, and brought him prisoner before the King. He was threatened with death unless he used his influence over his brother, who was siding with the English. Ahsanúllah Khan pleaded for the Rájah that he was not responsible for his brother's conduct: that for some time there had been an ill-feeling between the brothers, and in consequence of this, the Rájah Ajit Sing had taken up his residence at Delhi and left Patiála. The Rájah threw himself at the King's feet and implored his protection. The King gave orders for his immediate release.

June 11.—Kúli Khán, formerly an artillery man in the service of the English Government at a salary of twenty-eight rupees, distinguished himself by his exertions, keeping up a constant fire from the bastions at the English; the whole city was full of his praises. The King, cheered by the prowess of this man, ordered one hundred *maunds* of gunpowder to be prepared. Saltpetre and charcoal were purchased. A report received that the Lieutenant-Governor of Agra, hearing that Delhi had not fallen, had ordered his *dák*[1] to be laid. The Commander-in-Chief was reported to have come down from Simla to join the army, and was expected to be before Delhi on the 12th. A confidential report was received this day by the King that when the news of the Mutiny reached the Queen of England she ordered 24,000 troops to be despatched. About two o'clock to-day the English established a battery at Kaband and opened fire at the Cashmere Gate. The fire of the King's artillery prevented the English from completing their design; the English lost all courage, and were much disheartened. A force of 2,000 men was ordered to the Cashmere Gate. Two cavalry sowars arrived in the city and begged for reserves to be sent up at once, as the King's troops were hard pressed. Reserves were ordered up, but the attack which the English had intended was abandoned, and they had retired to their encampment. It was reported to the King that it was the intention of the English chiefs to attack the Kúdsia Bágh; 21,000 men were kept under arms in readiness all that night. The artillery fire of the English caused destruction this day in the city, killing many people on their housetops and injuring many houses. Four English were found this day concealed in the house of a *Khansamah*, and were killed by the mutineers.

June 12.—Piári Lál was taken forcibly before the King, and charged with supplying sulphur to the English. Certain

[1] A *dákgharri* is a posting carriage. Ordering his *dák* to be laid meant making arrangements to leave Agra.

sowars arrived from Badli Serái, to announce that five companies of Sepoys, 300 sowars, and 6,000 rupees of treasure might be immediately expected. The treasure shortly afterwards arrived ; the troops escorting it were ordered to encamp in the Shumru-Ke-Begami Gardens. The King expressed his anger at the apathy of the mutineers, who were making no serious attempt to drive off the English ; the King chided the chief at not having gained a single victory.

June 13.—The whole force was mustered, including the sappers and miners, and the King's Bodyguard, and marched out of the Cashmere Gate to give battle to the English. Certain thieves plundered the house of a Thanadár in Chaora Mohalla, and wounded several of the household. The Thanadár seized one of the thieves. A sowar arrived from the battlefield and reported that the Sepoys had reached the Kaband, and came under the artillery fire of the English. The mutineers having lost twenty cavalry and sixty Sepoys by the fire, the whole force was retreating, the regiments reported as having set the example being the mutineers from Umbálla.

June 14.— Buldeo Sing, the brother of Lachman Sing, Thanadár of Alipúr, was seized and brought to the Kotwáli. He was accused of sympathizing with the English. He was shot, and his body suspended from a tree. Thirteen bakers residing at the Cabul Gate were dragged from their houses and killed, on being suspected of supplying bread to the English. The shop of Jamna Dáss was plundered because he sold *attah* at a high price. The mutineers committed many other oppressive acts this day. About three o'clock in the afternoon 6,000 Sepoys with twelve guns marched out of the city. A fight ensued, in which loss occurred on both sides. Reserves were sent up. Heavy artillery fire lasted the whole night. The houses near Sadut Khán's house suffered severely from the English fire. The city people were angered and put to great difficulties. Reports came of the oppressions practised by the Gújars on travellers. The city people began to be anxious, and were perplexed at the situation. On one hand there were enemies among their own countrymen, both inside and outside the city, and on the other there was the overhanging shadow of the coming attack of the enraged English. A Mahout deserted with his elephant from the English camp, and made his way to the Palace. The King took the elephant for himself. On the morning of this date, Nawáb Mahabúb Ali Khán passed away to paradise. Elephants and troops accompanied the body to the grave. The dead was buried at the Masjid of Karím-ulla-Shah, near the Khanum Bazár, with great pomp and ceremony. The body was followed by all the nobles of the city.

June 15.—Seven cannonballs fell early this morning in the King's palace. The King threatened to leave the city and retire to the Kútub, unless the troops left the city. Under pressure, ten thousand mutineers were let out of the city at midnight to attack the English camp. Many fell on both sides, but the troops could make no way against the heavy fire of the English, and returned in great disorder to the city. The city people were apprehensive that the Magazine would be blown up by the English fire. More troubles for want of supplies. Shopkeepers seized and harassed. Fifty coolies sent to pull down the house of the Maharájah of Indore. Proclamation sent to all Durbáris to attend the King's Durbár on the third day after the death of Mahabúb Ali Khán. A sowar arrived from Nímuch to report the approach of 500 mutineers from that station.

June 16.—Hakim Ahsanúllah Khán, Mir Fateh Ali (officer in charge of the throne), and Bodhau Sahib (*sic*), and other nobles went to the Masjid and offered prayers in honour of the late Mahabúb Ali Khán. A sowar reported that there had been an engagement between the Sepoys and the English, in which 200 men had fallen. A body of cavalry came in from Nímuch with treasure. Seven persons who had been imprisoned on charges of friendship with the English were this day released. Three men, taken to be spies, were killed by the troops. A woman and a resident of Mulliwara were killed in the city by a stray cannonball from the English lines.

June 17.—A proclamation was issued selling the Bank House[1] and some opium. Several *kaharies* and *khatris* petitioned the King regarding the oppressions practised by the soldiers, and the stoppage of provisions from entering the city. On this the King sent for the chief of the mutineers, and threatened to take poison, unless greater discipline were enforced and the oppressions discontinued. The chief promised immediate compliance, and said that there should be no further occasion for similar complaints. An order was issued to Kazí Faiz-ullah-Bég to prepare provisions for the troops that were about to attack the English. Forty cannonballs were picked up this day fired from the English camp. Many persons were killed by them. A very large cannon was taken from the Magazine, and mounted, to reply to the English fire. The chief attended the Durbár, and reported that three batteries had been constructed—at Dir Chuki Hill, and also on the Idgáh—and that they intended to attack the English. Later on in the day the English attacked the Idgáh Battery,[2] and drove the mutineers out of it, capturing two guns. Seven carts laden with lime were despatched for repairs to Selimgarh. Several

[1] The Bank House was the property of Mrs. Dyce Somba, afterwards Lady Forrester.

[2] Major H. Tombe, B.H.A., commanded in this affair.

persons, desiring to send letters, presented themselves before the King, and asked permission to do so. It was refused. A cannon, lying at the door of the Palace since the time of Sháh Jehán, was taken by the mutineers and mounted at the Lahore Gate. It being a long-range gun, it was intended to annoy the English troops marching from Agra.

June 18.—Rumour spread that the "2nd Regiment" at Nasirabád had mutinied and murdered their officers, and had arrived at Delhi with treasure and ammunition. We learned from some of the men that the Maharájah of Jeypúr had supplied them with rations on their march under great pressure. They stated that the Maharájah would give no assistance to the King. It was reported that Lala Pershad was recruiting for the English. News reached the Palace that the native troops at Cawnpore had murdered their officers, and were on their way to Delhi; also that 1,500 Europeans came *via* Jeypúr *via* Nasirabád to Agra.

June 19.—The officers of the Nasirabád troops attended the King's audience, and agreed to attack the English next day.

June 20. — The Nasirabad troops attacked the English, and a severe engagement followed, in which many were killed on both sides; a shell set fire to a house. A proclamation issued to send provisions to the army at Singharh. Again the troops attacked the English, and continued the engagement until the evening. A cannonball entered the house of Ganésha Lál, a shopkeeper, killing his servant. A Jathni of Dhiráj Pahárí took a house in the Billí Mohalla. Seven Sepoys went to his house to plunder: the neighbours turned out in force; a fight ensued, and several of the Sepoys were wounded. Reinforced, the Sepoys returned to the attack, and further plundered the houses of the sons of Umed Sing and Ram Sahai Mull. Many persons were killed by the cannonballs which fell into the city.

June 21.—Several thousand mutineers attacked the English camp this morning; the engagement lasted a long while, but there was no victory. All the night cannonballs flew into the city. A sowar came to announce the arrival of three regiments of foot and cavalry from Jullundur, who offered their services to the King; they were ordered to encamp outside the city. Nine carts of provisions for the English were intercepted and brought into the city. It was rumoured that the mutineers from Bareilly and Cawnpore were marching on Delhi. A force left the city in the afternoon to attack the English.

June 22.—The three regiments from Jullundur arrived, and were encamped in the Kúdsia Bágh Garden. Their officers attended the Durbár, and complained that they had been attacked on the road by the forces of Patiála, which they had defeated, taking one gun. They explained that they had reached Delhi by a roundabout way through fear of the English, whose forces were daily increasing. The native officers were boasting that they had murdered the Collector of Nasirabad, and had taken his elephant, which they had brought with them. The King flattered them, saying they were great Bahádurs, whose like was not to be met with. About fifty Sepoys entered the house of Jogul Kishore, son of Kaniya Lál (news-writer of Hyderabad), with a view to plunder, but were deterred by Mirza Mogul. They then plundered the Mohalla of Mir Ashik.

June 23.—A gun constructed in the reign of Sháh Jehán was taken, and mounted. When ready a he-goat was tied to the mouth, and twenty-five *seers* of sweetmeats placed inside, and a necklace of flowers hung round the muzzle. Several Brahmins and astronomers were summoned, and directed to consult their almanacks as to whether the mutineers would be victorious. The astronomers replied that great disturbance would last for a year. Several thousands would die, but the shadow of Peace and Security would spread over the land from 1916 Sambat. Beyond this the astronomers would say nothing. News arrived that two regiments of native infantry at Calcutta, afraid of losing their caste, had fled to Nepaul. News came that a Brahmin had been hanged outside the city of Alighur, under orders of the Collector, for spreading a rumour that a battle had been fought at Delhi between the English and the mutineers, in which there had been great slaughter. News arrived of fresh troops from Bombay coming to swell the English force, and that twenty regiments of English for India had started from England. An order was issued to the Kotwál to supply sweetmeats and provisions for the troops, who had gone out to attack the English. All day there was fighting. About four p.m. the troops returned to the city. A proclamation by beat of drum was issued, that such a cannon would be fired that night that the concussion was expected to level all the streets and dilapidated houses in the city. People were warned not to sleep in such houses.

June 24.—The Sepoy sirdars attended the King's Durbár, and reported that they had engaged the English the whole day, till bugle-call on both sides stopped the firing. They also complained that as they were returning to the city, a shot was so carelessly fired by Kúli Khán from the city that three Sepoys had been badly wounded and several camp-followers killed. He (Kúli Khán) had been placed under arrest, and was brought before the King. He was charged with being in collusion with the English. It was rumoured that Luckman Séth was enlisting troops for the safety of Agra, and had sent bodies of men there. Hakim Ahsanúllah Khán reported that the mutineers were plundering the town, and had entirely depopulated Dip Cháh Pahárí Mohalla, and Tellewari. It was rumoured that the Cawnpore troops had gone to attack the English at Meerut. A battle had been fought, with some loss and no result. News received of the arrival of 1,500 English from Nasirabád at Agra.

June 25.—Hakim Ahsanúllah Khán, Nazir Hassan Mirza, Mahbúb Ali Khán, Mozuffer-ul-Dowlah, and the chief city officers presented themselves at the audience to pay their respects. The sirdars of the Sepoys also attended. The bad behaviour of the Sepoys was referred to. Hakim Ahsanúllah Khán was accused by Ali Khán and Kadir Baksh, in charge of the Serais, of releasing the bad characters who had been captured red-handed for plundering, and had taken bribes from them. They pleaded for better arrangements for the peace and security of the city, and represented that all trade was at a standstill. A zemindár came in from Bagpat and presented a nazzar of one rupee. He reported that one thousand Sepoys of Maharájah Surdíp Sing were plundering that portion of the city where he lived, and were constructing a bridge over the Jumna river. He asked for a body of troops to drive them out of the place; the King referred him to Mirza Kizr Sultán. The King also issued an order to have Ali Khán and Kadir Baksh turned out of the city for calumniating Hakim Ahsanúllah Khán. The King's orders were this day issued to Abdul Sulíf Khán to send Nawab Mustaffa Khán under safe escort to Delhi. Four hundred Jehádis from Gurgaon and other districts arrived at Delhi, and presented themselves before the King. Cannonballs were falling into the city all day. A syce and several persons were killed. The traders of Churi Mohalla petitioned the King in person that gunpowder was being manufactured in the house of the Shumru Begum, near their houses; they expected any moment to be blown into the air. The King consoled them, and promised to stop the manufacture. A council of war was held, consisting of Makhan Lál, Hakim Ahsanúllah Khán, and Nawáb Ahmed Kúli Khán. The King addressed the sirdars of the Sepoys, pointing out that they were destroying the kingdom that had lasted for 500 years, and remarked sarcastically that when they went out to fight the English they returned "topsy-turvy." He offered up a prayer, saying: "Alas! this is the will of God that I and my kingdom shall be destroyed." "I wish you all to leave the town." News reached the Palace that the Collector of Bijnour had made over charge of the city of Najibabád to Nawáb Mahmúd Khán, and had himself gone to Rúrki. News arrived that the Bareilly force was at Shahjehanpúr.

June 26.—One hundred men from Bhopál, and two hundred from other places, this day came into the city. The King received them. They were ordered to encamp outside the city. A man came from Benares; he also was ordered to live outside the city. Two regiments of infantry and 200 cavalry, and two guns, were sent to engage the troops of the Maharájah of Jhínd. Mirza Mogul was thrown out of his buggy in driving back from the Delhi Gate, and received a slight injury. News received that the Gwalior contingent, having murdered their officers, were marching on the city. It was reported to the King that the troops who had left the city to fight the English, were returning, as the air did not agree with them (*sic lit.*). The King issued orders to the effect that the troops, having failed to drive away the English, should leave the city, and go elsewhere. It was rumoured that 5,000 wine-distillers had joined the English troops.

June 27.—An engagement began early this morning at Kúdsia Bágh and Idgáh, lasting all day, and many persons were killed. A petition was received from Bagpat that the troops of Jhínd had been defeated, the bridge they had been constructing was broken down, and the troops sent from Delhi would return early the next day. An order was issued to Hakim Ahsanúllah to move the gunpowder manufactory from Begum Shumru's house. Four hundred men were assembled outside the Cashmere Gate. The English artillery fire told heavily upon them. It was rumoured that the Commander-in-Chief of the English had that morning been killed in the fight, and his body buried before the Cashmere Gate. It was rumoured that there had been a quarrel between the English and the Gurkhas. Thirty sowars of the Gwalior contingent reached the city, and reported that they were the advance-guard of the whole Gwalior contingent. They were ordered to encamp outside the city. The King informed Mirza Mogul that the royal treasury was empty, and no further pay would be issued to the troops. The force returned from Bagpat, and reported that they had brought the Thanadár and Matsadi back in custody, as they had been supplying provisions to the English. It transpired that the troops sent for the protection of Bagpat had plundered the city. The English this day failed in blowing up one of the city bastions. They had mined the Customs House with this object.[1]

June 28.—The whole number of the leading inhabitants of Delhi waited on the King to pay their respects. A letter was received from Mirza Mogul, saying that the 25,000 rupees given for the pay of the Sepoys had already been distributed, and 2,500 rupees was still due. The King ordered the balance to be sent. A man was caught digging a mine in a house in the Palace, in connivance with the

[1] Quite imaginary; the English were never near enough to do anything of the sort.

English,[1] to blow up the Palace wall; he was blown from a gun at Selimgarh, as a warning to others. Several persons were killed by cannonballs falling in the city. The officers of the army complained of the inconvenience they were subjected to in camping during the rains outside the city. The King permitted them to reside in the city till the rainy season should pass. All the troops encamped outside the Delhi, Lahore, and Turcoman Gates returned to the city, where they occupied the Civil Courts, the Mahommedan College, and the houses in the city. Badges engraved with the King of Delhi's name were this day issued to the Guards occupying the Police Station, the Kútub, and other places.

June 29.—The King held a levée, which was numerously attended: the prospects of the war were discussed for several hours. The officers of the regiments from Nímuch reported that two regiments of native infantry, 600 cavalry, and one battery of artillery, with one lakh and some odd thousands of rupees, would arrive in the city in a week. Representative officers from the Bareilly force presented themselves, and reported that the force would arrive in Delhi in the course of three days. A letter was received from Wallidád Khan, of Bálagarh, asking the aid of one regiment of foot and some guns from the Bareilly force: he was told to raise a force to preserve peace and order. Mitan Lál, Matsadi of Bág Begum Shumru, received notice that all his employer's property had been confiscated by the State, and that all rents in future were to be paid into the Royal Treasury. A note was written to the officers of the regiments, asking for a guard to be put over Luckmiput Seth's house, as it had been plundered by the Sepoys. Reports made to the King that all the wood lying on the banks of

[1] All imaginary.

the Jumna was being taken by the Sepoys to cook their dinner with. Orders issued to prevent this. Report received from the Thanadár of Shahdara Police Station that the Bareilly forces would arrive to-morrow. Orders passed for collection of provisions. Representative officers of regiments from Benares present at the audience. They reported that their regiments were halted at the tomb of Safdar Jang, awaiting orders. They were told to halt until further orders, and that provisions would be sent there for them. Four hundred rupees collected as rent of shops in the Chandni Chowk, and paid into the treasury. A man was apprehended, being found in possession of ammunition stolen from the Magazine. Petition received from Rájah Nahár Sing, chief of Bulubgarh, that, if permitted, he would send all the property of his cousin, Nawul Sing, to Bulubgarh. Permission granted. Twenty sowars arrived from Cawnpore, and reported that for several days a fight had raged between the English and the natives. All the English had in the end been put to the sword, and the city was in the possession of the troops. Mirza Mogul held a council of war at his house. It was rumoured that four spies visiting the English camp had been seized and examined. They told the English that the man sent to fire the mine under the city walls had been blown away. On hearing this the spies were shot. The forces of the Nawáb of Jajjar wished to join the religious cause. Military guards placed at all police stations.

June 30.—Engagement with the English at Sunéri Mundai. Officers of the forces engaged attended the King's levée, and expressed their loyalty and their determination to fight the English to the best of their ability. They boasted at some length of the prowess of the Sepoys. Five hundred fanatics returned with an elephant they had taken from the English, and presented it to the King. A mine was discovered being dug near the Cashmere Gate. The man caught was hung before the Kotwáli on a tree. A proclamation was issued that all friends of the English would be treated in this manner. A man disguised in the garb of a fakir was seized at the Ajmere Gate, and being suspected to be a spy from the English camp, he was killed. It was rumoured that a force of 200 English had set fire to and burned down the Mohalla of Tellewaria, Dheragpahári, and Saidepúra. One Englishman rode up to the Lahore Gate, and fired at the sentry with a pistol; he then rode away. A heavy storm of wind occurred this day, in which the Jumna Bridge sank. Several carts laden with goods, on their way to Bulubgarh, were seized, on the suspicion that they held ammunition; they were taken back to the city, but, on being searched, nothing was found, and they were released. The Bareilly force was reported to have reached Ghaziabád. Orders issued to repair the Darogah Bridge.

July 1.—Hakim Ahsanúllah Khán, Nawáb Hassan Ali Khán, and other sirdars attended the audience. Two messengers arrived from Bíjah Bai as the bearers of a nazzar of one lakh of rupees for the King. The messengers complained that the Gújars had plundered them of the letter of which they were the bearers near Furidabad, and that they had torn up the papers. The King ordered them to be given a present of one rupee each. News reached the Palace of the arrival of the Bareilly force on the banks of the Jumna. The broken bridge prevented the Delhi force from crossing over to the Delhi side of the river. Four hundred coolies and two companies of sappers and miners were sent to repair the bridge. Mir Fateh Ali appointed to repair the bridge. The King examined the Bareilly forces across the river through a telescope, and remarked upon the elephants and cavalry. Khán Hassan Ali reported that six shells had been fired from the city into the English camp, of which three had burst on the main road and one in the camp. Orders were issued for the dispatch of 100 shells to the native batteries. Hakim Ahsanúllah ordered to hasten the reconstruction of the Jumna Bridge. Heavy fire poured into the city. Many casualties among the inhabitants reported. The English fire was chiefly directed on the battery commanded by Kúli Khán. Two artillery-men and seven others were killed; one gun dismounted and rendered useless. Expectations of an attack from the English. The King summoned all the leaders and ordered them to take a large force to meet the English outside the gate. A force consisting of several thousand men marched out of the city and took up its position at Idgáh and Dum Dumma. The Nasirabád contingent were employed in mounting heavy guns in the batteries. Munshi Kishen Lál appointed Bakhshi of the Chowkidars (paymaster of the police or municipal watchmen). The bridge was reported ready for the passage of the Bareilly force on the morrow. Mahommed Kúli Khán ordered to receive the force and welcome it. Nawáb Bahádur Jang borrowed a sum of 6,000 rupees from the Nawáb of Jajjar for the pay of the troops. Two men ordered to pull down the houses in the Sunéri Mundai.

July 2.—Nawáb Ahmed Kúli Khán went out to receive the Bareilly force. Hakim Ahsanúllah Khán, General Sannad Khán, Ibrahim Ali Khán, Ghulám Ali Khán, and others were present. Mahommed Kúli Khán, with Mahommed Bakht Khán,[1] commander of the Bareilly force, solicited orders

[1] Bakht Khán was the chief native officer of a field battery of artillery, all the gunners being natives. It was rather a famous battery, as it had served at Jalalabad under Sale in the first Afghan War, and had a mural crown as an honorary decoration on its guns. Bakht Khán had served in it at Jalalabad. He was much sought for after the Mutiny, but he was never found or heard of. He was not killed in action, or we should have heard of it; and one or two of the guns were never recovered: they will turn up some day.—*Note by G. H. M. Ricketts, C.B.*

for the employment of the force. The King's orders were that the inhabitants of the city must not be plundered. The King said it was no use his giving orders, as they were never obeyed, and he had no one to enforce them, but his decree was that the English should be caused not to exist. Mahommed Bakht Khán offered his services as Commander-in-Chief of the forces, with a view to enforce general discipline. The King grasped his hands in token of friendship. On returning to the troops Bakht Khán acquainted the Subahdárs with the King's acceptance of his service, and asked them whom they would obey. The Subahdárs swore allegiance and obedience to Mahommed Bakht. After the levée the King gave the General a private audience. The General pointed out that he was the descendant of the same family as the King of Delhi, and asked the King to satisfy himself that this was true. The King replied there was no necessity for inquiry, for a greater man than the General did not exist. The General replied: "I shall be entitled to the honour of Bahádur when I shall have driven the English out of Delhi and Meerut." Orders were issued to the Darogah of Nawáb Abdul Rahman Khán, of Jajjar, to vacate the Kalla Mahall in favour of the troops. The order was carried out. The General Bakht Khán visited Prince Mirza Mogul, and after a long consultation returned to camp. A shield, a sword, and the title of General were bestowed on Mahommed Bakht Khán, and he was appointed Commander-in-Chief of the whole of the forces. A proclamation was issued ordering the attendance of all officers in command of regiments to receive instructions from Mahommed Bakht Khán. Mirza Mogul was appointed Adjutant-General. Mahommed Bakht informed the King that if any of the Princes attempted to plunder the city, he would cut off their noses and ears. The King replied: "You have full authority. Do whatever seems good unto you." In accordance with this order, the Kotwál of the city was informed that if any more plundering took place he would be hanged. Soldiers plundering were to be arrested. Mahommed Bakht Khán reported that he was ready outside the city with the following force :—

> Four regiments of foot,
> Seven hundred cavalry,
> Six horse artillery guns,
> Three fieldpieces,
> Fourteen elephants,
> Three hundred spare horses taken from the Government Stud at Hanpir,
> One hundred Jehádis.

The force had received six months' pay in advance. He reported also that he had treasure to the extent of four lakhs. He declared he would not trouble the King for any assistance, and if his troops were victorious he would pay in any surplus money to the King's treasury. The King ordered 4,000 rupees to be distributed among the Bareilly troops for festivities (*siafut*). All officers commanding detachments of troops were ordered to place themselves under General Bakht Khán's orders. Similar orders were issued to the Agra force. The General ordered a proclamation, by beat of drum, that all shopkeepers were to keep arms, and that no one should leave his house unarmed. Persons having no arms to apply to headquarters for them, and they would be given them free of charge. Any soldier caught plundering was to have his arm severed from his body. All persons having ammunition to give it over to the Magazine, under pain of severe punishment. The police officers were ordered to cause all the respectable inhabitants of Delhi to attend the General's levée. The General inspected the Magazine, and ordered the stores and material to be properly arranged. Complaints were made that the house of Rai Ransurám Dáss, deputy collector, had been plundered. Reports received that several thousand men of the Rájah of Bikanír had arrived at Hánsi Hissár, had attacked bands of soldiers and had killed a great number of them, and had restored peace and security in those places. They were about to march to Rohtuk. The postal line was open from Hissár to Sarésar. Dispatches from Lucknow that the troops had risen and had surrounded all the English in Muchí Bawan. Dispatches received from Gwalior that the contingent wished to mutiny, but were kept together by the influence of Maharájah Jya Jee Rao Singhia, who counselled the soldiers to remain with him and not to join the army at Delhi. At eight o'clock this night General Bakht Khán visited the King, and long remained in consultation with him, Zínut Mehal, Hakim Ahsanúllah Khán, and Ahmed Kúli Khán.

July 3.—Haksan Ali Khán, Rajah Ahmed Sing's son, and other sirdars attended the King's levée. A petition was presented by the city residents complaining that General Mahommed Bakht Khán had summoned them to attend at his house and had sent the summons through the police. They felt hurt and maltreated. They prayed that the order should be recalled, and if they (the petitioners) were wanted and were politely summoned by letter they would attend. The General, being called upon for an explanation, said that he had not sent for the bankers of the city, but had sent police to warn them to be ready armed. On this same date (July 3) orders were issued by the King to Bakht Khán to arrange for the monthly payment of the King's servants. The General was empowered to fine all those plundering, and to give compensation (*tawán*) to the plundered victims. He was also instructed to arrange for the civil administration, the police, and revenue departments. An order issued whereby the royal princes were relieved from all further duties connected with the army. A sowar of the 4th Cavalry reported to the General that two European soldiers had pursued him from the English camp: he had killed one of them near the Lahore Gate, but the guard at the gate had taken away his arms and horse. He also reported that 200 carts with provisions had been sent by Patiála to the English, and were then on the road. To intercept these, two regiments of foot, one battery of artillery, and some cavalry were started off at once. The General asked the King's sanction for the repairing of his tents. Twenty thousand troops were assembled on parade near the Jumma Masjid and Lál Díghí. Khuda Baksh Khán, the Naib Kotwál, came to the parade with an order for the troops to stand at attention. They were then marched through the Cashmere Gate and the Selimgarh and Lahore Gates, and halted. The General and his staff went to the Palace, taking with them two European sergeants. The General reported that they had accompanied his force from Bareilly, and had made themselves very useful. They had also, it was stated, prevented the Europeans at Bareilly from blowing away natives. They were ordered to go to Selimgarh, Cashmere, and Lahore Gates, and report on the batteries. Report received that the Collector of Gurjawan had marched with a mixed force from Jeypúr, and had severely punished the villagers of three villages near Bithúr, who had joined the mutineers. A spy brought in news that the English force numbered 9,000 Europeans. News came that the Lieutenant-Governor of the North-West Provinces had written to Luckmiput Seth of Muttra for twenty lakhs of rupees. He had replied that he had gold to that amount, but not silver. Reports received that the troops at Kalpí and Udeypur had mutinied, murdered their officers, and were marching on Delhi.

July 4.—Mirza Kizr Sultán presented himself at the King's audience, and complained that the princes were going about oppressing the people in the city. General Bakht Khán received the title of Farzand.[1] The sons of Ahmed Sing, Hassan Ali Khán, and Halmed Ali Khán waited on the King. The Thánadár of Sháhwarah sent in a letter saying that twenty sowars were required there to maintain order. Ten men were sent. A letter was written to Moulvie Ahmed Ali, Vakíl of the Rájah of Bulubgarh, demanding an explanation of the fact that a cart belonging to Farukh-u-dín had been plundered within the Rájah's territory. General Bakht Khán issued a proclamation calling on all the residents to assemble at the Chandni Chowk to hear an order read. The two regiments sent out to intercept the provisions for the English, returned with two carts they had captured. Nine sowars of the Patiála force were killed. A battery was opened at Alipur. The English made a night attack, with a loss to the Sepoys of eight hundred men. Twenty thousand men assembled in answer to the orders of yesterday, but before the General arrived the crowds dispersed. Four hundred men arrived at Nampur and Naghena to join the King's forces, and took up their quarters in the Fatehpur Mosque.

July 5.—The King gave audience to Ahsanúllah Khán and Ahsan Ali Khán. Imani Begum, wife of Mirza Bulahi, son of Bahádur Shah, late King of Dehli, attended, and represented that the night before Abu Bakr, in a state of intoxication, came to her house with several sowars to seize

[1] Shah Alum first gave this title.

her, and fired several shots with rifles and pistols, and beat a number of people of the Mohalla. The police arrived, but Abu Bakr attacked the Kotwál with a sword, had him seized and taken away in custody, insulted him, and finally plundered her house. The King was very much displeased, and took away from him all military rank. Orders were issued for his arrest, but in the meantime he escaped. The King ordered all the Princes to keep away from his levées. He issued orders to all the sirdars to note that he had disgraced the Princes, and they were to be treated as ordinary persons if they were found committing any oppression. It was proclaimed that special constables not acting according to orders would be regarded as offending against the estate. Five companies of Sepoys arrived from Jutapur, and reported that Mán Sing had gathered 50,000 men, armed with all sorts of weapons, and had placed them under the orders of General Bakht Khán. Report came that the English had established a battery at Chandrawne. General Bakht Khán sent out a force to intercept provisions: twenty carts fell into their hands. They were brought as far as Zia-u-dín Garden, where the English caught up the Sepoys and recovered the carts. Dispatch received from Nasirabad that Colonel Lawrence had reached Abú, and had reassured the inhabitants. One thousand Sepoys were sent to Dholpur for the safety of the town. They were engaged by the force from Jeypur. The troops of Indore and of the Nawáb of Jadra, stationed at Moridpur, deserted without orders. News came that Kishwar Lál, son of the Vakíl of the Maharájah of Hindora, had died of cholera at Bikanír. From Multan news came that the English had attempted to disarm the troops; they had refused, and had threatened the English, who had all run away and taken refuge in the fort, and the Sepoys had gone off to Lahore.

July 6.—Bahádur Ali Khán, chief of Bahádurgarh, presented a nazzar of eleven rupees, and complained that his ancestral estate had been seized by Bahádur Jang Khán. He asked for justice. Yakúb Ali presented a nazzar. The Sepoy officers attended the audience, and reported that a force had been sent out to cover the bridge over the Hindun river, but owing to the want of provisions, and the heavy fall of rain, they had returned. Complaints were made that the General provided his own troops with supplies, but made no arrangements for the rest of the army. The King referred the complainers to the General. The King openly censured Mirza Abdulla and the other Princes for their bad behaviour, and ordered them to disgorge the money they had forcibly taken from the bankers, otherwise their allowances would be stopped. Main-u-dín Khán, the former Thánadár of Pahar-ganj, and Hyder Hassan Khán, were summoned, and ordered to give up the property that they had plundered, otherwise they would be severely dealt with. Two petitions from the General were received complaining of the sufferings of the troops owing to the unseasonable weather. Orders issued for the troops to be housed. The General also asked for permission to maintain fifty chuprassies (office messengers). Peitah Sing was ordered to supply the chuprassies. A statement of the strength of the forces in Delhi was ordered to be sent in daily, in order to prepare the pay account. A soldier at Selimgarh had his head taken off by a cannonball. Orders issued to exclude all armed men from the Dewan-i-Khás (Hall of Audience). Youths without turbans were also to be excluded, as being both distasteful and disrespectful to the King. Ahmed Khán, Resaldár of the 4th Cavalry, with several sowars, deserted from the English, bringing with them several thousand rupees; they made their way into the city in the evening. The King sent for the General

Bakht Khán, but owing to pressure of business he could not attend. The King sent a *táwíz* (a charm worn round the arm) to Ahmed Kúli Khán, with a verbal message to cover it with iron and bind it on his arm, and he would be victorious. Report said that three companies of Europeans and three guns had marched from Agra, and would encamp that evening at the tomb of Safdar Jang Khán, and would march in the morning for Alipur. The King visited the Asud Battery, and inspected the arrangements. Two spies were sent to Jeypur to ascertain if any force were coming from Bombay. Orders issued for the whole of the troops to parade in the morning. Three spies from the English camp were to-day taken in Mahommed Bakht Khán's camp, and were executed there. Two men carrying bottles of brandy in a dirty bag were arrested. An elephant from the English camp was captured and brought into the city. Orders issued to all the police officers to the effect that Mahommed Kúli Khán had been appointed Magistrate over the city with full powers.

July 7.—Amin-u-dín Khán, Mirza Zia-u-dín Khán, and Mir Hamed Ali Khán waited on the King. A letter was received from Wallidád Khán, chief of Bulubgarh, saying that he had been attacked by the Collector of Bulandshahr and several hundred European soldiers, but that he had defeated them at Mainpur, twelve miles from Bulubgarh, taking three guns, and had driven them back into the fort. If the King would send him some assistance, he would destroy that Collector Sahib altogether. The King ordered a regiment and one gun to be sent to his assistance. The Kotwál was ordered to arrange for the commissariat in communication with the General. Rajah Nahár Sing, of Bulubgarh, sent an urgent letter saying that he had been ordered by the Nímuch force to have in readiness 700 *maunds* of *attah* (flour), *gram* (a pulse for feeding horses), and other articles of food, and asking for instructions if he were to obey this order. Seventy men from one of the cavalry regiments from Lucknow reached the city, and were attached to General Bakht Khán's force. Several high-caste soldiers complained to the King that the General did not supply their wants, and they were discontented; they asked to be put under the command of Mirza Mogul, and to have the money they had brought with them restored to them. The King promised that in future they should be carefully looked after. Orders to this effect were issued, and it was said in writing that it was expedient to make the troops contented. An order was issued to Luchmenarain, Vakíl of the Nawáb Bahádur Jang Khán, to send two maunds of opium at once into the city; payment was promised. The troops were paraded from the Delhi Gate to the Ajmere Gate; the General spoke kindly to the men and comforted them; every regiment received a message from the King, that each man who went out to the battlefield, and each man who distinguished himself, would receive a grant of five *bighas* of land, and receive honorary posts. After the parade the General rode to the Magazine, and examined the park of artillery; he was satisfied with the inspection. Two petitions reached the King from the General: the first was to the effect that he had consulted with the native officers about sending troops to Bulubgarh, and would verbally report the result; in the second dispatch it was stated that he would arrange for the distribution of pay to the army. A dispatch received from the Nímuch force saying that they had been victorious at the fight at Hodel over the troops from Jeypur, who had fled. They asked for one company of sappers and miners, and six guns, to attack the fort at Agra. The petition was sent on to General

Bakht Khán. Orders issued for police reports to be made daily to Ahmed Kúli Khán. Hakim Ahsanúllah Khán complained that he had been superseded by Ahmed Kúli Khán. The King consoled him, and changed the order to the effect that the reports should in future be made to Ahsanúllah Khán. Reports received that three Marwara bankers and a Musalmán had been arrested by some English soldiers from Mehal Bhali Bhatharí, and had been taken to the camp; that the Marwaris had been released, but the Musalmán had been shot. It was reported that five lakhs of rupees, sent by Maharajah Narenda Sing, chief of Patiála, had reached the English camp safely.

July 8.—The King entered the Dewan-Ááam and held a levée. Nine thousand rupees were sent to Mirza Mogul as four days' pay to the troops. A dispatch was received from Khán Bahádur Khán, son of Hafiz Nahamut-ulla Khán, chief of Bareilly, saying that he had made himself master of Bareilly and Shahjehánpur. The King wrote him complimentary letters. A dispatch received from the Peshawur forces intimating that 20,000 men were willing to join the King and would shortly arrive. All the cavalry ordered from Mahalab Bágh to Lál Díghí to the house of Khán Ali Khán. Namchund Dáss Korwalla and other shopkeepers arrested Sadut Khán and brought him before the King. He was released after the payment of 6,200 rupees as "nuzzer." Mahommed Azim Khán, son of Shahzada Jehán Aklar, asked for armed assistance to bring his family from Sarésar, as the English were marching upon that place. General Bakht Khán was instructed to render the assistance asked for. Five butchers were caught taking meat to the English camp on a bed; they had their throats cut. Great dissatisfaction in the city in consequence of this brutal act. It was reported that forty gun *khalassies*, with some guns sent by Captain Louis, Commissary of Ordnance at Furidpur, had reached the English camp, but ten of these men deserted and had presented themselves before the King. They reported that there were 400 English at Naini Tall, that the Nawáb of Rampur had taken possession of Moradabád and Umrút; and that Nawáb Mahommed Khán, chief of Nujibabad, had taken possession of Bijnozur, Nampur, Nagíma, and Adampur, also that Colonel Lawrence had reached Nasirabad from Mount Abú; that all the Vakíls of the Rájahs of Rájputána had gone to meet the Colonel, who had sent for 1,000 men from the Rájah of Pertabgarh, and that the Rájah of Jadra was encamped at Nímuch to protect it; also that 500 cavalry and foot-soldiers had been summoned from Jodpur. It was reported that twenty Gujars had been beheaded by Rao Tulla Rám for committing dacoities. It was reported that the English were still at Lucknow, entrenched at Muchee Bakwan, and had undermined the ground all round their position, but that the mine on the river-side had been injured. The English force was gathered at the Bailey Guard, and had armed the Ferozepur Gate. Reports received that a mutiny and disturbance had taken place at Benares and Allahabád; that the English were in good state at Allahabád, but had gone into the fort.

July 9.—According to custom the King entered the Durbár. Several relations of Nawáb Mahabúb Ali Khán presented a nazzar of four rupees. The butchers of the city complained that five of their companions had been murdered, and that they had received orders not to open their shops. Mirza Mogul was ordered to inquire into the grievances. It was proclaimed by beat of drum that anyone caught cow-killing would be blown away from a gun, and that anybody who was found objecting to the killing of a goat would be punished.

It was rumoured that General Bakht Khán had attacked the English with ten thousand men, both cavalry and infantry, and that an engagement was taking place at the Chowní Bastion, and that the English position at Tehari Hazarí had been taken. General Bakht Khán charged with cavalry into the English lines, cutting down a great number of officers and men. The artillerymen, it is said, recognized Bakht Khán; the Jehádis took part in the engagement. Part of the English camp was being plundered when the gunners turned the fieldpieces upon the Sepoys, and shot them down, wounding and killing a great number. The Sepoys then retreated back to the city. In that day's victory, twenty horses, seventy camels, and a great deal of valuable property were seized.[1] Thirteen cavalry and twelve infantry soldiers were taken as prisoners. Several Europeans who were concealed in the *serai* of Mahabúb Ali Khán were killed, and their heads exhibited as evidence of the victory gained, and laid before the King. The King, on seeing the heads, expressed himself as much pleased, and gave a reward of 100 rupees to those who had killed the Europeans. Two artillerymen of Kúli Khán's battery were shot, for not firing on the gunners, on account of cowardice.

July 10.—The King visited the battery at Selimgarh. Nawáb Ahmed Wallidád Khán presented a petition, asking for assistance to help him to realize his revenue. Orders were sent to Mahommed Bakht Khán to despatch troops at once, in order to bring the defaulting tenants to their senses. The Treasurer reported that there were only 175,000 rupees in the treasury. Letters received from Fazand Ali Khán and Nazir Hassan Ali Khán, nobles of Lucknow, saying that they had murdered all the English in that place, and

[1] It is not clear if the plunder fell into the Sepoys' hands or not, but I understand that the horses, camels, and prisoners fell into their hands.

secured the possession of several districts lately in the hands of the English. After reading the letter, the King ordered a letter of congratulation to be addressed to them. It was reported that the English were about to attack the line of entrenchments; a large force of infantry and cavalry was at once placed under arms, and held in readiness to resist them. It was subsequently found that the English had only sent out a burial party, to collect the bodies of those who had fallen the day before. General Bakht Khán asked for horses to be sent out to bring in the wounded Sepoys. Orders issued to Hákim Hassan Khán to do so at once. Orders issued to General Bakht Khán to send out a force to Chandrawul, to prevent the English from making a bridge.

July 11.—The King held a levée, and received all the nobles in the city. He then visited Mirza Mogul, and remained an hour with him in confidential conversation. On his return to the Palace, he gave an audience to General Bakht Khán and fifty officers. The General expressed his regret that the King had censured him in a letter which he had received. The King denied that he had sent him any such letter. The General asked that in future all letters from the King should be sealed with his seal. The King assented, as also to another request that wounded Sepoys should receive a pension as well as a grant of land. Bakht Khán represented that he was a native of Sultánpur in Lucknow, and related to the royal family of Oude, and requested the truth of his statements might be inquired into. The King replied that there was no necessity to do so, as he was assuredly of a noble family. The General replied that he asked for a formal inquiry, as he should press his claims to some mark of distinction when the English should be expelled from Delhi, Meerut, and Agra. The General issued orders to Nawáb Abdul Rahmán to vacate the Kalla

Mahall, which he did. He then visited Mirza Mogul, and remained in conversation with him a long time. Orders issued to the Chief of Rewári to collect all the revenue, and pay it into the Treasury. Orders issued to Hákim Abdul Hak to send ten troopers to Shahdara Police Station to notify that, if anyone should receive the new coin he would be punished. Five troopers arrived from Cawnpore, and reported to Mirza Mogul that five thousand Sepoys were on their way from Cawnpore to Delhi. Orders issued to the Kotwál to prepare all the available tents for their use, and report the number to the Commander-in-Chief. Mirza Ahmed, Vakíl of the Rájah of Náhur Shanker, reported that provisions were ready at Bulubgarh for twenty thousand men of the Nímuch force, who were expected there *en route* for Delhi. Orders issued by the Commander-in-Chief to the whole force to hold itself in readiness to fight if it became necessary. It was rumoured in the city that several hundred men had killed three Englishmen who had come to the city to take service with the King. A few English soldiers had arrived at Mehdipur in the Bulubgarh district, and had warned the residents to leave the place, as there would be an engagement there in a few days. It was also rumoured that 12,000 English were marching from Bombay to occupy Delhi, Meerut, and Agra. It was reported that the Gujars of Shunkuri, to the number of three thousand, had made friends with and joined the Sepoys, and, after plundering several villages, had gone on towards Meerut. The English had sent out a force against them of one company of Europeans and two guns, and had dispersed them, after killing several hundred men. The English lost two serjeants and sixteen Sepoys, who were killed, and the village of Shunkuri had been burned.

July 12.—The King visited the Mahálab Garden. On his return he received Hamid Ali Khán, Hassan Ali Khán, and his son, Saádut Ali Khán, Hossein Mirza Nazir, and Mozuffer-ul-Dowlah. After the presentation of nazzars, Mozuffer-ul-Dowlah presented a petition from Mehdi Ali Khán and Basur Ali Khán, sons of Aga, a noble of Lucknow. They begged for a letter assuring them of the King's approval of their conduct, as they said they had killed all the English at Cawnpore. They intended going to Lucknow and Benares on their way to Delhi, where they would join the King's forces. The King ordered the letter to be made over to Hákim Ahsanúllah. Several relatives of Sháh Shújah-ul-Mulk (deceased), late Governor of Cabul, were presented at the audience by Mirza Mahommed Azim Khán. Ahmed Ali Khán, Faiz Ali Khán, a noble, and Moulvie Ahmed Ali, inhabitant of Bulubgarh, were presented to the King. They declared their loyalty to the King and to the Mogul Dynasty. By a written order they were told to remain with all their retainers and soldiers. Yúsúf Ali, a noble of Rámpúr, came and reported that he had taken possession of certain districts. He was also told to remain at Delhi with his followers. The city Kotwál came to say that he could only get thirty tents, which he had sent on to General Bakht Khán's camp. The police officer stationed at the Cashmere Gate requested, at the same time, that the King would give orders concerning the property of deceased persons which he had in his keeping. General Bakht Khán wrote a petition begging the King to demand four lakhs of rupees for the pay of the troops from the Nawáb of Jajjar. The petition was numbered, and orders were issued accordingly to the Nawáb. Seven deserters from the English camp came to Mirza Mogul, and reported that the English had only 2,000 native troops, and that these were dying owing to insufficient food; that all their ammunition was exhausted, and that the Rájah of Patiála had ceased, since several days, to supply food to the commissariat. Three hundred cavalry came in to-day from the adjacent districts, and reported themselves to General Bakht Khán. A trooper came in from Cawnpore, and reported that three regiments of foot and four of cavalry were hastening up to Delhi. Ahmed Khán, Resaldár,[1] deserted from the English camp and came to his house in the city. Mahommed Bakht Khán, hearing this, ordered him to be seized, as he thought he was a spy. He sent him and two sergeants who had come from Bareilly to the Kotwáli. Two Europeans found concealed at Pahárganj were killed by some troopers. Some camels, laden with grain from the English camp, were captured and taken into the city. To-day it was rumoured in the city that the forces of the Rájah of Ulwar had attacked the mutineers from Nímuch, but that his troops had been defeated and two guns captured. The troops from Nasirabád expressed a wish to-day to appoint Mirza Jaimul as their commander. Some Játs, who had carried off three cannon belonging to Wallidád Khán, offered to return them, as he was a relative of the King. The army, this day, expressed a wish to be led against the English. A tax of eight annas a maund on sugar was ordered to be levied. Ten sowars of the Rajah of Bulubgarh's force, who were going to join the English, were captured near the tomb of Safdar Jang. They were escorting a buggy, and had several letters. A man stated, at the King's Durbár this morning, that the troops from Jhánsi, Muttra, and Nímuch, having joined, had attacked Agra. There had been a severe engagement three miles from the fort, where the English had

[1] Of the 9th Bengal Irregular Cavalry. He offered to enter Delhi as a spy, and got an advance of 1,000 rupees and deserted with the money in his pocket.

constructed a battery. The English had been beaten, and had been pursued up to the fort, which they eventually abandoned, as they found they could no longer hold it. On hearing this, Mahommed Bakht Khán was much pleased, and caused the victory to be proclaimed by beat of drum throughout the city, stating that the English were now no longer left at Agra.

July 13.—The King entered the Dewán-í-Khás by the Kaspura Gate. All the nobles of Delhi and the chiefs of the native army paid their respects. The victory of Agra formed the general subject of conversation for a long time. A regimental band played music expressive of good news (*muzda*) before the King in celebration of the victory. The King presented the band with two gold mohurs. The King charged Hákim Abdul Hak Khán with helping to send the buggy and letter and the ten sowars to the English. Hákim Ahsanúllah, who was present at the King's levée with the view of helping Hákim Abdul Hak to meet the accusation, remarked that he, Abdul Hak, had thrown off allegiance to the Rájah of Bulubgarh for the last three years, and that he personally knew the Rájah wished to get hold of him in order to punish him. Ahsanúllah Khán expressed an opinion that he did not believe Abdul Hak had anything to do with the matter. Mirza Nosha and Mukarram Ali Khán read a *kasida* (a triumphal poem) in praise of the King's victory over the English. In the evening the King sent three dishes of food to the relatives of the Amir of Cabul. The youngest son of Hassan Ali Khán presented the King with a nazzar of four rupees. The Kotwál sent some boxes found in the house of some Khalassies evidently taken from the Magazine. A letter was written to Nawáb Abdul Rahmán Khán, of Jajjar, to send three lakhs of rupees; if he could not send five he was ordered to send three, and warned that if he disobeyed, a regiment would be quartered upon him to feed. Thirty-one guns were fired from the Selimgarh Bastion in honour of the victory at Agra. The same number of guns was fired from the camp of Mahommed Bakht Khán. The Sepoys plundered bamboos, beams, and wooden posts from Mir Mehdi's shop on the banks of the river; General Bakht Khán proclaimed that anyone caught plundering would be severely punished. Reports received that the English had fought an engagement near Fatehpur, and that they had been defeated by the native troops. Mahommed Bakht Khán distributed 500 rupees among the artillerymen in honour of the victory of Agra. The General waited on the King. A deserter from the English camp reported that supplies for the English were collected at Arab Serai; orders issued to intercept the same. Five hundred ladders were prepared by order of the General, to enable the Sepoys to escape over the wall, in case the English took the city and hemmed in the Sepoys.

July 14.—The King entered the Dewán-i-Khás through the Kaspura Gate. Mirza Hassan Ali Khán, Amin-u-dín Khán, Zia-u-dín Khán, and other noblemen, attended the levée, and paid their respects. Mirza Hassan Béy, nephew of Moulvie Sadr-u-dín Khán, presented a nazzar of five rupees, and Nasraf Kurram Ali Khán a nazzar of two rupees.

July 15.—The King, as usual, gave audience. Mirza Ahmed Ali Khán made his obeisance and reported the state of the city. Barkat Ali, Resaldár of Lucknow, reported that a force of 7,000 men, having killed all the English at the Bailey Guard, were now, with cries for justice, guarding the King's interests. Adjodya Pershád and Thákur Dáss, merchants, presented a petition to the purport that they had large stores of wine and spirits which had been taken possession of by the police. Some landholders, bad characters of Delhi complained that 200 cavalry had plundered a waggon and six camels. The King, after hearing their complaint, dismissed it, on the ground that it was false. A petition was read from the Nímuch camp, asking for artillery; an order was issued that no artillery could be spared until the English were driven from the Ridge. General Mahommed Bakht Khán represented that the *octroi* tax upon sugar and salt should be withdrawn, as the taxation would stop the importations into the city, and the army would suffer. The King replied that he thought the levy of *octroi* duties had been unwise, and they should be withdrawn. The King informed General Mahommed Bakht Khán that the officers of the army had urged him to appoint three Generals of Division; the General replied that it was necessary to do so. Two companies of the Grenadier Regiment from Umbálla came in, and reported that the Rájah of Patiála had shot down a thousand Sepoys who were marching through his territory towards Delhi. Two artillerymen and two sappers deserted from the English camp to-day, and, on the recommendation of Said Hassain Darogah, had been enlisted. Some person who had been watching the English camp with a telescope was arrested. Mirza Mogul presented the King to-day with an excellent telescope. The King's principal wife (Zenut Mehal Begum) visited her own house to-day for some purpose. Mirza Mogul and officers were summoned by the King, and ordered to select three Generals of Division, placing eight regiments of infantry and two of cavalry under each. Under these arrangements the Bareilly Brigade alone remained under General Bakht Khán's command. Arrangements were made for systematically attacking the English camp. Wallidád Khán, the Collector of the Revenue, petitioned that he had been surrounded by enemies, and asked for assistance. After reading the petition, the King ordered it to be made over to Hákim Ahsanúllah Khán. It was reported to the King that Mahommed Bakht Khán had sent for Saligram the banker and had demanded money of him. The banker had replied that all his papers and several thousands of rupees had been plundered, and he was ruined. He was allowed to leave, but a number of soldiers were placed on guard over his house. The same day information was received that the English were constructing a masked battery near the Masjid, and that it had been armed. Information was received that Captain Robinson, Superintendent of Sirsa, was coming in command of a force sent by the Rájah of Bhawalpúr, and with some elephants of the Rájah of Bikanír, and that a small force of English had been sent to guard the road from Alipur to Karnaul. Information was received from Jajjar that Nawáb Bahádur Jang had pledged jewellery to the amount of 16,000 rupees with the Nawáb of Jajjar, and further, that on a subsequent occasion, he had again sent jewellery to the value of 13,000 rupees, which the Nawáb had fraudulently taken and spent. Bahádur Jang believed this, as he had very good evidence of the Nawáb's bad faith, and had accused him of misappropriating the money and of spending it in paying his troops. The following rebel force was reported to be at Jajjar: the 8th and 11th regiments of foot, nine companies of artillerymen. These would arrive on the 24th, at Karnaul. The Rájah of Bulubgarh had taken into his service 200 troopers who had lately been in the employ of the English. Information was received that the tribes near Gujerat had plundered the city and had killed five hundred persons. Nawáb Mahommed Khán Walli has taken possession of the treasure from Bijnúr.

July 18.—The King entered the Dewán-Ám, or public hall of audience, and received the salutations of the nobles who were present. A letter was written to Madan Sing, a landholder on the banks of the Jumna, to stop murdering and plundering people, which he admitted he had been doing. Haidar Hassan Khán, the Darogah of the artillery lines, brought two men, spies, who stated that the English force was about six thousand men in camp. Orders issued to Hassan Ali Khán to write to Jajjar at once for three lakhs of rupees to be sent without delay. The rebel forces from Nasirabad and Delhi engaged the English to-day. The fighting continued for some time. The English were overpowered, and retreated, leaving their guns on the field of battle. The rebel force from Jhánsi, elated with success, attacked the English with great vigour, and killed three camels. The rebels intended to carry off the guns, but they were so firmly fixed in the ground that it was found impossible to move them, especially as they were bound together with heavy chains. A counter-attack of one thousand native troops from the English camp against the rebels recovered the ground lost in the morning, and drove the enemy back. About seventy English soldiers concealed themselves in the *serai* of Mahbúb Ali Khán. Several hundred infantry and cavalry of the rebel forces surrounded them. When the English saw they could not be rescued, they came out and made off, but were all killed. The rebels lost two hundred men.

July 19.—The King went to Selimgarh. After that he gave an audience. The rebel guard, according to custom, received him with a royal salute. A relative presented him with a nazzar of two rupees. Faiz Ali Khán Fozdar also presented a nazzar of two rupees. Fifty artillerymen lately in the employ of the Rájah of Jeypúr presented themselves, and represented that the Rájah had sheltered Europeans, and that the Pundit was always deceiving the

Rájah by telling him to side with the English, but that Ráwul Sheo Sing and the whole army was anxious to join the rebels, and, as soon as an opportunity occurred, intended to seize the Rájah and bring him into the service of the King. Orders were issued to them to report themselves to General Mahommed Bakht. Twenty troopers joined the rebels to-day from Gwalior. They were ordered to report themselves to Mirza Mogul. General Mahommed Bakht reported to the King that the English sergeant and two English soldiers who had been brought to Delhi by the —— Regiment had been executed in the river-bed of the Jumna. The King, as if under divine inspiration, suddenly said: "If I be altogether victorious, after the victory I shall go to Agra, and make a pilgrimage to Ajmere, and visit the tomb of Salim Chaste (?), if the Most High be willing and will fulfil all my desires." Orders issued to Ahmed Kúli Khán to attend the audiences daily. The King remained till a late hour discussing the insubordinate conduct of the rebel Sepoys belonging to the Delhi and Meerut Regiments. Ali Ahmed Khán, Vakíl, and Faiz Mahommed Khán, of ——, attended the Durbár. They presented two gold mohurs, and represented, on the part of their client, that his family had served the King's ancestors, and that he would immediately join the King with a force of 400 men. He was desired by letter to come at once. It was rumoured that Sir T. Metcalfe, accompanied by artillery and two hundred cavalry, was encamped at Ráni Serai, and that two hundred Sikhs were at Alipur. It was also stated that the landholders and grain-dealers of Pánipat were supplying the English camp with provisions, and that the English were throwing up a battery at Sabzimándi, and further, that two hundred English had gone in the direction of Meerut to collect material. From Newari came information that Ráo

Túlla Rám had taken a large force with him to collect revenue, but he had been told by some five thousand men that they had already paid the revenue to Nawáb Ahmed Ali, chief of Farukhnagar. They asked for assistance; the Ráo had replied that he had no power to render them assistance, but, if they wished to oppose the Nawáb, he would become their chief. Eventually Ráo Túlla Rám ran away! Orders issued to General Mahommed Bakht Khán to receive five lakhs of rupees from Muttra; he was to return quickly with the money, and pay the troops. Abdul Hak, the Revenue Collector of Gurjawan, was appointed a police superintendent. Azim Ali Khán, Resaldár, was sent by the King's orders to bring in treasure from Jajjar. The King received a report that the army had gone out to fight, but that the English did not care to engage. It became an artillery duel. One artilleryman was killed and two wounded of the King's forces, and one bullock belonging to a battery was killed.

July 20.—Hassan Ali Khán, Mirhad Ali Khán, the sons of Ahmed Sing, deceased, together with many other nobles, attended the King's Durbár. A number of evil-minded landholders of Bágpat attended, and reported that two hundred Europeans, with two guns and five hundred native infantry, had gone to Bágpat with the intention of building a bridge there, and were collecting the Land Revenue. Orders were issued to General Mahommed Bakht Khán to take such steps as he thought best to oppose the English. A number of sappers deserted from the English camp, and their officers attended the Durbár, and reported that the English fighting strength was 6,000 men. If they were attacked by the whole force in Delhi, the King would probably be victorious; but if there were any delay, the English would obtain reinforcements from England, and the

King's forces would not be able to prevail against them. A number of cavalry troopers sought service; the King replied he had no money to pay for their services. Several unarmed soldiers applied for muskets; the King replied he had no reserve arms to give them. Muthra Dáss, treasurer of Bijnúr, sent the King several Sepoys that he had caused to be arrested. He presented the King at the same time with a nazzar of five rupees. Another person also at the same time paid a nazzar of five rupees. Mahommed Khán, son of Nawáb Najibabád, presented a petition on the part of the Nawáb, asking for a written expression of the King's commendation for having taken from the English Najibabád, Rámpur, Bijnúr, Dusnaria, Nagina. The petition was ordered to be sent to General Mahommed Bakht Khán for reply, as the King would not commit himself. Ghulám Nabi Khán presented a letter from the Nawáb of Jajjar to the purport that, owing to the rebellion, it was impossible to collect revenue; but, as far as lay in his power, to the extent of three lakhs, the King might draw upon him. The Thánadár of Negumboda forwarded certain property belonging to deceased Europeans which he had discovered in the house of one Rám Gopál. The King, after inspecting the property, ordered it to be made over to the Begum. The Thánadár of Sháhdara sent in five landholders concerned in murders. They were ordered to be kept in confinement. Four deserters from the Sepoys were sent under arrest to the King by General Mahommed Bakht Khán. The King ordered them to be imprisoned. Fifty Sepoys were enlisted, and sent to assist Nawáb Wallidád Khán, the Revenue Collector. As they were passing the Calcutta Gate, they were stopped by the guard, who suspected them of deserting under pretence of acting in the service of the Revenue Department; so they deprived them of their muskets. A Resaldár, with several troopers, wanted to get away to-day to Gwalior; they were also stopped by the guards at the Calcutta Gate, and their weapons were taken from them and they were plundered.

It was rumoured to-day that, in the recent fight with the English, a woman dressed like a Sepoy had acted with great bravery; when the rebel Sepoys ran away, she remained opposed to a number of English, and killed one English soldier. Two regiments of infantry and five hundred cavalry, with six guns and ammunition carried on camels, started this day, under orders of General Mahommed Bakht Khán, for Bágpat, to prevent the English from building a bridge. Four regiments of foot and one thousand cavalry, with six guns and ammunition, went off to Alipur to cut off the commissariat supplies. Some troops also marched outside the city for the purpose of attacking the English and distracting their attention, and till midday they carried on a desultory artillery fire. After twelve o'clock the force returned to the city. During the afternoon it was rumoured that the rebels had that day gained a great victory, and that the English had fled towards Alipur. There was great excitement in the city. At once the city rose, and about three thousand horsemen rushed out to share in the victory; they were augmented by some four hundred Mahommedans of high and low birth, and altogether by about six hundred fanatics armed with clubs, swords, spears, and guns. In high spirits they rushed out of the city, intending to plunder the English camp. When they neared the English camp and found that the English were there as usual, they were mightily "sold," and returned very crestfallen to the city. The rebels, however, kept up the firing till the evening. News came from Meerut that the English strongly held that place, and had apprehended Mirza Haider Sheikh, son of Sulimán Sheikh, and had hanged him. Information reached General Mahommed Bakht Khán that several native regiments were coming. A camel sowar and a messenger came from Lohára to get news, to ascertain if the troops coming were rebels, or drafts from the English camp. Information came that the English cavalry and infantry regiments had reached Gwalior. Ghulám Mahommed Khán, with one hundred cavalry, reached Delhi. News also came that the revenue-payers had refused to pay Ráo Túlla Rám, of Rewári, any revenue, as they were partisans of Ghulám Mahommed Khán. Ráo Túlla Rám had come to Delhi, to obtain authority to enforce payment, and to gain possession of the village.

July 21.—The King visited the fort of Selimgarh, and inspected a newly raised regiment of foot numbered 56, after which he gave a public audience. Mir Said Ali Khán, Mirza Zin-u-dín Khán, Mirza Ulla Khán, and other nobles were present. Several landholders of Rajnahar Sing, chief of Nahab Gari, complained to the King against their chief. After hearing their petition the King made over the petition to Hassanullah Khán, with the observation that the Rájah had shown disloyalty and ingratitude. A camel sowar arrived from Gházibád and stated that 200 cavalry and three companies of sappers were marching from Benares, and would arrive in the city next morning. Eighteen cavalry-men deserted from the English camp and joined the rebels. A resaldár of the Jhánsi force came to-day to the King and complained that he had never received pay nor reward for his services. The King replied that the Jhánsi force had appropriated three lakhs of rupees, not a penny of which had come into the royal treasury. From what source could he grant pay and rewards? The resaldár was ordered to report himself to Mirza Mogul. Mir Said Ali Khán presented the King with a waist-sash. The King divided it in half, and sent half to General Mahommed Bakht Khán. Six hundred Jehádis from Tonk arrived and appeared before the King to-day; they reported that two thousand more men were on their way to join the King. The King replied: "I have no money to give you." One company of infantry arrived from Sahárunpúr, and were ordered to report themselves to Bakht Khán. The King sent General Mahommed Bakht Khán seventeen trays of food from the royal table. Mahommed Khán, chief of Najíbabád was ordered by letter to send money and horses for the King's use. It was privately told me that Mirza Mogul intended to review the whole army three or four days from then. Orders were to-day issued to General Bakht Khán to attack the English vigorously and simultaneously at Sabzimándi, Alipur, Mubárak Bágh, and at other points, so as to ensure their total discomfiture. He was to tell off the infantry and cavalry into brigades, and was to take immediate steps to do this. Letters were sent to the chief of Jajjar warning him that if he did not send the money demanded from him at once, the King would take other steps to enforce his orders. The revenue collector appointed by the King sent in 3,900 rupees collected by him. One hundred cavalry deserted from the English camp and came into Delhi. They were ordered to encamp outside and under the fort. The force sent into Bágpat in accordance with the representation of certain landholders returned and reported that, though they had searched everywhere, they had seen no English; the landholders had, therefore, been arrested, and had been brought back to Delhi for inquiry as to why they had made false representations. It was rumoured in Delhi that a European force had retaken Cawnpore and had killed the son of the Péshwa.

July 22.—The King entered the Public Hall of Audience through the Kaspura Gate. General Mahommed Bakht Khán was present, and complained that certain evil-disposed persons were spreading a report that he was in collusion with the English, and that when the King's troops were attacking the English, he (the General) was in the habit of slinking home and of leaving his men to fight without orders. The King replied that he was quite certain of the General's loyalty, and regretted the vexation he had suffered from such slanderous rumours. He (the King) had no cause of enmity against the English, but he felt he would be exalted by that army which had rushed to his protection. Mirza Abu Bakr, Mirza Rawas, and Mirza Abdulla were present at the Durbár. General Mahommed Bakht Khán rose from his seat, went behind the King, and whispered something in his ear. The Princes, who were present, took objection to his doing so, and openly charged him with bad manners in thus violating the customs of good society, by whispering into the King's ear in their presence. The General apologised, and, after flattery from him to the Princes, the matter dropped. The General suggested that the King should order the troops to harass the English with daily attacks. He (the General) would undertake to guard the bridge of boats with part of the force under his immediate command, and he would also attack the English in the morning with the remaining portion of his troops. The General then asked for a private audience in the King's apartments. He went, accompanied by two Moulvies, and presented a petition, which the King signed. The General then left for Selimgarh, and examined the batteries and bastions. After this he visited Mirza Mogul, and suggested that a general parade of the army should be ordered to take place a few days from then, at which he should order every man to be sworn by oath that he would continue to fight against the English, giving those who were faint-hearted, leave to return to their homes. If any of those who took the oath were found skulking on the field of battle, they should be severely dealt with. A general order to this effect was issued. Information reached the King that cavalry from Benares would arrive in the city. The English artillery fire began to tell upon the city, and a number of the city people were killed. I heard also that the English had cut down all the trees in Mir Said Ali Khán's garden, and had constructed a battery there. News also came that a thousand English soldiers, with a great number of camels and several thousand Sikhs, were encamped at Karnaul, and that a long train of ammunition and stores had reached the English camp. It was also reported that the English had blown away three Mahommedan fanatics from the guns at Agra, and intended to blow up the whole city. It was said that Lál Juti Pershád had petitioned the Lieutenant-Governor at Agra to the effect that all who were concerned in the rebellion were assuredly deserving of punishment, but that many of the Hindus were not seditious, and to punish the innocent with the guilty was very unjust; and he begged that the blowing away from guns should be stopped. News came that men were being hung every day. It was also reported that Lál Juti Pershád had promised the Lieutenant-Governor of the North-West Provinces that he would advance as much money as was required. Information was received that a banker was in the habit of visiting the English camp daily with supplies. To-day it was known in the city that the English had issued orders to the Revenue Collector of Koti Kasim, to Akbar Ali, Nawáb of Patudi, and to the Nawáb of Jajjar, that they would be held responsible for the collections of revenue due within their states, and were warned not to pay money to the King. Orders issued to Makand Lál to prepare a burial-place (?) for Nawáb Mahbúb Ali Khán, deceased. Hakim Ahsanullah Khán presented himself before the King, to lay before him the affairs of the kingdom. One item was the petition of Wallidád Khán to the effect that Abdul Latíf Khán was conspiring against him, and trying to oust him from his position. He requested that in the future the King would not hold direct communication with him. Azim Ali Khán, Resaldár, reported that the Nawáb of Jajjar had promised to send three lakhs of rupees on the following Wednesday. A petition was read in open Durbár from Rao Tulla Rám, noble of Rewári, to the effect that he was sending his brother with a confidential communication to the King, and begged he might be heard and a favourable answer sent. Orders were sent to Mahommed Akbar, the chief of Patudi, to send in the revenue from Sashpur and other villages. A hundred cavalry troopers from Gwalior reported themselves. In the course of the afternoon Mirza Mogul and other princes reviewed the whole force outside the city walls, and the orders of General Mahommed Bakht Khán were read. The unanimous answer of the army was, that they would continue to fight the English to the bitter end. News came that the Rájah of Sashpur was dead, and that the Vakíl of the Rájah, who had been on bad terms with the Ráni, had become reconciled to her.

July 23.—The King went to Selimgarh Fort and gave orders that the cavalry regiment, 600 strong, coming from Benares, was to be met with all proper ceremony, and paraded before him. When this was done the regiment was ordered to encamp outside the Ajmere Gate. The King then returned to the Palace and entered the private apartments. Mir Said Ali Khán and Hassan Ali Khán attended the King. The landholders of Klanore brought an elephant belonging to the English which had fallen into their hands; the King, after inspecting the animal, ordered it to be taken to the elephant stables. The Agent for Rao Tulla Rám, noble of Rewári, presented a nazzar of one gold mohur on his master's behalf, and five rupees on his own, and transacted some business connected with the estate of Bhora. Matters connected with Nawáb Said Ali Khán, of Farukhnaggar, were also explained to His Majesty. Gopál Sing and Dokul Sing presented five rupee nazzars, and were ordered to report themselves to General Mahommed Bakht Khán. Orders were issued to the Revenue Collector of Kot Kasim to bring all his accounts for the King's personal inspection. A dispatch was received from the force marching from Nímuch that they had reached Jáloul, and would shortly arrive to drive the English from the Ridge, and would retake it.

July 24.—Mir Said Ali Khán and some of the Sirdars (Chiefs) held a consultation regarding the insubordination of the soldiers. The Chief Police Officer of the city personally reported that he had brought 2,800 lbs. of sweetmeats for the delectation of the soldiers; the King inspected the same. Mirza Abu Bakr represented to the King that if he would authorize him, he would take 2,000 men and go out to collect the revenue of the villages in the direction of Gurgan. His Majesty replied he would take time to consider. A deputation of officers represented that they were in great want of pay. Mirza Akbar Sultán summoned all the wealthy bankers of the city, and extorted a sum of 8,000 rupees from them. In this matter the principal movers were the Begum Zenut Mahal, Ahsanullah Khán, her minister, and Mahmud Lál. Mirza Ali Baksh sought an interview with the King, and privately advised him to open negotiations with the English. The King replied he was powerless and unable to do so. He was warned that if he failed to do so it would be injurious to His Majesty: there the matter dropped. Some 200 fanatics from Nujíbabad arrived and halted outside the city. Mirza Mogul waited on the King, and with an escort of 100 cavalry visited the city and distributed 100 rupees among the fakirs. The King sat at night in the Council Chamber and conversed with Hákim Ahsanullah Khán until a late hour. The King sent cooked food and a piece of fine linen to his instructor in religion, Moulvie Hassan Asgorie.

July 25.—His Majesty sat in the Public Hall of Audience and received the nobles. Ghulám Mahommed Khán, the Revenue Collector of Kot Kasim, was ordered to pay in the balance due of 3,000 rupees; the Collector stated his inability to do so. Gungarám Harkara (messenger), Háfiz Abdul Hákim, and Jewan Lál, were directed to take several hundred cavalry and realize the money from the landholders. Samnud Khán, Resaldár, presented himself before the King, offered a nazzar of one rupee, and reported the affairs of his part of the country. A deputation from the Nímuch camp waited on the King and complained that there was no room for them in the Arab Serai where they were located, and asked for better quarters; their petition was ordered to be sent to General Mahommed Bakht Khán. Azim Ali, Resaldár, petitioned the King that the demand for money from his master, the Rájah of Jajjar, might be withdrawn, but said he would send in a few thousand rupees, which was all he had; some of this would be sent in the course of a few days, and the rest a little later. His Majesty, after hearing the petition, directed Hákim Ahsanullah Khán to prepare a reply. One hundred and fifty cavalry of the Gwalior contingent, who had joined the Nímuch rebels, presented themselves at the Palace to ask for quarters to be assigned to them, but in the meantime the King entered the private apartments. Information was received that a man armed with a written authority from the English to raise money had been for some days in the house of Alap Pershád, Agent of the former Nawáb of Jajjar, and was on his way to Muttra, travelling in a bullock-cart. When he reached the Delhi Gates, the guards searched the man and found the paper in question; they then confiscated his cart and severely beat the man. After this some 400 of the soldiers went to Alap Pershád's house and charged him with concealing Europeans, and on this pretence they searched and plundered his house, and those of seven other persons, and carried off property to the value of 50,000 rupees. As soon as General Mahommed Bakht Khán heard of this he sent off several hundred men to stop the outrage, but these soldiers would not interfere with the plunderers. Gordohon Dáss, resident of Luttu, was leaving the city in a cart, and had with him for his own protection some cartridges, gunpowder, and bullets; the guard at the Delhi Gate searched his cart, and arrested him on the ground that he was taking ammunition to the English. On this pretext several hundred Sepoys went to this man's house and extorted 2,000 rupees from him by intimidation; one soldier was wounded. Information was received that four regiments of native infantry, 1,700 cavalry, with several lakhs of rupees, several fieldpieces, and forty elephants, under the command of Heera Sing, Ghosh Mahommed Khán, and Sadhari Lál, were in the Nímuch camp, and in the morning would encamp below the breastworks. During the night several residents of the city and Palace were killed by the fire from the English camp. Ghulám Mahommed Khán visited General Mahommed Bakht Khán.

July 26.—Mirza Zin-u-dín Khán and Mirza Amín-u-dín Khán were present at the audience this morning. The rent-collectors of the Shah of Lucknow gave in a petition to His Majesty to the purport that they were intent on realizing the revenue, which they would send to the royal treasury as soon as it was realized. Amanut Ali, police-officer, lately in the employ of the English, presented himself at the Durbár, and, after offering a nazzar, represented, on behalf of Nawáb Hassan Ali Khán, that he had been engaged in raising ten thousand men for the King's army, and on this account had not been able to come to Delhi. A letter was received from one of the chiefs of Lahore, in which it was written that Sir John Lawrence had issued a proclamation in the Punjab, which declared that the King of Delhi had offered large rewards to anyone who would kill Sikhs, and bring in their heads. Several Jehádis from Tonk were introduced to the King by Samnud Khán: each presented the King with a nazzar of two rupees. Rao Tulla Rám and Rám Sing, noble, uncle of the chief of Rewári, were presented at the Durbár, and represented several matters. Some cavalry soldiers stated that they had carried off a number of chargers from the English camp. Mirza Mogul inspected a cavalry regiment, 800 strong, in the Nímuch camp. The officers presented him with gold mohurs, a horse, and an elephant with trappings, as nazzars, but Mirza Mogul declined their presents. In accordance with the petition of General Mahommed Bakht Khán, he was invested with the rank and title of Governor. The King informed the General that he was much pleased with his conduct. In return, the General expressed his gratitude and offered a nazzar of ten gold mohurs, and promised that Joan Bakht should be recognized as the Heir Apparent. Thakúr Gopál Sing, son of Dhobul Sing, sought an interview, in order to represent certain matters. Mirza Abu Bakr, Mirza Abdulla, and Mirza Kwáss entered the audience chamber, and informed the King that 252 lbs. of oil were consumed every night in the English camp, and that all this quantity went from the city. A trooper committed suicide to-day, on the Jumma Masjid, by shooting himself. The King received information that when the Nímuch troops were approaching Bulubgarh, Dewán Sunpuk Rao went ten miles forward to meet them, and, with much suavity and politeness (with a touch of dissimulation), accompanied the force to Futiabad, when he was allowed to leave. The King received private information that it was rumoured at Meerut that the English intended to punish the rebels on the 1st of August.

July 27.—Awala Pershád and Munshi Ratnal attended the audience, and complained to His Majesty that the Sepoys had plundered property to the value of £10,000 from their houses, on the pretence that they had concealed Europeans. The King ordered the complaint to be inquired into by Mirza Mogul, and arrangements to be made to recover the property taken away by the soldiers. An urgent dispatch was received from the police-officer of Bakhtghari, that a body of 2,000 men were assembling with the intention of plundering the city. Orders were issued to General Mahommed Bakht Khán to send a force to scatter these insurgents. Orders were issued to Moulvie Sirdár-u-dín Khán to preside over the criminal courts, but the Moulvie declined to do so, saying he could not undertake the office as long as the English remained unconquered. To-day two Sikhs came on behalf of the chiefs of Lahore to say that 200,000 cartridges had been safely delivered to the troops in the Nímuch camp. Orders were issued that these were not to be wasted, as the supply in the Magazine was running short. A native deserter came in to-day from the English camp. General Mahommed Bakht Khán held a parade to-day, and warned the soldiers not to harass and plunder the people in the city. Those who transgressed this order would not be allowed to participate in the coming victory. Two native artillerymen, deserters from the English camp, came in to-day. They stated that there were very few fighting men left in the camp, but that the English were very strong in artillery and siege trains. Orders were issued to the officers of the Nímuch force to present themselves before the King at once. They sent back a message that they would be present on the morrow. Important news to-day that 20,000 Europeans had landed from ships, that Cawnpore, Benares, Fatehgarh, Allahabad, etc., had been reoccupied by the English, that there had been some insubordination in the army of the Rájah of Patiála, and that several hundred mules laden with ammunition and stores had been escorted by the Rájah's troops and safely delivered in the English camp. It was reported to the King that the English had constructed an armed battery of eighteen guns at Hirsul, another at Barampari and Alipur, also in the garden of Nawáb Said Ali Khán; and that they were digging a deep ditch a mile in length near the garden of Mehaldar Khán to stop any advance, and to prevent any attack on their camp. The English had also sent 800 cavalry, escorting some guns, to prevent the Sepoys making a bridge over the canal, and they were said to be inspecting the country with the view of selecting a suitable battlefield where they might destroy the rebels.

July 28.—The King inspected the Fort of Selimgarh, and he proceeded afterwards to the Hall of Public Audience. Mir Said Ali Khán and Hákim Abdul Hak, the sons of Rájah Ahmed Sing, deceased, also Hassan Ali Khán and other nobles, were present. There was a great gathering of officers. The General Mahommed Bakht, Sirdhari Lál,

Ghosh Mahommed, and Heera Sing were present. The latter related the fight with the English at Agra. The recent report of the English reinforcements was discussed. Kamund Lál petitioned that he might be allowed to take the body of his deceased mother through the Calcutta Gate of the city. The petition was granted. Rao Tulla Rám, of Rewári, wrote asking that he might obtain a grant of the village of Bhora. The petition was made over to Ahsanullah Khán for report. The King ordered letters to be written to the General and officers of the army that no cows were to be killed within the city during the festival of the Eed, and if any Mahommedan should do so he would be blown away from a gun; and whoever, on the part of a Musalmán, helped to kill a cow, would also be killed. Hákim Ahsanullah Khán demurred to such an order, and said he would consult the Moulvies. The King, on hearing this, became very angry, closed the audience, and retired to the private apartments. Some troopers brought in six ponies they had captured. Fifty cavalry came in from Cawnpore, and reported that the English had retaken the place. They brought with them an elephant which they presented to the King; they also reported that the Nana Sahib Péshwa had run away. The officers of the Nímuch force presented the King with twenty-six elephants; they were ordered to be sent to General Mahommed Bakht Khán. It was reported that the English had captured several grass-cutters belonging to the Bareilly camp, and had questioned them as to the number of Sepoys, and had chaffed them as to why General Mahommed Bakht Khán did not come out to fight; and after cutting off their ears and noses had let them go. According to the King's orders Bakht Khán had it proclaimed that cow-killing in the city was forbidden. Mirza Mogul convened a council of war at his house; he also deputed a force of 200 cavalry for the protection of his mother. He then went to the Ajmere Gate. The King ordered that Ghulám Nubee Khán, representative of the Nawáb of Jajjar, should be excluded from the Durbár, as his master had not sent the money demanded from him. Ghulám Mahommed Khán, noble of Farukhnagar, presented a certificate for the King's signature appointing him Tehsildár of Bhora. It was reported that Mahommed Bakht Khán had issued orders for the arrest of Rai Rám Sing, uncle of Tulla Rám of Rewári, on the ground of a series of complaints prepared by a number of the inhabitants of Rewári against him, but, being warned, Rám Sing left the city before he was caught. It was reported that Bombay troops had arrived at Rewári.

July 29.—A Durbár was held to-day in the city by Mirzas Amin-u-dín Khán and Zia-u-dín Khán, and other of the principal men in the city. General Bakht Khán came as a representative of the King. Kádir Baksh, Subahdár of the Sappers, addressed the meeting and charged Bakht Khán with neglecting to attack the English. "Many days had passed and the General had not led his forces to fight; the result was that the English were collecting every requirement for successfully attacking the city." The General lost his temper, but was restrained by the King, who remarked that the Subahdár had spoken truly. Nothing definite was settled. The officers of the Nímuch force represented that they were short of tents; they were referred to the General. A landholder appeared and presented a nazzar of a rupee. Salaries of the King's officers were distributed to-day to the amount of 120,000 rupees. His Majesty sent four trays of meats from his table to General Mahommed Bakht Khán. News reached the King that several thousand Sepoys from Lahore were investing Patiála. Several Sikhs, retainers of the Rájah Narunder Sing, deserted from the English camp and appeared at the Durbár, and they reported that the English were badly off for artillery horses, but had plenty of guns. Five hundred soldiers, foot and horse, from Fatehpur, arrived, and were ordered to report themselves to General Bakht Khán. The General this day issued orders to Hassan Ali Khán to go and realize three lakhs of rupees from the Rájah of Jajjar, under threat that he would send a force to compel the Rájah to pay. News came to the Palace that troops from Bombay had reached Madhu Ganj, and were pushing on for Delhi. Ramjí Mall and Jítmall, bankers, were ordered to pay five lakhs to the royal treasury, and threatened if they did not comply. A regiment from Nasirabad joined the Nímuch force.

July 30.—The King went this day to see a fakir in the Fahatab Garden, and talked to him for some time regarding the fighting. After seeing him, His Majesty consulted Mir Said Ali Khán and Hákim Abdul Hak Khán; after that he entered the private apartments. An unpleasant incident occurred. The son of Nawáb Mahommed Mir Khán, deceased, was seated during the audience. After the King had left, Mir Said Ali Khán said to him: "It is very improper that you should remain seated whilst all the other nobles stand in the presence of the King, and you, too, must in future stand, and not take a seat, or it will not go well with you." Certain fanatics (Jehádis) represented to the King that they had no food, and were starving. His Majesty's reply was that the treasury was empty. Wallidád Khán, Nawáb of Bulubgarh, sent a petition to say he had collected 200 horses and several fieldpieces that had fallen into his hands, but he wanted infantry to convoy them. The King directed General Bakht Khán to send a regiment of foot, four hundred cavalry, and two field guns, to assist the Nawáb. The General, however, wrote to the Nawáb that he must first send him a present of one thousand rupees, and then he would despatch the force to his assistance. Gobind, the Nazir, complained to the King that General Bakht Khán had ordered him to give up his house for the use of the soldiers; the King issued instructions to the General not to harass the petitioner. A messenger from Jeypur presented himself, and after offering a nazzar of one rupee, communicated to His Majesty that the soldiers of the Jeypur army were dissatisfied with their Rájah, because he had concealed eleven Europeans within the private (female) apartments of the Palace, and that they intended, when the Rájah next appeared in public, to arrest him and take him prisoner to Delhi to appear before the King. The Rájah, it was said, had enlisted 2,000 Rájputs for his protection, and had mounted cannon around his Palace. The soldiers in their petition asked for a royal letter approving their conduct. The King dictated a written reply, that whoever was loyal to the King should in due time be rewarded. Letter received from the Rájah Nakir Sing, of Bulubgarh, through General Bakht Khán, praying that whatever fault he might have committed, he might be pardoned. Two cavalry deserters came in from the English camp, and stated that they had been sent from Meerut to bring in commissariat stores from Saharanpur, that they had been attacked on the way by Gujars (robbers) and the stores all plundered, and that the petitioners now wished to join the King's forces. Three shawls and twenty-one rupees were sent to Dewán Makand Lál on account of the death of his master, as a token of sympathy. At four o'clock in the afternoon Ramjí Mall, banker, and Puttia Mall, merchant, waited on the King at the Durbár, and after making their obeisance Ramjí Mall placed his turban at the King's feet, and pleaded that he had not a penny in the world left. His banking firm was at Lucknow, and his house had been plundered; he had nothing to give the King. His Majesty replied, "I ask you for money as a loan; I do not want to take it as a tax. See, my friend Jeoti Persha had advanced 30,000 rupees to the English; on what grounds do you demur to lend me money?" The King told Puttia Mall that he must advance 50,000 rupees. Orders were issued that the Nímuch force was to march in the morning in the direction of Alipur. Several citizens were killed to-day by the English fire, which reached the city. There was a quarrel between officers of the Bareilly and Nímuch forces; General Bakht Khán went to the Nímuch camp and brought about a reconciliation.

July 31.—Nawáb Ahmed Ali Khán, Chief of Farukhnagar, sent a petition reminding the King of his connection with the Royal Family, and of the fact that he held a *jaghir* of two *crores* of rupees yearly, given to his ancestors by the Moguls; he complained that he was about to be attacked by Rao Tulla Rám, of Rewári. At the same time a letter was read, sent by Rao Tulla Rám to Ghulám Mahommed Khán, with the words: "Are you intoxicated that you think the English are going away from Hindustan? They will most assuredly return and will destroy you." It was also stated in this letter that Rao Tulla Rám had sent some money to Rewári, which some landholders had seized; also that he had grossly insulted the Begum, and had not up to the present time appeared before the King. His Majesty desired that letters should be written to the Chief of Farukhnagar to send money to the royal treasury; also to Rao Tulla Rám. The children of Rájah Mahid Sing petitioned that seven villages given to their father by the King had been taken by the English, and prayed that the King would order them to be restored. A chief of the fanatics (Jehádis) arrived from Tonk, and presented a nazzar of five rupees. Juhir Lál, the keeper of the royal jewels, produced seven changes of raiment to be worn during the Eed festival. Mir Feraz Ali represented that the Jehádis were dying of hunger. The King replied he had no money to feed them. Feraz asked that they might be fed by the city people under the King's orders; the King highly approved of this proposal. A number of the officers of the Nímuch force appeared at the Durbár and reported that they had marched to Alipur at two o'clock in the night, and reached Bisari Bridge about eleven o'clock, where they came under artillery fire. They quickly destroyed the entrenchment thrown up by the English; they then mended the bridge, and returned, and had an engagement with the plunderers (English) in which about two hundred men on both sides had fallen. The King cried, "Bravo! well done!" and gave the officers great praise. It was also said that when the Nímuch force was crossing the bridge the English sent out reinforcements, but General Bakht Khán diverted and engaged their attention, and retreated on Alipur. The Revenue Collector appointed by the King at Ghaziabád sent in a petition to say that a collector on the part of the English with 100 soldiers had come there; but he had enlisted himself for the purpose of collecting the revenue, and at a convenient moment, with the assistance of fifty troopers, he had arrested eighteen revenue *burkundazes* (collecting staff) and seized five horses. The following items of news were circulated: that the English had hanged sixty-four men at Meerut on the 29th; that the Nána Sahib had killed 1,500 English soldiers who had reached Cawnpore, and had retaken possession of Cawnpore. Several residents of the city were arrested on the false pretence of concealing English. It was also stated that the Nímuch force, with two guns and

400 men, had gone towards the Ridge and Alipur, but when they found the guns could not travel, they had returned. A Moulvie said to the King to-day that, if he would permit him to recite a verse of the Koran over the entrails of a goat, then the guns of the English would become useless. Certain zemindars of Buri Basari petitioned the King that the English were demanding revenue from them. If the King would only give the order they would not pay a single pice, but would slaughter the English.

August 1.—The King held a Durbár. Hákim Ahsanullah Khán attended, also the other nobles. The King and all his courtiers went to public worship and prayer, and distributed six suits of clothing and three strings of jewels, and scimitars, to the Moulvies at the Jumma Masjid, Chota Masjid, and at the Eedgah, and four dresses of honour and three strings of jewels to Mirza Ahmed Sultán and Mirza Jehandád Khán, at the durbárs held at the Eedgah and Jumma Masjid, and at the former place the King sacrificed a sheep. Mirza Janwan Bakht and Hákim Ahsanullah Khán, also Rájah Ajít Sing, noble, of Patiála, Nazir Hassan, Mirza Mozuffer-ullah, Captain Dilwar Ali Khán, and other officers, presented nazzars in accordance with their rank, in value 8 gold mohurs and 120 rupees. News came to-day that the Nímuch force had had a fight with the English at Basi. Many were killed and wounded, and, on account of the rain, the whole force had suffered great inconvenience. His Majesty then entered his private apartments. The Begums presented nazzars. I heard privately that in the morning the English, with a battery of six guns, had attacked the Sepoys, and had beaten them back. Soldiers sent by the King's officials came with an order demanding 50,000 rupees from Munshi Sultán Sing, and 25,000 from me, and smaller sums from others. They were very importunate, and an altercation ensued. At last Lalla Sant Lál persuaded them to go away. He also interceded for us with Hyder Hussein Khán, who commanded the artillery. We also entreated Hákim Ahsanullah Khán, Lalla Bhola Náth, and others. The Hákim said the matter rested with General Bakht Khán, the Commander-in-Chief; he himself was unable to interfere; we must pay something to obtain release. Lalla Shám Lál, the Vakíl for the Heir Apparent, did his best for us. Mirza Ilahí Baksh made them believe we had no money, and it was useless to demand it.

August 2.—The Hall of Public Audience was filled this day with the brightness of the King's presence. Mirza Amin-u-dín Khán, Saadut Ali Khán, Vakíl, Fazl Hassan Khán, Ibrahim Ali Khán, Vakíl Akbar Ali Khán, were present; also General Samund Khán, Resaldár, Ghulám Nabi Khán, Vakíl, Hassan Ali Khán, and Moulvie Sadr-u-dín Khán. The value of the nazzars presented to-day was 126 rupees and 9 gold mohurs. The conversation turned for a long time on the fighting. Then the King recited some verse which he had composed, and which he sent to General Bakht Khán—

> "May all the enemies of the Faith be killed to-day;
> The Firinghis be destroyed, root and branch!
> Celebrate the festival of the Eed Kurban by great slaughter;
> Put our enemies to the edge of the sword—spare not!"

A petition was received from Rao Tulla Rám, with a nazzar of five gold mohurs. General Bakht Khán attended, and reported that, in consequence of the heavy rains, the troops that had gone in the direction of Basi had found the whole country flooded, and had returned. The King, on hearing this, became very angry and said: "You will never capture the Ridge." The same day the King summoned all his officers to the Hall of Public Audience in the evening, and addressed them:—"All the treasure that you brought me, you have expended; the Royal Treasury is empty and without a 'pice.' I hear that day by day the soldiers are leaving for their homes. I have no hopes of becoming victorious. My desire is, that you all leave the city and go to some other central point. If you do not, I will take such steps as seem to me most advisable." In answer to this address the officers tried to cheer His Majesty, and exclaimed: "By the help of God we will take the Ridge yet!" At that moment a round shot from the English entered the Selimgarh Fort and killed a Sepoy. A lengthy order was issued to me to the purport that I must present myself with 50,000 rupees. I recited the following verses in my mind:—

> "God rescue me from this trouble;
> No one but He knows what is passing in my mind."

Ahmed Mirza incited the princes against me, asking them to put a guard over my house day and night. Soldiers, horse and foot, were sent by Hyder Hossein Khán to trouble and importune me. At last Sant Lál took them to the Palace and executed a reconnaisance.

August 3.—Ghosh Mahommed Khán, an official of the Nímuch force, waited on the King. He refused to see him, saying he had no leisure. The officers of the Criminal Administration presented nazzars to Nawáb Kuli Khán, Vakíl. Mahommed Akbar Ali Khán of Patudi presented a gold mohur on behalf of his mistress the Begum. All the officers of the Army, in accordance with the orders of Mirza Mogul Beg, attended the Durbar. The subject of conversation was, for a short time, the last engagement. Ten troopers arrived from Fatehgarh and joined the rebels. A petition was received from the troops at Gwalior to the effect that 2,000 men were ready to march to Delhi if the King would give the order. He said in reply: "The Royal Treasury is empty." Some Jehádis from Nasirabad sent a petition saying 6,000 men there were of one mind, but that the English had retaken the city. The King dictated the reply: "Say there are 60,000 men in Delhi, and they have not yet driven the English away from the Ridge; what can your 6,000 do?" General Bakht Khán came to the Durbar and complained that the soldiers no longer obeyed his orders. The King replied: "Tell them, then, to leave the city." A courier presented a scimitar to the King, and said: "This scimitar belonged to the Prophet." A crier went about the city proclaiming that the Akúnd of Swat was marching to Delhi with 1,400 Jehâds to serve the King. No one prevented him from doing so. Mirza Mogul went out for a ride with an escort of 200 cavalry as far as Jingpur. This afternoon, while one hour of day remained, there was an earthquake. It was told me privately that Akbar Khán, the Chief of Patudi, was in the city in disguise. Mirza Mogul, through the persuasions of Lalla Sant Lál, came to me. I told him all about myself, that I really had no money. All my salary went to pay my ordinary expenses. I had worked all my life honestly, and had amassed no money. I had no money now unless my salary was paid. The King had it in his power to do what he liked. The Mirza charged me with sending news to the English, with causing Brahmins to pray for the restoration of the English and for the defeat of the King, and with calling the Sepoys "faithless traitors." He said: "All I can do for you is to reduce the amount you have to pay."

August 4.—Whilst the King was in the private apartments a deputation of officers came with the complaint that Hákim

Ahsanullah Khán was in communication with the English, and that it was he who had caused the proclamation to be made that 1,400 Jehāds from Swat had reached the halting-place, and would arrive in the city to-day. The officers stated that from inquiries they had ascertained that the men were Pathans enlisted by the English, who, to make themselves masters of the city, were coming to fight the Purbeahs and kill them. The King replied to the officers that he had no information of any such proclamation, and was certain that Hákim Ahsan was not concerned in any such treachery. On the contrary, the King knew the Akúnd had deputed a trustworthy agent to act as his deputy, and had placed his own sword in his hands with an order to destroy the English in the name of God and the Prophet. So convinced were the officers of the Hákim's treachery, that they went in a body to his house to kill him, but Hákim Ahsan was not at home, having been warned. The King sent for the officers and Mirza Mogul, and after flattering the former told them that he was satisfied that the man who had made the proclamation was an agent of the English; he also told them that he had appointed Mirza Mogul and General Bakht Khán to command them; they might select which of the two they preferred. He would confirm their choice, but it was intolerable that the residents in the city should be harassed and threatened by the soldiers, who had come to the city with the avowed object of destroying the English and not their own countrymen. These soldiers are always boasting that they are going out of the safety afforded by the fortifications to destroy the English, and yet are always returning to the city. "It is quite clear to me," said His Majesty, "that the English will ultimately recapture this city, and will kill me." The officers seemed impressed with the King's words; they besought him to be brave of heart, and they invited him to put his hand on their heads, for without doubt they would be victorious. There were about 150 officers present, and as they passed before him he placed his hand on the head of each man. Then His Majesty uttered a prayer and said, "Go with haste and be victorious on the Ridge." The King rose, and after they had gone he entered the fort of Selimgarh, and ordered them to fire shells from the batteries; then he returned to his own private apartments; from thence he sent a written order to Mirza Mogul to be watchful that no harm happened to Hákim Ahsanullah Khán. The King ordered pay to be disbursed to the soldiers. He further requested that every officer of any position in the Army should be summoned to appear before him. General Bakht Khán, in accordance with this command, came to the Durbar, and explained that the officers had gone out with an escort of 400 cavalry and the local zemindars to make themselves acquainted with the various positions they were to occupy, and he added: "Now I shall be victorious; if God wills, I shall prosper. My plan is to attack the English at Alipur." A message came to the King from Gwalior that the whole army was willing to place itself under his command. "Reply," said the King impatiently, "as I said before; there is no money for their support. We have here 60,000 men in the city, but they have not been able to win a clod of dirt from the English." Hassan Ali, Resaldar, presented a petition to the purport that if the King would authorize him he would assess every landholder from Delhi to Hardwar, and by this means raise at least five lakhs of rupees. English shot and shell killed and wounded many citizens to-day. The Sepoys were paraded before the Delhi and Ajmere Gates. These troops were divided into three brigades under Mirza Mogul, Ghosh Mahommed Khán, and General Bakht Khán. The men were warned to be on the alert against the strange men reported to be the Jehádis; the guards were to be careful they did not enter the city: they were said to be encamped at Ram Serai, and to be really native levies raised by the English, and not friendly Jehádis. The Generals exhorted the men to be of one mind, and if they were so the attack on the English could not fail to be successful; they would be victorious, and the English would be slaughtered. I communicated with Nawáb Hossein Ali Khán Bahádur, through Lalla Gopie Nath, to use his influence with Ahmed Mirza to desist from troubling me. Hyder Hossein Khán, Commandant of Artillery, again sent me an order for payment, brought by a mounted orderly. Sant Lál replied. Budri Messur came to me and said that Sir John Metcalfe, with some horsemen, had been in Tilwara in pursuit of rebels, and was much grieved to hear of the sad condition of myself and other loyal natives in the city. He wished me to keep up my heart, as the English would soon retake Delhi. The delight this information produced in my heart was as new life which a seasonable shower gives to a garden. As the soldiers sent to extort money used to create much disturbance at my house, Lalla Jíwunchund and other relations and friends deserted me, thinking it most prudent to keep away from me. I had a visit from Hákim Ghulám Naksh Band Khán, who cheered me by saying he would use his good offices in my behalf with Hákim Ahsanullah Khán.

August 5.—His Majesty sat this day in the Public Hall of Audience. Hákim Ahsanullah Khán was present with other nobles. A letter of congratulation was read from Lucknow, bearing the signatures of Kudrat Ali Khán, Rájah Hírat Sing, Rájah Khán Sing, and others, saying: "We have killed all the English here, and 1,600 have been slaughtered at Cawnpore. We have now seated the son of our beloved Mistress the Begum on the Throne. We are also in want of *skhu* and ramrods, which please send." The King ordered the letter to be made over to General Bakht Khán. A letter was received from Fatehgarh from Syud Ali, saying: "We have killed all the English here, and we have a force of 8,000 men willing to act under my orders, and I am awaiting the King's orders." Certain Sikhs presented a petition complaining that they were in the habit of attacking the English entrenchments, but had to return, as the Purbeahs would give them no assistance and would not co-operate; they prayed the King to form a regiment of Sikhs from amongst the regiments of Delhi, and to entrust them with two field guns, that they might attack the English with some chance of success. They were encouraged, and told not to despair of victory. The sapper and miner regiments also complained that they laboured at erecting batteries in the open, at much loss of life, to protect the King's soldiers when fighting, but that these abandoned them at night, and the batteries were destroyed night after night by the English. The King called General Bakht Khán's attention to this complaint. The Jehádis complained that they were the only people who went out to fight the English in earnest; the others were like people sitting down and making no exertions. They were told to carry their complaint to Mirza Mogul. Orders sent to Rájah Dévi Sing, Rájah Saligram, and Rái Gunjaram by Fazl Beg jointly to pay into the Treasury 50,000 rupees. General Bakht Khán informed the King that the troops would attack the English to-morrow. Rájah Bholam Nath waited on the King and presented him, in accordance with the Eastern custom, with ornaments to be attached to His Majesty's wrist at the time of the full moon in Sawun. Two hundred cavalry were sent to Jajjar to bring in three lakhs of rupees, and fifty men were sent to Kútub and fifty to Kot Kasim to bring in revenue collectors. It was stated that as the English were running short of shot and powder they were cutting out stone balls from the rocks. Certain Cashmeries, servants of Mahárájah Golab Sing, were arrested by some cavalry and taken to General Bakht Khán; they stated that Captain Ropeston (*sic*) had enlisted 1,000 horse and foot at Ghoharia, and was collecting revenue. A Frenchman came to the King and offered to make grapeshot. The King visited the Bastion Batteries, and ordered a continuous artillery fire to be kept up upon the English camp and upon those batteries which were sending balls into the city.

August 6.—A letter was written to-day to the Mahárájah of Patiála to send the King six lakhs of rupees. It was entrusted to Samund Khán to send the letter under an escort of 100 troopers. Mahommed Azim, son of Prince Akbar, was ordered to Hissar to collect revenue. Petition received from Bahádur Ali Khán that he was halting on the other side of the Jumna with a force of 1,000 men awaiting orders. He was directed to cross over early the next morning and encamp outside the Ajmere Gate. The Punjabis living on Saadut Ali Khán's Canal promised to pay to the King 41,000 rupees. It was reported that Sirdarhi Lál, Commander of the Nímuch force, and Mahommed Bakht Khán, commanding the Bareilly Sepoys, had joined their forces together, and had attacked the English at Alipur, at the Ridge, and at the Mutali Bridge; and that the English had beaten back the troops that had gone out at the Cashmere Gate, and had beaten them as far back as the Residency; they were retiring, having lost sixty troopers. One hundred men and two resaldars were killed. The fighting continued the whole day; the wounded returned to the city. When Bahádur Ali, with his 1,000 men, were crossing the river, he was met by Mirza Mogul and presented with a gold mohur. News came from Lucknow that on the 22nd July several thousand English soldiers had reached the city, and after severe fighting had established themselves there. News came also that the English had taken Benares.

August 7.—The King visited the Selimgarh Fort, and then entered the Public Hall of Audience. Mirza Amin-u-dín Khán, Mirza Zia-u-dín Khán, Hassan Ali Khán, Rahamat Ali Khán, and Mir Said Ali Khán attended the Durbar. A nazzar was presented on the part of Nawáb Ali, of Guzerat. Bahádur Ali Khán, of Kumaon, attended and presented some gold mohurs, and some of his sirdars gave thirteen rupees. Ahmed Mirza, addressing Mirza Mogul, requested him to inquire why Zia-u-dín was not present the day before. An altercation then ensued. Mirza Amin-u-dín Khán defended Mirza Zia-u-dín, calling Ahmed Mirza a blackguard, and using other opprobrious epithets. Mirza Ahmed appealed to the King to protect him from insult. The King said he was pained at such language, that Ahmed Mirza was a great chief. A petition received from some landholders of Baroda Zillah, Meerut, that they were willing the King should collect the revenue, if he would render them assistance. The petition was made over to Mirza Mogul. Ghosh Mahommed, one of the officers of the Nímuch force, presented himself, and reported details of the fight of the previous day. The following persons met in the guard-room of the Fort: Mirza Mogul, Mirza Kizr Sultan, Rájah Dévi Sing, Saligram the banker, Ramji Dáss, Rai Gunjaram. A subahdar of a sapper and miner regiment warned them that, if arrangements for paying the mutineers were not speedily made, the soldiers would plunder the city. The above-named persons, after consultation, promised to raise one lakh and fifty thousand rupees for the pay of the troops. This afternoon the gunpowder manufactory carried on in the house of Símurd Begum, in Chariwalla Ward, exploded, and four hundred and ninety-four persons were blown up;

only thirteen escaped. The King was in the Selimgarh Fort at the time, and it was told him that the soldiers were coming to plunder the Palace. Hassan Ali Khán came running to the King, who was standing in the porch of the gateway of the Palace, and reported that the soldiers were under the impression that the explosion had been arranged by him, and that they had gone in a body to plunder his house and kill him. Whilst he was speaking, others came running up, and said that more than a hundred cavalry troopers were hunting for Hassan Ahsanullah. The King commanded him to be hidden behind the throne in the throne-room. The King then ordered the gates to be closed, and Hákim Ahsan to be taken for concealment to the underground place of worship. Samund Khán, Resaldar, explained to the men that he was not in the Palace. The King also gave verbal orders to Mirza Mogul to protect Hákim Ahsan's house and stop the plundering. The Mirza tried to carry out his orders, but with little success. The females happily managed to get away, and eventually escaped violence at the hands of these soldiers. Mirza Mogul arrived on the spot, and with some cavalry drove the plunderers away. For greater protection, he brought away on fourteen camels and in two carriages and three waggons the personal effects which had been rescued, and placed them in the Palace, and the King ordered these goods to be locked up in a safe place. The whole day there was fighting between the Sepoys and the English. At night the Sepoys surrounded the Palace, and demanded Ahsanullah to be given them. For hours His Majesty resisted their demands. At last, finding himself helpless, he agreed, on the condition that his life was spared. This was agreed to, and the Hákim was handed over to the soldiers, and confined by them in the room kept for the custody of the Crown jewels. The King then summoned all his sons around him, and told them to remain by him and protect his life. Mirza Kizr, Mirza Mehdí, and Mirza Abdullah remained with him all night. There was a panic in the city; every shop was closed. The Mahommedans passed every hour in fear, and fully expected that the soldiers would kill the King and massacre the citizens.

Nazir Ali, formerly in Mr. Simon Fraser's service, and now in charge of a police-station, came to arrest me with a letter from Mubarik Shah, Kotwál, accompanied by a hundred soldiers with unsheathed swords. They got into the house by a rush, as the gate was being opened for the water-carriers to bring in water. The ladies of the family were seated, nursing Maharaj Lál, who had been operated upon for stone, and was suffering dreadful agony. They ran for their lives on seeing the soldiers, leaving several articles of jewelry and a box containing *pan*. I was then arrested and placed in a palanquin, and taken under a guard of soldiers with drawn swords to the Kotwáli (head police-station). I found there Mubarik Shah, who treated me with respect. He was previously a Customs officer, who had now transferred his allegiance to the King. He told me that my fears were unfounded,—not to be afraid, as he, too, was a servant of the English. He showed me an order, issued by order of Mirza Kizr, addressed to him, ordering my arrest, together with Munshi Sultan Sing, Chutthun Lál, and Sant Lál. To deceive us, the order stated we were all required for consultation. I and Munshi Sultan were then taken to Mirza Mogul. On arrival a Subahdar, who was standing, tried to stab me with a dagger, shouting out: "This is the man who sends news to the English." I was rescued by the crowd (really by God), who explained I was summoned to be made to pay money. This gave some peace to my mind. I was then taken upstairs to Mirza Mogul. There

I saw a great crowd of people assembled in a strange, irregular fashion. On one side sat Mirza Mogul, reclining on pillows. There were present Hamid Ali Khán, Raj Saligram, Hákim Abdul Hak, and other officials of the King's Court. In front, stretched on a bed, was the notorious Kooray Sing, Brigade-Major of the rebel Sepoy army. There was not a semblance of court etiquette. The King's officials were moving here and there without order. Lalla Saligram (treasurer), Ramjí Dáss Goorwala, Lalla Girdhur Lál, Zorawar Chand, and about twenty-five other bankers, were sitting there under arrest; I was directed to sit in the row with them. Lalla Gham Lál, Lalla Nashi Lál, Lalla Sant Lál, my friends, came there to get me released. Shortly afterwards, Mirza Ahmed Jín went up to Mirza Mogul and whispered something in his ear, upon which the latter summoned Sant Lál, and, with a great show of condescension and leniency, told him I was to pay five thousand rupees down at once, or I should be imprisoned. The demand for money was made in the same way from the others, and at last we poor writers were threatened, guns being placed on our shoulders and fired. But our hearts remained firm—by divine impulse, doubtless. We made up our minds to die rather than yield to the threats of these rebels. We were kept in suspense as to our fate, while the rebels deliberated from the morning till four in the afternoon, when Mirza Ilahí Baksh appeared quite unexpectedly, like the Huzoul Khizour, to point out a path to the forlorn traveller, or like the God-sent rain to refresh a parched tree. He by favour of God cheered me. He induced Mirza Mogul to grant him a private interview, and, I believe, used such arguments on our behalf, that we were but poor clerks, living on the pay we received; that English rule was not yet abolished. The English might retake the city, and these poor clerks might prove of assistance to him should he then fall into the hands of the English. Mirza Mogul replied that I was sending information to the English, and offering prayers for their success. Mirza Ilahí Baksh argued that we only had been faithful to those whose salt we had eaten. Ahmed Mirza and the sons of Mirza Jajun argued, on the other hand, that a heavy payment should be exacted or our houses confiscated; the latter hoped that, if I should be put to death, my house would fall into his possession. The proceedings went on till evening. The ornaments taken from my house by the soldiers were recovered from them and taken to the house of Mirza Mogul, where they were weighed and valued at two thousand rupees. This amount was ordered to be deducted from the sum demanded from me. Next pistols were brought in, and an order was given for a gun, with a view to intimidate us. But finding me resolute in my determination not to pay, and being befriended by Mirza Ilahí Baksh, my tormentors took a recognizance from him, and allowed me to go with him. The good Mirza, in the extreme kindness of his heart, took me straight to my house in safety, and advised me to change my residence and keep myself concealed, or the rebels would find me out again. He told me he was my security, and, through God's favour, the rebels were powerless to harm him. Thus God, through His mercy, saved my life. I can never repay the kindness Mirza Ilahí Baksh showed me in this emergency, nor can words express the feeling of my gratitude to him. My tongue only can express the thankfulness I owe him. If each hair on my body could speak, with each one would I glorify and praise him. I learned afterwards that, when I was arrested, Lalla Sham Lál wrote to Mirza Ilahí Baksh that now was the time to render me assistance, as I was a servant of the English and he a well-wisher. The Mirza's child had died that morning, and he hurried through the funeral ceremony to come to my rescue. A more sincere friend will never be found.

August 8.—This morning every nobleman waited upon the King; but he said that he would not hold an audience that day, that he was very indignant at the way he had been treated. To some of his courtiers he said: "Every princely house has its vicissitudes, and my turn is now coming." To his sons he gave orders to use every influence, and to employ every means, to save Ahsanullah's life and obtain his release. The Begum sent word to the King that she, too, was suspected of negociating with the English, and that she had been warned that the soldiers intended to plunder the Palace. The King sent two hundred troopers to guard her house and Ahsanullah's. It was reported that the soldiers had made a bonfire of all the property taken from the latter house. The King had tried to prevent this, but no one paid any heed to his orders. The King sent for the accountants attached to his household; but, through fear of death, no one would leave their houses. Mirza Abdullah was sent by the King to Hákim Ahsanullah to beg of him to eat some food. Every door and every window throughout the city were closed; the householders remained in perfect silence within through fear. Throughout the day the Sepoys fought with the English. Great pressure was again put upon me and Munshi Sultan Sing for the payment of two thousand rupees each, but we gave nothing.

August 9.—The King visited the house of prayer. Shah Nizam-u-dín, son of Meah Kali Sahib, the King's Teacher, came to the Durbar, and told Mahommed Ali Akbar Khán that fifty troopers had arrived at Patudi, saying they had been sent to bring three lakhs of rupees to the King; and, to extort the money, they had seized the son of the chief, and were keeping him in confinement. The King replied: "I did not send them to bring the money; the soldiers deserve severe punishment." Rájah Nazir Sing, chief of Bulubgarh, sent a petition and a nazzar of five gold mohurs. The King accepted the money, and ordered these words to be written on the back of the letter: "I have accepted the money on account of your bad name." Orders were issued to Mirza Mogul to withdraw the guards from Ahsanullah's house. A great number of officers assembled in the court, and said: "We are satisfied that the Hákim had nothing to do with the explosion of gunpowder." Six suits of clothing were given to Makund Lál by the King on account of his mother's death. General Mahommed Baksh Khán reported that a Gurkha from the English camp had been taken prisoner. The house of Moulvie Sadar-u-dín Khán was attacked to-day by fifty soldiers; but, seeing that there were seventy Jehádis ready to oppose them, they retreated, but carried off two colts from the house of Ahsanullah Khán. Several hundred people are reported to have died from the effects of the explosion of the gunpowder factory. The wounded were removed to-day to Brahmin Khán's *serai*, and placed in the Imambara. Six Gurkha soldiers were made prisoners and killed. It was reported in the city that the English had raised two regiments of sappers in Lahore, who had arrived at Delhi, and that gunpowder was being manufactured in the house of Mr. Manson, a European in cantonments.

August 10.—The King went to the house of prayer. Hafiz Dawu-u-dín Sahib and Nazir Hassan Mirza waited on His Majesty, who expressed his anger and disapproval of the excesses committed by the soldiers. The King again pressed the release of Hákim Ahsanullah on Mirza Mogul.

A company of infantry and a squadron of cavalry were to arrest Munshi Choton Lál and Munshi Sultan Sing, on the charge of sending information to the English, but the men avoided arrest. Hákim Ahsanúllah was released to-day. Mirza Abdullah, son of Mirza Shah Haraj, attended the Durbar, and told the King that Mirza Amín-u-dín Khán and Zia-u-dín Khán had amassed a large sum of money, but they had not assisted in any way to pay the Army. The King remained silent. Later on Mirza Abdullah, taking with him an escort of two hundred men, went to Mirza Amín-u-dín's house and asked for money. Amín-u-dín replied: "I have no money; but, if you are come to my house with a force to take my property, then, in the name of God, I am ready for you." And, calling his retainers, he made so great a show of force that Abdullah, seeing he would be overpowered, retired. Mirza Abu Bakr arrested all the bankers in the city, and demanded money. A letter was received from Ráo Tulla Rám, of Rewári, in which he made certain representations regarding Ghulám Mahommed Khán and Nawáb Ahmed Ali Khán, chief of Farukhnagar. Hákim Ahsanúllah Khán attended the Durbár and presented a gold mohur, and expressed his deep gratitude to the King, by whose favour alone his life had been preserved. He asked for the restoration of his property, which the soldiers had plundered. The King ordered Mahommed Lál to take five thousand rupees, and get the scattered property together again. Mirza Kizr Sultán came to the Durbar with a proposal that all persons known to have servants to the English should be confined, as they were sending information to the English camp.

August 11.—The King, to mark his respect and sympathy for Hákim Ahsanúllah Khán, desired the Princes to escort him to his house. In accordance with this order, he was escorted by Mirza Mogul, Mirza Kizr Sultán, and Mirza Abdullah. On arriving at his house, he showed them how he had been plundered and his property destroyed and burned. Mirza Mogul witnessed a parade of the troops outside the city. General Ghosh Mahommed Khán waited on the King; General Bakht Khán and the Princes were also present. The King consented to some compensation being paid to the families of the men blown up in the gunpowder factory. There was severe fighting all day, but the English remained masters of the field.

August 12.—The King sat in the Council Chamber. The King desired Moulvie Sadar-u-dín Khán to let it be known that he would not again sit in the Public Hall of Audience until the soldiers returned the property plundered from Hákim Ahsanullah's house. Later on a deputation of officers from the Nímuch and Bareilly forces waited on the King, and had a private audience, and gave the King some secret information, in consequence of which the King visited the Selimgarh Fort. He consulted with Mirza Amín-u-dín Khán and Mirza Zia-u-dín Khán, whom he came across accidentally. This night an English force approached the artillery park near the Bara Nindwar, but, finding the Sepoys on the alert, they retired. News reached the city that the forces of the Rájah of Indore had rebelled, that the Rájah had taken refuge with the English, and that 13,000 of his rebellious soldiers had started for Delhi. It was also reported that the son of Rájah Buni Sing, deceased, had succeeded his father, and had been recognized by the English.

August 13.—His Majesty went to the place of worship. Letters received from the Nawáb of Farukhabad, Bareilly, and Amínpur, stating that they had possessed themselves of their properties, and asking for the King's written approval. The prayer was granted. The Princes attended the King's audience. His Majesty objected to the practice, recently assumed, of wearing pistols in His Majesty's presence, and forbade it in future. Swords might be worn, and they were sufficient protection. Hassan Ali Khán complained that the soldiers at the Ajmere Gate had taken away a camel, two scimitars, and two changes of raiment; he asked for their restoration. Mirza Mogul was directed to enforce restitution. There arrived from Lucknow 100 cavalry troopers, escorting four wagons of ammunition, sent to General Bakht Khán at his request. Mirza Mogul and other officers met at the guard-room of the Fort, and for a short time remained in consultation. A petition came from Mahommed Ali Akbar Khán to the effect that he was suffering great annoyance from the cavalry soldiers. The King replied: "It was wrong of you to kill your soldiers. You have the authority to govern your own country; do so." The English attempted this night to scale the Tilwara Bastion, but, finding the Sepoys on the alert, they retired. The soldiers to-day restored the property taken from Hassan Ali Khán. News came that Bega Bhai had sent a notice to the Lieutenant-Governor of the North-West Provinces that she could no longer control her troops, and they had joined the Indore force, and were marching to attack Agra. On hearing this, the Lieutenant-Governor had sent off 100 European soldiers and four elephants for the purpose of preparing a battery. The news of the rebel advance had created great fear in Agra, so that thousands were leaving the city, and the English were borrowing large sums from the bankers and taking every precaution.

August 14.—The King entered the Hall of Public Audience. Hákim Ahsanullah and others attended. General Mahommed Ghosh made a private report to His Majesty, who replied: "Unless the English are driven from the Ridge, you will never be victorious; the Indore troops are coming. You have the Nímuch force; you must attack the English at Alipur." Food from the royal table was sent to-day to General Bakht Khán. One Nujíb Adín sent a letter from Agra. It alleged that the English intended to blow up the Jumma Masjid, and prayed the King to take steps to prevent it.

August 15.—Public audience. Hákim Ahsanullah, Nazir Hassan, and Aurbadhin Sahib were present. The last-named said there was a bad spirit extant among the princes. Certain resaldárs petitioned that Ráo Tulla Rám had prevented them from joining the King at Delhi; that he had collected several thousand rupees from the bankers and others for the pay of the Army, and then had appropriated the money; and they asked the King permission to bring the money by force to Delhi. The King sent them an order to this effect, and another to Ráo Tulla Rám to give up the money. Complaints were received at the same time against the oppression of Ráo Tulla Rám and Azim Khán, purporting to have been sent by landholders. Information was received that Azim Khán had collected 8,000 rupees from Gurjawan, and had gone to Patudi, and, after leaving that place, had taken the road to Jajjar; after taking several thousand rupees from the Rájah, he had gone to Rohtuk; then, putting all the money together, he had gone to Hissár. The King, on hearing of Mahommed Azim Khán's movements, was very indignant, and sent off urgent letters to him to send the money at once to Delhi, and in future to oppress no one. The King addressed a letter to the Maharájah of Gwalior, to join him at once with his forces and his treasure; he wrote also to the Bhai Sahiba. To-day nearly three hundred Sepoys, despairing of their pay, and disheartened at the result of the rebellion, brought their firearms to the King, and left the city through the Calcutta Gate for their homes.

Muna Lál, Deputy Collector, reached the English camp safely. A trooper killed a foot-soldier to-day at the Delhi Gate, after an altercation. A court-martial was held to try the man, under the presidency of Mirza Mogul. News was received that the Nawáb of Jajjar, with two field-guns and an escort of cavalry, had gone to Patudi to take charge of the administration.

August 16.—Moulvie Fazl Hak attended the audience. He presented a nazzar of a gold mohur, and conversed with the King upon the situation. Petitions were received from the Rájah of Bulubgarh: one was addressed to the Begum, another to the King asking pardon for any offence he might have given to His Majesty: the King sent an autograph letter of pardon. Nawáb Ahmed Ali Khán, Chief of Farukhnagar, petitioned the King that he had tried to collect the revenues of Bhora in accordance with orders, but was unable to do so, the reason being that Rao Tulla Rám had warned the villagers not to pay, as the King had given him the village. The petition was made over to General Bakht Khán. The Chief of Jajjar sent in 7,000 rupees, with a petition stating that he had tried to raise the three lakhs of rupees which the King had demanded for the pay of the Army, but he had failed to raise that sum within his territory; he had, however, raised one lakh, of which he was sending only 60,000 now, and would send the remaining 40,000 within fifteen days; in the meantime he asked the King to send him an autograph letter, that he might show the purpose for which the money was wanted. In the meantime he asked the King to have his house in the city vacated by the soldiers, who had taken possession of it for a barrack; also, he begged that Mahommed Azim, who had been sent to plunder his territory, should immediately be recalled and no one again sent to his territory without his permission; further, he prayed for a royal assent in writing to be sent him confirming him in the possession of his territories. The petition was ordered to be made over to General Bakht Khán. Mirza Mogul received information that the principal battery of the English had been left without a sufficient force, as they had sent out the greater part of their men to oppose the rebels in a different direction. As the English flag was flying over the battery Mirza Mogul conceived a plan for spiking the guns and carrying off the flag, for which he ordered out the whole force at his command; one regiment of a thousand strong was directed to make a rush for the battery. But it appears Mirza Mogul was wrongly informed, for the Sepoys met with such a fire from the guns that they lost heavily. The English sent out a force of two thousand strong to Hissár to attack Mahommed Azim Khán.

August 17.—Public audience. Some of the Sepoys caught a pedlar crossing the Bridge with 300 rupees; they took him to the King, who gave them seventeen rupees for their trouble, and the rest was paid into the treasury. Four troopers were sent to Jajjar with letters demanding payment of money. Kasim Ali, resident of Allahabad, presented a nazzar. Hákim Ahsanúllah read the King a letter of gratitude, and returned to his house. A requisition was made for three lakhs of rupees for the pay of the troops by Mirza Mogul and Mirza Kizr Sultán, on Mirza Zia-u-dín Khán, Mirza Aminulla Khán, Moulvie Sadar-u-dín Ali Khán, Hákim Abdul Hak, Raza Khán, Sudar Mirza, Kázi Fazl Ali, Badr-u-dín Khwaja Ali-u-dín Khán. General Mahommed Bakht Khán complained to the King that the Princes had collected money from different bankers for the pay of the troops, but the troops had not received one pice. On hearing this, the King gave orders to Mirza Kizr to hand over all the money received to the General, and in future, when money was requisitioned, it was to be paid to the General, in the presence of the citizens. Certain landowners of Nareli came and complained that because they had killed three Englishmen their village was to be destroyed; they asked for the King's protection. The King refused any assistance. The landowners of Darna brought a cart laden with cannonballs, which they had found broken down on the road to the English camp. It was reported that out of six grass-cutters caught to-day by the English two had escaped and four had been shot. The troops went out to fight about four in the afternoon, and continued fighting until sunset.

August 18.—The King visited the Selimgarh Fort, and held a council of war. Ghosh Mahommed reported it was his intention to attack the English the next day, in conjunction with the Bareilly force. Mirza Baksh and Nawáb Ahmed Kúli Khán asked for a pass to enable them to pass to and from the Palace; it was granted. Moulvie Fazl Hak reported that it was said in the English newspapers that a general massacre would follow the capture of the city; the city would be razed to the ground, and not a voice would be left of the King's household to utter his name or to give him a drop of water. "It is worth your Majesty's while," said the Moulvie, "to devise some means to induce the Sepoys to cease their opposition to the English, for they cannot prevail against the English." The King replied: "Look to your troops; go out yourselves to fight, and lead them against the English." The Moulvie replied: "Alas! they will not listen to the commands of those who cannot pay them their wages." The King replied: "Use your troops, then, to collect revenue." Mirza Amín-u-dín Khán, and others on whom a requisition for money had been made, waited on Mirza Mogul, and represented to him that they had not got the money to pay up. They repeated their inability to pay, on which the Mirza Mogul said to his Silver Stick in waiting, "Arrest that man," pointing to Amín-u-dín Khan, "and put him under the guard till he pays the money." Amín-u-dín, roused by this impertinence, drew his swòrd, and challenged anyone to touch him. Turning to the Prince, he said: "If you send troops to my house, I will defend it to the last!" Leaving Mirza Mogul's house, he went to the Palace, and told the King what had happened, and that he would be killed rather than have money extorted from him. The King asked him to be seated, and told him he would be protected from these demands in future, which pacified him. General Bakht Khán was present at the interview, and said the demand was unjust, for the pay of the Army should be demanded from the Army. The King said to the General: "Do not demand money except from the soldiers in the city." Orders were sent to Mirza Kizr not to concern himself with money matters. Orders were sent to the bankers to negociate directly with General Bakht Khán. Information was received that the residents of Sabzimándi had sent a petition to Sir John Metcalfe, telling him of their utter destitution, and had received a reply to be of good cheer and to keep up a brave heart, for the English would soon be able to relieve them. The sons of Bhoali Shanker received a warning that their absence from the King's audiences had been noticed, and they were suspected of being in communication with the English; and advising them in future to attend. Mirza Kizr Sultán reported to the King that the Jagirdars of Lohára were in sympathy with the English and in communication with them, and were refusing to give money on that account.

August 19.—It was reported that 600 cavalry had left

Delhi disheartened, and through fear of the English. Abdul Hak Khán, son of Moulvie Fazl Hak, and Moulvie Faiz Ahmed left for Gurjawan to collect revenue; Ahsan Baksh, with a force, started for Alipur with the same object. The Bareilly force declared itself discontented with its General (Bakht Khán). The ill-feeling arose out of the fact that the General gave two mares that had been captured by his troops as a present to his father-in-law. The soldiers had chaffingly said that no one was entitled to prize-money, except the King; if they shared plunder with the General, why did he not share with his soldiers the lakhs of rupees he had seized? From chaff arose bitter feelings. The English shot three Sepoys outside the city. The Princes visited the King, and held a long consultation with him on the feeling among the soldiers. Mirza Kizr Sultán rode down to the Bareilly camp. The General offered him a nazzar of an elephant, a horse, a gold mohur, and five rupees. Mirza Mogul sent down 1,000 rupees, collected from some bankers, and a message to say that the payment of the soldiers was receiving the earnest attention of the King and of his councillors. General Bakht Khán summoned Dévi Sing and Saligram, bankers, and on their refusing to grant money had them placed in confinement. Mirza Sultán extorted 25,000 rupees from some other bankers and sent the amount to the General. A number of soldiers surrounded the house of Allanath, and demanded 1,000 rupees, or they would kill him. Mirza Mogul hastened to the house, and got rid of the soldiers.

August 20.—After being in confinement ten hours Dévi Sing and Saligram paid 6,000 rupees and were released. General Gon Shunker and General Talyar Khán came to the King, bringing a Sikh who had been taken prisoner. He was told to repeat the information he had given. He then stated that Bakht Khán was in secret communication with the English, and it was understood he had arranged to draw off his force to attack Alipur, and then the English would attack Delhi unopposed. The King remarked that the man was a spy, with a mission to create ill-will in the Army. He was then asked how many regiments there were, how long they had been in camp, and the name of the General commanding them. The man in answering all these questions feigned madness, and said he had come to see Mirza Mogul and Said Ali Khán; he then offered a gold mohur, and said that he had revealed all the secrets of the war. The King remarked that the man was a bad character. News came that the English were constructing a battery in the Metcalfe compound, preventing food for the Sepoys from crossing the bridge into the city, and were keeping up a heavy fire from it into Selimgarh, but no harm had been done. The King ordered the fire from this battery to be silenced. However, the guns bearing on the bridge became silent,[1] but the guns of the Cashmere Gate continued fire; during the night there was no firing. A deputation of the officers came and represented that the men were starving; the King assured them that that would be speedily remedied. One, Mir Kazim, of Allahabad, was promoted to the rank of Subahdar. Mirza Ilahí Baksh objected, saying it was not right that anyone should be promoted to such a rank without having proved his bravery in the field. The General reported to His Majesty that he would attack the English in the morning. Badhan, son of Mahommed Mir Khán, divided 2,000 rupees among the Jehádis to-day, and chaffingly told them not to let the enemy see their backs, but to fight to the

[1] The account is not very clear whether the English stopped firing or that their battery was silenced.

end. News came that Bahádur Jang Khán, of Dardari, had arrived there, and had taken possession of the city. News also received that as 200 of the followers of the Rájah of Ulwa were escorting 350 maunds of sugar, purchased by the Rájah, and two camels laden with goods, Ráo Tulla Rám fell upon the caravan, and had taken 1,400 rupees from the men before allowing the caravan to proceed. Mirza Zia-u-dín Khán and Mirza Amin-u-dín Khán called a meeting, and addressing it, said: "If there were any persons present who preferred death to being plundered by the Sepoys, let them bind themselves to resist further exactions." The bankers of Lál Koti and Chandi Chouk were called on to sign a document to the same effect. When the Sepoys heard of this they determined to kill the originators, but finding the whole city was against them, they thought better of it. The Bareilly camp lost a number of camels; rewards were offered for their recovery. Akbar Ali Khán, Chief of Patudi, with the assistance of cavalry and artillery from Jajjar, returned to Patudi, and took possession of the city. It was rumoured to-day in the city that the English had given back Lucknow to the Nawáb, who had taken over the administration, and peace and order had been restored.. News came that the Gujars of a neighbouring district, in two gangs, were plundering and looting the country-side in every direction.

August 21.—The King held a Durbár. General Bakht Khán informed His Majesty that he had brought seven elephants and two hundred horses for his inspection. His Majesty went at once to the porch of the gate of the Palace, and, after inspection, selected seventeen horses, and ordered the rest to be taken away. Under the King's orders two batteries were prepared, one at Asinapur, the other at Agharauda, with three guns each. Five companies of

Sepoys and one hundred cavalry of the Jhansi force, and three field-guns, were sent off to Walid Khán, Chief of Balagarh. A force of three hundred cavalry and foot came to the city from Jadree, and reported that the Jeypur force had mutinied, and were marching for Delhi. Ahmed Ali, Resaldár, returned from Jajjar, and complained that he had gone to the Nawáb for payment as he had been ordered; but, whilst there, a letter had come, purporting to be from His Majesty, not to entrust the money to Ahmed Ali. The King denied any knowledge of sending such a letter, but admitted that a like letter had been sent to Patudi. There was a rumour that Narunder Sing, the chief of Patiála, intended to join the English in the camp before Delhi. The rebels took away all the timber from my garden.

August 22.—After the morning audience the King visited the Fort of Selimgarh, and ordered the battery to fire a few rounds. He said to the artillerymen: "It is much to be regretted that, in place of your silencing the English fire, I see their batteries getting nearer every day." The gunners answered: "No fear, your Majesty; we are getting the better of them." The King turned away, and went to the Hall of Public Audience. Ahmed Ali Khán, Resaldár, asked His Majesty's pleasure in reference to the bond which the Nawáb of Jajjar had given; he was directed to go and realize the money, and in case of default the troops had orders to attack the Raján's fort. The son of Nawáb Mahommed Mir Khán represented to the King, on the part of several bankers, that twice had the Sepoys extorted money from them, and again were now demanding money from them. The King replied: "If the Sepoys would only leave the city, and employ themselves in collecting the revenue, I should be in a position to pay them, and to protect the lives and property of the citizens." On the part of the bankers it was said: "The pay of so large a force amounts to lakhs. It is impossible that we can ever find the money to pay it." The King advised their representative to go to Mirza Mogul. Gunga Pershád, the City Police Superintendent, brought Samund Khán, Resaldár, before the King, under an armed guard. It was rumoured in the city that the Bareilly force would march in the morning to Alipur. The King went to the Selimgarh Fort, and after a time returned to the Palace. I changed my residence to the house known as Radhakshunwala.

August 23.—Again His Majesty visited the Selimgarh Fort, and ordered the batteries to elevate their fire so as to reach the English camp, and, after watching the fire for some time, he returned to the Palace, and sent off a further force of one hundred cavalry and a company of infantry to get money from Jajjar. Fifty troopers from Jadra came, bringing the heads of five Englishmen, whom they had killed at Indore, and presented themselves before the King. They informed him that five thousand men had killed all the English at Indore, and had dismounted the heavy guns from the fort, which the men were bringing across the river Chumboul, and were marching on Delhi. The deputation petitioned the King for letters to be given them: one assuring the Indore soldiers of the King's approval of their conduct and offers of protection; the second, a written order to Rána Bhaganat Sing, chief of Dholpur, to supply Commissariat. The King expressed his anger that General Bakht Khán had not marched upon Alipur. The officers of the Nímuch force accused Bakht Khán of negotiating with the English, and of withholding his soldiers until the English should receive sufficient reinforcements from England. The King was induced to issue an order that General Bakht Khán should not be admitted to the Palace.

The officers of the Nímuch force then suggested that they should be allowed to disarm the Bareilly troops, which they offered to do with four regiments of infantry and one of cavalry. The King gave no answer to this proposal, but later in the day he issued orders to all the officers to obey neither the orders of Mirza Mogul or of any other General, inasmuch as His Majesty had appointed a Court of twelve members, six to be appointed by the King and six by the Army, for the future conduct of the siege. The Army was to obey all orders issued by the Court. A letter was intercepted to-day purporting to have been written by the record-keeper of the Commissioner's office, conveying information to the English. In consequence of this Mán Sing Mahafiz was arrested; all his property was plundered and carried off to the Palace, where it was placed in custody in the verandah of the Hall of Public Audience. Mirza Amin-u-dín Khán and Mirza Zia-u-dín Khán hired one hundred men of the cavalry for the protection of their houses.

The Kissenganj Battery was hotly engaged all day. General Mahommed Bakht Khán, in the presence of all the principal officers of the Army, and of Mirza Mogul, swore upon the Koran that he had opened no negotiations with the English. Information came that Prince Mahommed Azim, who had gone with a force to Hissár, had been beaten in an engagement with the English, and the Prince had been taken prisoner and hanged. It was also rumoured that Mirza Bul, the father-in-law of the King, who had gone to Soniput, had been taken prisoner by the English. Several foot-soldiers attended the Durbár, and complained that no opium could be purchased in the bazars, and from this cause many were dying. The King ordered some of the drug to be sent at once for the use of the soldiers.

August 24. — The King went this morning early to Selimgarh to see a place where it was reported some unknown persons had been digging for treasure. On further excavations being made it was found that some small field-pieces had been buried there, but no money. After giving orders to have the guns dug up, and watching the artillery practice, the King went to inquire into a complaint made by some bankers against the Princes of extorting money from them for the third time. General Bakht Khán reported that he was going to attack the English, and came to take leave of the King. His Majesty said: "Go, may God protect you! Show your loyalty by attacking the English; destroy them, and return victorious." An order was sent to Ráo Tulla Rám, Chief of Rewári, to send opium for the use of the soldiers. Information was received from Soniput that the English had ordered the residents to clear out of the town, but the men had refused. The English had sent a force, and there had been a skirmish, with loss to both sides. The English had made the Tehsildar Fazl Hassan Khán a prisoner, and had hanged him. Also, it was said that Golab Sing, the Commissariat collector, and Sirdar Kandar Sing had been guarded by Patiála troops to Rohtuk to collect revenue. It was reported that 400 English soldiers were lying sick and wounded at Umbálla.

August 25.—His Majesty went on the river, in a boat manned by some men of the Sapper Regiment, and watched the artillery fire directed on the English from the Fort. Ahmed Mirza came in great haste to the Fort and reported that 150,000 rupees were on their way to the English camp, along the Bágpat road. Six hundred cavalry and two guns were sent off in haste to intercept the treasure. Mirza Mogul, for some reason, was offended, and would not leave his house. More demands were made for pay by deputations of officers. The King went into his private apartments, and brought out jewelry and gave them to the officers, saying, "Take this and forget your hunger"; but the officers refused, saying: "We cannot accept of your Crown jewels, but we are satisfied that you are willing to give your life and property to sustain us." The Nímuch Brigade marched to Alipur. Some of the officers reported that they were in hopes of beating back the English. The Begum Zenut Mehal went to the Lál Kotí. Mirza Kwáss and Feroz Sháh reported that they had made arrangements with a banker for the supply of money, and they would pay the troops. The King expressed his pleasure. A man was arrested who was inquiring what time the Ajmere Gate was closed at night and opened in the morning. He was suspected to be in the pay of the English. He was given fifty rupees as a bribe to hold his tongue, and was released. A city spy, resident at Chota Daria, was caught by the English, who, after closely questioning him as to the state of things in the city, let him go.

August 26.—The King sat in the Hall of Public Audience. A trooper named Ashraf Khán entered the Hall, and, saluting His Majesty, proceeded to relate how, the Bareilly Brigade being encamped at Elipalam (*sic*), the Nímuch Brigade unexpectedly arrived. General Bakht Khán held a consultation with the officer commanding the Nímuch force. He advised him to halt there (as the English force was only a short distance off) and join forces with him, proposing to make a joint attack the next day. The Brigadier of the Nímuch force would not agree to this plan, but pushed on to Bakhtghara, intending to encamp there for the day and rest his men. While the camp was being pitched, and the men had piled their arms, and many had taken off their belts and accoutrements, they were suddenly attacked by the English from two directions with a heavy fire of artillery and musketry. Taken unawares, the Sepoys bolted, leaving twelve guns and their ammunition. The loss, Ashraf Khán went on to say, was a thousand killed and wounded. The King on hearing this news was greatly disheartened, but several of the Councillors suggested that perhaps this man's statement was not true, and probably it was greatly exaggerated, and there was no cause to be anxious. Another informant stated that he knew the English had gone to Alipur. The King regarded the information as very serious. He summoned the following persons to his Council Room: Mirza Mogul, Mirza Koash, Mirza Kizr Sultan, Mirza Abu Bakr, Mirza Abdullah, Mirza Abu Nisr. After consultation, His Majesty directed a force to be sent off at once, under the command of Captain Wallidád Khán, to take the English camp in the absence of the troops. All the available troops were collected and put under arms. Then Ghosh Mahommed, the General commanding the Nímuch force, arrived, and on being told of the news received, disclaimed all knowledge of any engagement with his troops, saying that he had received no information and doubted the truth of what he had heard. On being assured that his troops had been defeated, he asked for reinforcements. One regiment of Sikhs and four of cavalry were placed under his command. The force marched, but after going a short distance met the defeated force returning, so, covering their retreat, they returned to camp. An explosion occurred in the Kissenganj Battery, by which twenty-four Pathans were killed. Mirza Mogul in the meantime had started with all his force to attack the English camp, but returned without making the attack, with the loss of seventeen men killed. The guns which Mirza Mogul had mounted in different batteries kept up an incessant fire all day, viz., from the Mulahi Bridge, under command of Mirza Koash, and from Kissenganj, under command of Mirza Abdullah. A petition received from the Nawáb asking for a letter and some mark of dignity. King's Bodyguard, 11 killed, 30 wounded; other troops, 100 killed. In the city, great anxiety and distress.

August 27.—Buldeo Sing, the banker, who had promised to advance money for the pay of the troops, made his obeisance to the King and presented a nazzar. Mirza Koash was also present, and expressed great zeal for His Majesty, who appointed him Commander of the Cavalry. A number of the city people captured two camels, eight grass-cutter's ponies, one grass-cutter, and forty goats, from near the English camp, and brought them into the presence of the King. All the jewellers in the city came to His Majesty to complain of the extortions of Mirza Kizr Sultan. The King promised that they should be protected from further demands. One Tsree Bing, from the Nímuch camp, related how the English first captured two guns, which he, with great bravery, afterwards retook, with the assistance of certain landholders. He accused the Bareilly troops of quarrelling with the Nímuch force, and returning to Delhi without co-operating with them. He prevailed upon the King to give him the command of five hundred cavalry and four companies from each regiment to attack the English with. The King sent a messenger to General Bakht Khán telling him he had been false to his salt, in turning away from the field of battle. A clerk made a proposal to the King to arrange for the pay of the troops, if all the revenue collections were made over to him. Ahmed Khán, son of the younger Begum, enlisted 100 men, under the orders of General Bakht Khán. It is reported that the Maharájah of Patiála has joined the

English in camp. Sent the Purcha (*sic*) to the English camp. The matter now rests with the Government.

August 28.—Hákim Mahommed Ali Khán, son of Hákim Nasar Ali Khán, attended the Durbár, and presented a nazzar of four rupees. He told the King that the Resaldár sent to Jajjar for money had taken with him a man of very bad character of the name of Kalandar Baksh, who had used very bad language to the Nawáb and so angered him that he refused to pay any money. The speaker suggested a nobleman of rank should be sent, when the money would be paid. His Majesty deputed Mirza Kuda Baksh, and sent by him an autograph letter to the Nawáb. A man offered the King a remedy for gunshot wounds, alleging that he cured them. The King ordered the medicine to be first tried on goats in the Mahalab Garden. Amír Rahmán Khán presented the King with a box from China, and Mirza Sultán with a horse. Abdul Laluf Khán, a pleader from Cawnpore, presented a nazzar of two rupees on his own account, and four gold mohurs on the part of his clients who had come from Cawnpore with five hundred foot and horse to take service with the King. A petition was received from the Rájah of Bulubgarh, with a present of a horse. Mirza Koash was appointed commander of two regiments of foot, viz. the second Grenadiers and the 4th Regular (Nizamat) Cavalry. He was directed to pay the men, in accordance with an agreement made by him. The force from Nasirabad, which had gone out as a support to the Nímuch Brigade, returned and reported that they had been unable to ascertain their whereabouts. Four native cavalrymen, deserters from the English camp, came in to-day, but they were suspected of being spies, and were not admitted into the city. During the night the English attacked the Kissenganj Battery. The whole Sepoy force was put under arms in expectation of an assault from the English. Four landowners represented to the King that the Nímuch force had beaten the English, and was ready to attack the English, but it had no supports. His Majesty did not believe this story, so he directed that three of them should be kept in the guard-room, and the fourth he ordered some cavalry to take with them to ascertain the truth. The King promised the men that they would be well rewarded if their statement were true. If false, they would be executed. In accordance with the orders of the Court, Munshi Aga Khán, Munshi Saádat Ali, Ramsahan Mall, and Jehangir Chand, city bankers, were put in prison, and money demanded from them. By order of Mirza Koash, Parka Mall, banker, was also imprisoned till his money was forthcoming.

August 29.—The King sat in the Hall of Public Audience. Hákim Ahsanúllah, Said Ali Khán, Nazir Hassan Mirza, Mozuffer-ullah, and other noblemen were present at the Durbár. A communication was read from the Gwalior force stating that the men would very shortly arrive at Delhi. It was rumoured that more than 1,000 men were killed in the attack at Kissenganj, and one English officer. The Sepoys proposed to cut off his head and exhibit it in the city as an evidence of their victory. As they were doing this there came such a storm of shot and shell that the men fled. There was a heavy fire kept up all day both of musketry and artillery, but neither did the English succeed in rescuing the officer's body, nor did the Sepoys succeed in cutting off his head. Three camels arrived, sent by Rao Tulla Rám of Rewári. The King in reply urged him to send money as soon as possible. His Majesty sent an order to Mirza Mogul not to demand money from Ramjí Dáss Goroal, as he had already contributed. Some one stole fourteen camels belonging to Bahádur Jang from the rear of the

English camp, and took them away. A letter was sent to Bahádur Jang to trace out and send back the camels, which were attached to the Nímuch column. Orders were sent to the Nawáb of Farukhnagar to have two thousand matchlocks made. Mirza Abdullah, son of Mirza Shahir, deceased, reported that a company of sappers and four companies of Sepoys had separated themselves from the English, and had joined the Nímuch column. A letter came from General Mahommed Bakht Khán, stating that many persons were giving the King advice about the war which was of no value; yet His Majesty was displeased with his generalship. He proposed in the future to concern himself only with the command of the Bareilly column. The King replied: "No one has censured your conduct, and I am quite satisfied to leave the chief command in your hands." A woman employed in the powder factory was arrested, and put in confinement, because a fellow-workwoman had heard her say she had been offered six hundred rupees to blow up the factory. A postal runner from the English camp fell into the hands of the Sepoys; he was questioned closely in Durbár as to what was going on in the camp. He boldly expressed the opinion that the Sepoys would never prevail against the English, the time for that had passed; but even suppose they did prevail, the position of the English at Agra was perfectly secure. In revenge for his outspoken opinion the Courtiers sentenced him to death. Mirza Khorshed Alum was directed not to enter the King's apartments. He might attend the Durbár. The King issued orders to Doláli Mall, head of the Commissariat, to issue one seer of flour, ¼ seer lentils, half a chillah of clarified butter, one tolleh of salt, and one pice to each soldier of the army; but this officer pleaded his inability to do so for want of money. The Agent of the Nawáb of Rampur attended the Durbár. It was stated to-day that there had been a fight between the Gujars and the landowners in the Farukhnagar territory, and more than one hundred people had been killed.

August 30.—The Agent of the Nawáb of Rampur sought private audience of the King, which was fixed for after midday. Kudrat Ali Khán, Resaldár, represented that he had brought three hundred persons with him. At the same time, Rahaman Khán, son of Nawáb Noagish Khán, informed the King that he had raised a force of five hundred cavalry. He presented a nazzar of twenty rupees and one gold mohur. A Subahdar of Lucknow presented five rupees as a nazzar, with a petition in which it was written that all the English had been killed, and he had brought ten thousand men under his command. "Very shortly I will come to the King's assistance with money and troops." The followers of Kudrat Ali Khán presented each two rupees as nazzars, and Kudrat Ali Khán a nazzar of two rupees sicca struck in the King's name. At the time of presentation it was stated that money of that kind was current in Lucknow. After the Durbár was over, the King remained some time in private audience with Kudrat Ali Khán. Mirza Kizr Sultán was directed to go to the Kútub to collect revenue with a force of 400 cavalry. Kuda Baksh, of Nusapur, was directed to proceed to Jajjar to bring seven thousand rupees, and to take an escort of five hundred cavalry with him. Doláli Mall, chief of the Commissariat, petitioned that he was no longer able to serve out rations to the troops. Munshi Saádat Ali and Munshi Aga Khán, having paid up twenty thousand rupees, were released. Ramsahan Mall paid six thousand rupees, and was released. His Majesty went to the Hall of Public Audience after midday. Khán Bahádur Khán, agent of the Chief of Bareilly, presented gold mohurs on the part of his master and himself, and offered an elephant with a silver howdah, a horse caparisoned with a golden cloth, and a copy of the Koran, for acceptance. The agent of the Chief of Rampur also presented a nazzar of 100 gold mohurs, together with a petition.

August 31.—The coat and shoes of the Prophet Mahommed were brought this day with great ceremony from the Masjid of Nulub-u-dín, escorted by a company of infantry and four elephants. The King received these holy relics with great reverence, and presented a nazzar of one gold mohur and five rupees, and ordered the relics to be taken back, sending at the same time a dress of honour consisting of six pieces, with three different kinds of jewelry, as evidence of respect for the season of the Moharram (to Kulup-u-dín ?). He also sent three pieces of cloth, one jewel, a piece of gold cloth, two shawls, and an embroidered cloth worn over the side of a turban, to the doorkeeper of the Jumma Masjid. Both persons expressed their gratitude and thanks, and each presented a nazzar of two rupees to the King. The King also gave a rupee and four suits of clothes to the boys who accompanied their parents. A spy reported that the English were preparing more batteries on the Ridge, and would destroy the whole city and the troops encamped outside the city walls. The King, on hearing this, ordered the Military Court to sit and consult what should be done. More complaints from the Sepoys that they were starving, as the shopkeepers had refused all supplies for want of payment. Mulahi Lál Muthridi, a trader, reported that no more sulphur could be purchased, and the manufacture of gunpowder must cease. He suggested that urgent letters should be sent to the Nawábs of Farukhabad, Jajjar, and Bhoali to supply this, and His Majesty said: "No, refer this matter to the Military Court; they are responsible." Mirza Kizr demanded sulphur from all the traders, giving them the option either to supply the sulphur or money for its purchase, which would be extorted from them. The traders replied: "We have neither money nor sulphur." It was to-day proclaimed by beat of drum that if anyone were in want of wood they were at liberty to cut down the trees in the Nodsare Gardens, as they screened the fire of the guns from the Selimgarh Battery. The members of the Military Court summoned the bankers, and asked them for money (not demanded authoritatively). The bankers replied: "The Princes have already taken three lakhs and seventy thousand rupees from us, and we can give no more." The Court was displeased at this answer, and issued a proclamation that no more money was to be given to the Princes. Mirza Mogul went out to inspect the troops with an escort of two hundred cavalry. On his arrival at the parade ground the troops fired three volleys as a salute: instantly there was a panic in the city. All the shops were closed, and the inhabitants concealed themselves, thinking the English had entered the city.

SEPTEMBER 1: THE BEGINNING OF THE END.

The King held his Durbár; Ahsanúllah Khán, Mirza Amín-úllah Khán, Mirza Zia-u-dín Khán, and five hundred officers and nobles attended. Those named were loud in their complaints that Mirza Mogul and Mirza Kizr had taken several lakhs of rupees from the people in the city, and had given nothing to the Army, and prayed the King to insist on their disgorging some of the money, threatening to arrest and imprison them. His Majesty sent for the two Princes, and told them what had occurred. They replied that 40,000 rupees only had passed through their hands, that the statement about the three lakhs was absolutely false. Mutual recriminations followed. The officers again and again urged upon His Majesty to make some arrangement about the pay, threatening to plunder the city. The King replied: "There is no necessity to plunder. I will sell my horses, elephants, silver and gold ornaments of state, and pay the Army. If I do not do so, you can all leave and abandon the city, the more so as I never summoned you. If you intend to plunder the city, kill me first. Afterwards you can do as you please." His Majesty, rising, walked out of the assembly-room into his own private apartments. All the officers adjourned to the Public Hall of Audience, and remained there until six o'clock in an excited state, talking and haranguing with Hákim Abdul Hak, Mirza Ilahí Baksh, and Said Ali Khán, who went with a message that the first instalment of their pay would be issued next day, and the Begum Zínut Mehal would, from her own resources, within fifteen days disburse the balance due. After this the three regiments who had been kept waiting for orders to sack the city, returned to their quarters, and the officers, leaving three companies at the Palace gates, with orders not to allow any of the Princes to enter, gradually dispersed. Looking at the pay demand it was seen that the monthly cost of the Army was five lakhs and seventy-three thousand rupees. The King was reported to be much dejected. A report came from Mirza Bahádur Shah from Jajjar that Nadír Shah, Resaldár, had suddenly died from cholera. The writer was ordered to return at once to Delhi. A great exodus from the city to-day of all the clerk and writer class, through fear. A Sepoy guard was placed at the door of Munshi Sultán Sing and money demanded. The King very angry with the Princes. The Begum in fear of the Sepoys plundering the Palace. She sent three thousand rupees' worth of jewels to the King, and asked him to give it to the Sepoys, but the King refused, remarking, with a touch of sarcasm, that as long as he lived let the burden of indigestion and trouble fall on him. Samund Khán, Resaldár, received orders to go and receive six lakhs of rupees from Ellire. The Police-officer Shahdara sent in notice that there were two maunds of sugar lying unclaimed there. Mirza Mehdí was ordered to take an escort and bring it in. Two regiments of foot and twenty guns were sent down to arm the batteries during the night.

September 2.—His Majesty sat in the Hall of Public Audience. Mirza Ilahí Baksh, Moulvie Fazl Hak, Mir Said Ali Khán, and Hákim Abdul Hak, made their obeisance. Again the soldiers asked for pay. The troops to-day were paid in accordance with a detailed arrangement of Mir Said Ali :—Each Resaldár, twelve rupees; Subahdars, four rupees; Troopers, two rupees ; Sepoys, one rupee; Zemindars, three rupees. Kudrat Ali Bey sought an audience, and for a long time was in conversation with the King. Five cavalry soldiers from Lahore came in without arms. News came that the landholders of Kotkausor were rebellious. A force of two hundred English and two guns had gone to reduce them to order. The Zemindars had fled, but had been brought back, and warned to be on their good behaviour. It was reported also that several thousand Jehádis, under Moulvie Jelal-u-dín, had ventured to fight in the open, with the result that the Moulvie and several hundred of his followers had been killed, that the English had taken possession of Aligarh, that a regiment of Sikhs had arrived at Meerut and were encamped near the entrance to the city, and that the English administration was established as it was previously.

September 3.—The King sat in the Hall of Public Audience.

The landowners of Lole attended, and paid in 3,500 rupees as Government revenue. They complained that the troops had tried to take the money from them. The King expressed his pleasure, and gave the landowners a present of five *pagries* (head-dress or turban). Bashim Sing, Chowderí of Dadrí, presented a nazzar of ten rupees to the King, and spoke regarding a case in which he was interested. A *palki*-bearer who had deserted from the English camp, presented Mirza Mogul with a pistol valued at one hundred rupees. Mirza Mogul, Mirza Ilahí Baksh, Hákim Abdul Hak Káhín, and Mir Said Ali Khán had a long conference as to how to raise money for the pay of the troops. They sent for a list of Police-ratepayers, and with that for a guide, proceeded to make out a list, imposing such a rate as would raise four lakhs of rupees from the city people. Mirza Kuda Baksh reported that he had delayed his departure for Jajjar as he heard the English had taken possession of Gurjawan. The King on learning this recalled the letter he had written to the Nawáb. A petition came from the Rájah of Bulubgarh, complaining that "Hákim Abdul Khán is demanding four lakhs of rupees from me for the expenses of the war." The King replied: "The officer you complain against is acting under my orders. I will certainly require the money of him, and again I write to you to send the money without delay, also a contingent of five hundred foot-soldiers with two field-guns, and five maunds of opium; otherwise I will impose a fine on you of one lakh of rupees." It was reported to-day that the Sepoys had proposed to the Taj Mehal Begum to enthrone her in the place of Zínut Mehal Begum, whom they intended to imprison unless their pay was forthcoming within fifteen days. The soldiers surrounded the house of Sultán Sing to extort money. It was reported that there had been a stand-up fight between the

Mahommedans and the Hindus of Dasria, in which a number of persons were killed. Muthra Dáss, treasurer, was, it is said, plundered on his way to Delhi. Peremptory orders sent to Rao Tulla Rám to pay up the money which he had collected from bankers and shroffs in the city. The English intended to destroy the bridge in the night, but were forced back by a contingent of 2,000 Sepoys. The Sepoys caught a man to-day on suspicion of his being a European, but when the Sirdars heard the description of the man they ordered his release. Five companies of foot, two hundred cavalry, and two guns were sent off in the direction of Gurjawan to oppose the English. The Resaldár who was sent with Kallandar Baksh to Jajjar to get money, returned empty-handed, the Nawáb having refused to give so much as a single cowrie. The English threw up a battery in front of the Cabul Gate, but it was exposed to so hot a fire from the Cashmere and Cabul batteries that it was knocked to pieces.

September 4.—Mahommed Bakht Khán visited the King, and entered into private conversation with him. Certain officers of the Nasirabad camp, it appears, gave His Majesty a great deal of annoyance last night regarding their pay. In consequence of this the King ordered all the silver goods to be made over to them, saying: "Sell them, and divide the proceeds among yourselves for pay." The officers were still dissatisfied. Autograph letters were despatched to the Rájahs of Jeypur, Jhodpur, Bikanír, and Alore, that the King was in want of troops and was desirous of annihilating the English; but inasmuch as he had no reliable person to organize and administer the very important affairs of the empire at this juncture, he wished to form a Confederacy of States; and if the States he now addressed with these letters would combine for the purpose he would willingly resign the imperial power into their hands. The sugar sent for from Shahdara arrived this day. The force that had been despatched to Gurjawan appears, on reaching the Kútub, to have plundered a number of shops, and to have arrested a number of petty moneylenders who had taken refuge in a temple. The Sepoys also plundered all the property belonging to his relatives which was in Sir John Metcalfe's house and which had been placed in charge of a Jemadar, and servants appointed by the King for its safe custody. The Jemadar was arrested and taken by the Sepoys, together with the property, to the King, who, on learning what had happened, was very angry and ordered the servants to be released.[1] A man named Haidar, a petty trader, whose wife was a resident of Jallabhari, having dressed himself in an ornamental coat, and disguised a number of bad characters as soldiers, went to the house of one of the citizens, where he represented himself as one of the Princes, and having beaten the man, extorted four hundred rupees. When the soldiers heard of this they went in search of the rascal and apprehended him. They found on him 201 gold mohurs, 54 rupees, a pair of bracelets, a gold chain, and several golden breast ornaments. This day Wallidád Khán, chief of Balaghari, sent a petition to the effect that the English had occupied Aligarh, and were intending to attack him, but that God in His mercy had sent two regiments of foot, and some cavalry from Lucknow had joined his force. As these troops were on the march to Delhi an order to retain them was asked from the King

[1] The arrangements made by the King protected the Metcalfe property at the Kútub from May till September, when it was all plundered, except some cases of books which had escaped observation (and found their way back to England), having been placed in the dark inner lining of the dome. Whether the King protected the property for his own use eventually, or out of a friendly feeling to the owners, is a matter of speculation.

on the agreement that the Chief would pay them. His Majesty assented to the proposal, and a reply was returned. The Volunteer Regiment, the 28th Foot, brought their Commandant before the King and charged him with being in communication with the English. General Mahommed Bakht Khán defended the Moulvie, and the King ordered his release from arrest. His Majesty sent a written order to General Bakht Khán to pay the troops to the amount of twenty-six thousand rupees. The General replied he could not find the money, that he himself was so much pressed for money for his food that he had been obliged to sell elephants and horses. It was reported that Rána Bhagonaut Sing, chief of Dholpur, had sent fifteen hundred foot, some cavalry, and six guns to the assistance of the English at Agra, and they were encamped at the artillery ground sixteen miles distant. It was also stated that Sirdar Sing, chief of Bikanír, had enlisted and sent three thousand Rájputs to the assistance of Captain Robertson, and had written to say he was about to begin fighting. The Rájah of Nalagah, it was reported, had enlisted a thousand Gurkhas to assist the English. It was reported that the English were now in good heart, and the Maharájah Runbír Sing, chief of Jammú, was sending five thousand men to Lahore to assist the English. It was also reported that the magazine at Jhorpore had been struck by lightning and had exploded, and several thousand persons had lost their lives by it and a great part of the city was destroyed. Further reports told that Rájah Nazir Sing had sent six hundred muskets to the English. The English had written to the Nawáb of Jajjar to send 2,080 blacksmiths (*sic*), which order he had obeyed. It was rumoured that the English had killed all the Mahommedans in Aligarh, and had sent off two thousand Europeans from Cawnpore to the assistance of the Bailly Guard force at Lucknow; that there had been a fight with the English, in which the Sepoys had been defeated and had fled.

September 5.—The King held a council to-day, in which the position of affairs was considered. General Bakht Khán reported that the English siege train had arrived, and they were erecting breaching batteries opposite the Cashmere Gate. The King inquired, "What arrangements are you making for meeting the English fire? If you cannot oppose them you had better open the gates of the city at once." The General said: "I am removing the Magazine outside the city, and I propose to meet the English fire with forty guns, for which I am constructing batteries." The General further explained that he had arranged to employ two thousand cavalry to cut off all commissariat supplies from the English camp. The King inquired what stock of gunpowder there was, and an urgent letter was sent off to the Nawáb of Farukhabad to send without delay two thousand maunds of sulphur. Mir Said Ali Khán, Hákim Abdul Hak Khán, Mirza Ilahí Baksh, and Saligram the Treasurer met and consulted on the ways and means of paying the Army. Orders were issued to the police to appoint a "Pauch"[1] every day to fix the prices of food. A force was sent from the Nasirabad contingent to bring in revenue from Ghaziabad, but these orders were countermanded by Prince Mirza Mogul.

September 6.—The King sat in the Hall of Public Audience, and on hearing that the force ordered to Ghaziabad had been countermanded by Prince Mirza Mogul, His Majesty expressed his displeasure. An artizan exhibited a cannonball which he had made. General Mahommed

[1] A "Pauch" is a committee of five traders.

Bakht Khán made a complaint that, whereas the King's servants and other troops had received wages, the Bareilly force, on which the brunt of the fighting fell, had received nothing; that all his men were, in consequence, discontented. The King replied: "I have already caused one lakh of rupees to be distributed; the treasury is empty. How many lakhs of rupees have passed through your hands? Why have you not paid your men with some of the money?" A number of carts came from Shahdara into the city to-day laden with sugar. There was a very large gathering of officers at the Durbár to-day; they complained that there was no chief official to command or to issue orders. What should be done? For this reason there was "confusion worse confounded." The King replied: "You alone have the power to act. Whatever you think you are able to accomplish, that do." More cavalry arrived to-day from Lucknow. Intimation came from two foot-regiments from Lucknow that they were hastening to Delhi. The King gave as his answer: "Come, if you desire; if not, go elsewhere." Moulve Fazl Hak reported that the force from Muttra had gone to Agra, and after defeating the English had advanced against the city. It was reported that some European and Sikh regiments had joined the English on the Ridge.

September 7.—The King remained in his private apartments. Ahsanullah Khán Dád and General Mahommed Bakht Khán waited on His Majesty; the latter remained for some time in private conference. The title of Khán Bahádur, with a present of two shawls, was conferred upon the Khán Bahádur Khán of Bareilly. The patent was made over to his agent, who was despatched with it. A petition was received from the Chief of Bulubgarh, Nahir Sing, to the purport that sixty troopers had come with an order from the King to release Jumbít Khán. The Chief wrote: "Although I do not credit this order, the man has been released; but I have suffered great loss through these soldiers, who have taken several thousand rupees from me for their expenses." The King dictated a reply that he had never sent any soldiers, nor any such order, and the soldiers should be arrested and punished. A report came from the Morar force that owing to the want of boats it could not cross the river Chamboul. A petition received from the Nawáb of Farukhnagar brought by artillerymen. A sum of one thousand rupees received from Nawáb Amin-Al-Rahaman Khán, son of Noarish Khán, deceased, for which a receipt was granted. It was reported that the English had seized a number of buffaloes feeding in the Kudsalah Gardens, and had carried them off. General Bakht Khán attended with a deputation of ten of his officers, to inform the King that the men of his force had not received one pice of pay from the day that it had entered Delhi; that the men were very discontented and threatened to leave for their homes. The King replied they might do as they were minded, so far as he was concerned. Hákim Abdul Hak, Mir Said Ali Khán, Moulvie Fazl Hak, Badar-u-dín Khán, and every nobleman and chief citizen attended the Durbár. The police had also caused the attendance of every jeweller. They were informed that the citizens must raise eight lakhs of rupees immediately for the pay of the troops. The merchants replied that owing to the plunder and extortions and stoppage of all trade, it was impossible for them to raise the money required. After giving these orders the King directed Prince Mirza Mogul to exercise due diligence in the realization of the money, and notify the King's orders by beat of drum throughout the city. In consequence of this step being taken by the King the Military Council decided to attack the

English next day, and it was proclaimed that every citizen, Hindu or Mahommedan, who assisted in the attack, should share the plunder, and whoever made prisoners of Gurkhas, Sikhs, or English, would be handsomely rewarded. These orders were read to the troops on parade. Mir Said Ali Khán, Dewan Makund Lál, Bardar-u-dín Khán, Hákim Abdul Hak, with his sons, and Nawáb Kúli Khán, were all arrested and put in the Palace Guard-room, by order of the Military Court, till money was forthcoming for the pay of the soldiers. They pleaded that they were making arrangements to raise the money. It was reported that four hundred English soldiers with four guns had reached the camp, and the English were busy constructing batteries. It was reported that the English had levied a tax of one maund of wheat flour and one rupee in cash on every head of the population of the town of Panipat.

September 8.—The King remained in his private apartments. On the previous evening the English were busy finishing the construction of a battery in the Kudsia Gardens, and from there they opened fire, shot after shot being directed against the Cashmere and Mori Gates. All the Sepoys in the different bastions were hotly engaged. Shot after shot came flying into the city. On all sides it was being repeated : " Whatever it pleases God, we must await patiently." The King summoned the Military Court, and ordered them to release the persons in custody. On their agreeing to raise money by a self-imposed tax throughout the city for the pay of the Army, they were released. It was rumoured that the fire from the city bastions had silenced one of the English guns and a mortar. Shot after shot fell into the city, but did little or no harm. A Sepoy on the roof of Munshi Sultán Sing's house was noticed keeping watch. He then was seen to go into the house of a Hindu.

On suspicion that he was signalling to the English, he was killed. It was notified that all complaints would in future be heard by the Military Court at the office of the Press, at the Delhi Gate. The agent of the Nawáb of Bareilly, with his escort of soldiers of the Bareilly force, made an attempt to leave the city, but they were stopped by the guard at the Calcutta Gate. In accordance with the King's orders, the police proceeded to collect three months' rent from every shop and dwelling-house for the pay of the Sepoys. Imdad Ali Khán attacked the English with great bravery. He was surrounded, but managed to escape with considerable difficulty. All night the soldiers remained under arms.

September 9. — The King sat in the Hall of Public Audience, and inspected a horse from Faridkot. Imdad Ali Khán attended the Durbár. The King praised his bravery, and presented him with a horse from his own stable, in exchange for his charger, shot yesterday in battle. The King ordered the arrest of the Princes who had misappropriated money collected for the pay of the Sepoys. It was rumoured to-day that a force from Bombay had arrived, and was encamped at Kishen Dáss's Tank. A camel trooper was sent out to ascertain if this were true. He returned and reported that there was no such force encamped there. Munshi Joalla Pershád, Commissariat clerk, was ordered to prepare a die for stamping the current coin, with the following words: "The Coin of Bahádur Shah, King of Hindostan. By the mercy of God, the Golden Armament of the World." In accordance with directions given to Munshi Joahir Lál, Kalander Baksh, subahdar of the Sapper Regiment, waited on the King, and petitioned that the Governor-General, with several thousand troops, native and English, was marching from Calcutta to Delhi; that Joahir Sing, the nephew of Maharájah

Golab Sing, chief of Jammú, was hastening to Delhi, with six thousand of his troops; that Sir John Lawrence had started with several thousand newly-raised levies from Lahore; and that the English camp had so increased that it extended from the Ridge nearly to the city; that he (Kalander Baksh) had constructed an entrenched battery, and was prepared to fight the English as long as he had life. Wallidád Khán, chief of Bulubgarh, sent an urgent letter asking for troops to reinforce him; the King flatly refused, saying: "Fighting has begun again here in real earnest, and this is no time to send reinforcements elsewhere." The agent of the Nawáb of Bareilly waited on the King and stated that he wished to return to Bareilly to look after the collection of the revenue, with a view to sending money for the Royal Treasury, but that the guard at the Calcutta Gate had refused to let him pass. The King, after considering the matter, ordered that the agent should be allowed to leave the city; the guard, however, refused to obey the King's orders. Many men, women, and children were killed to-day by the cannonballs. The Sepoys proposed to construct a walled entrenchment near the Magazine. The Cashmere Gate was much injured by the breaching batteries. The King sent sixty maunds of sweetmeats to the Sepoys, and twenty-four rupees. In the course of the day the officers again pressed for their pay. Kadir Baksh, subahdar of the Sappers, reported that the English evidently intended to assault the city in the morning; it was so rumoured. News came that the English had entirely destroyed the village of Pakhoa, and had burned it, because the villagers had refused to pay their revenue. Five thousand rupees were found in a hide-skinner's house. The troops were under arms all day, behind the entrenchments.

September 12.—The King went to the underground

mosque, this day, for prayers. Hassan Ali Khán followed the King, and made his obeisance, as did also Nazir Hassan Mirza, and intimated that an agent from Lucknow would arrive the next morning, but that he had sent on a request that he might be received privately. His Majesty agreed to the proposal. Five thousand rupees were sent to the gunpowder factory to-day, for the manufacture of gunpowder. Samund Khán, Resaldar, left for Jajjar. The Nawáb of Jajjar to-day sent the salary of Hassan Ali Khán. Mirza Amín-u-dín waited on the King and reported that he had enlisted two hundred men to collect the revenue from Loharu. He asked for orders to the guards of the City Gates to allow him to leave the city. The King declined to issue the orders, as the Sepoys refused to obey his wishes. Mirza Mogul visited the Cashmere Gate guards, and made special arrangements for the battery in front of Mir Said Ali Khán's house. A petition, signed by several shopkeepers, was presented to the King, saying that they were in great fear of being impressed to work the guns in the batteries, as policemen had been told off to seize them for this duty. Through fear of being carried off, they had closed all their shops. The Military Court issued stringent orders against any of the leading class being impressed for duty on the batteries, but Chamars (skinners) and labourers were to be impressed. A Sepoy drew his sword to intimidate Mir Said Ali Khán for not paying the troops. Shot fell in the city throughout the night. A woman and one Joahir Lál were killed to-day by bursting shells, and two Sepoys were wounded. A proclamation was issued, that anyone refusing to pay three months' rent would be severely punished. The King passed the night in great anxiety; all his personal attendants remained with him throughout the night. A proclamation was issued by beat of drum, that His Majesty would himself lead an attack on the English this night and would destroy them, and inviting the whole city to rise and sweep through the English camp, and by their force of numbers kill every European soldier. The proclamation invited both Hindus and Mahommedans to bind themselves by an oath to do so. In consequence of this notice, upwards of ten thousand Mahommedans congregated near the Cashmere Gate, and waited till midnight for the arrival of the King; gradually this great assembly dispersed and went home.

September 13.—The King attended public worship. After prayers, Nazir Hassan Mirza introduced Mirza Abas Bey agent of the Court of Lucknow. He presented the King with a nazzar of two gold mohurs. His Majesty conferred on him the title of Safir-ul-Dowlah. The agent, in return, presented His Majesty with twelve gold mohurs, two horses nobly caparisoned, two elephants with clothing and Howdah of State, a pair of jewelled bracelets, a jewelled crown; with a petition asking for a patent of dignity and rank, and a title to his property and possessions. The Sepoys to-day completed a battery at the Magistrate's Cutcherry and at Mir Said Ali Khán's house. A shell burst in General Bakht Khán's camp, wounding several Sepoys, of whom two or three died. A barrel of cartridges was also blown up. Throughout the day and night the artillery fire was constant, cannon answering cannon. The residents of Kajuzi Mohalla, one of the city wards, and of Saádat Ali Khán's ward, left their houses, and sought refuge in a more distant part of the city. The whole city would have been deserted by man, woman, and child, if the city guards had only permitted them to leave. It required all the exertions of the police to induce some of the shopkeepers to open their shops. The English had constructed a battery in front of the Lál (red) Gate and made a breach in the masonry of the Cashmere Gates, and were in hopes that they would be able to enter the city by night-time. A friend of mine was arrested, on suspicion of giving information to the English. Seventy men, who had deserted from the English camp, got into the city, and took five Moguls as prisoners before the King. Muttra Dáss and Saligram, Treasurer, were placed in confinement. It was proclaimed in the city that to-morrow every citizen should attack the English camp. It was reported to-day from Meerut, that the English had enlisted a great number of Játs and Gujars, and had realized revenue from nearly one hundred villages, and peace and security had been re-established in that district, as also at Aligarh. A very heavy siege gun, to judge from the sound, was firing into the city all night. All passed a night of anxiety.

September 14.—The King remained in his private apartments. There was a rumour that the English would assault the city. Mirza Mogul ordered all the troops in the Palace under arms to take part in the defence. To-day it was apparent that Delhi was to become the scene of a severe battle. For the most part the Sepoys slunk behind the entrenchments. Eventually the English took possession of the Cashmere Gate and the Ali Burj Bastion. Some Europeans, Sikhs, and levies ventured as far as the Jumma Masjid, and drove back the Sepoys. Many thousand Mahommedans were assembled in the Jumma Masjid, and attacked the English, and killed a great many of them, so many that the soldiers retreated. A severe fight took place in the Begum's garden, where four hundred men fell.

About midday the Mahommedans ceased to oppose the English. They, together with the Sepoys, began to take refuge in the houses of the Hindus, whom they upbraided for not co-operating with them. The whole day, they were pouring abuse upon the Hindus, threatened to massacre both them and their families, when they should have defeated the English. The King endeavoured to mediate, and to pour oil on troubled waters, by proclaiming his intention of taking the field in person next day with a united force of all the Mahommedans and Hindus in the city.

FINIS.

APPENDICES.

FATE OF MR. DAVIS.

Mr. Davis has been previously mentioned. The fuller particulars connected with him are as follows. He was the head of the English Department of the Commissioners and Agents Office. When the Sepoys entered the city through the Rájghaut road, they were close to the house where Mr. Davis lived, together with his brother Tommy and his sisters. The Sepoys attacked the house. Both the brothers armed themselves with guns, and closing the door of the house, mounted on the roof.

My servant, whom I had sent to gather news of what was going on, found the house surrounded by soldiers, foot and horse. He saw eleven of them fall, shot from the roof of the house, and he saw one of the defenders fall backwards, wounded, while several of the soldiers were taken away wounded. The soldiers then retired. Subsequently Mr. Davis, together with many of his neighbours, took refuge in the house of a friendly native, and from there escaped to the underground apartments (*tái khana*) of the Maharájah of Kishengarh. Soheni, my servant, then communicated with them, proposing that they should change their clothes, and during the night he would conduct them to my house; but Mr. Davis objected, as the road and bazaars were crowded with soldiers who were patrolling the streets, looking out for Europeans, and it was improbable that they should reach my house safely. He proposed instead that I should send for the King's Vakíl, and through him communicate with the King, and point out that as I had charge of the account of the King's estate of Kot Kasim, His Majesty should be asked to claim Mr. Davis as his servant, and thus secure the safety at least of himself and his sisters. I immediately sent for the King's Vakíl, and begged of him to do this. The Vakíl laid the matter before the King, who sent an order for Mr. Davis to be brought to him; but before this could be carried out, Mr. Davis, together with the ladies of his family, and other ladies (amongst whom was Mrs. Thompson, the wife of Mr. Thompson, for many years a missionary at Delhi, much respected and beloved), were induced, with false promises from the soldiers who had surrounded the house, to come out of their place of concealment. Some were then killed, and others taken to the Palace. Two days and two nights the refugees were concealed in the underground apartments of the Maharájah's house, without food or water. On the third day, maddened by thirst, and seeing a water-carrier passing by with a skin of water, one of the men begged of him in the name of God to give him a drink. The man was carrying the water to the house of the Rájah of Bulubgarh. He came, and they opened the door and admitted him. The man gave them water, but when he got outside again he told some of the rebels, who were encamped in a garden, where the English were concealed. The house was immediately surrounded by a crowd of mutinous soldiers and scoundrels, who only became more bloodthirsty when they discovered it was impossible either to obtain access to the place, or from its situation to bring any effective fire to bear on its unfortunate inmates. They on their side saw every avenue of escape completely barred.

Such being the situation, the mutineers, finding force of no avail, resorted to craft, and made treacherous promises and solemn protestations to the refugees that if they would only come out, not a hair of their heads should be hurt, but they might confidently rely on being safely conducted to the Palace of the King, where they would be well treated. They succeeded in their object and induced the refugees to give themselves up.

There are two accounts of what happened after this. One is that the captives were told to sit down, and then and there were butchered in cold blood. The other, that the women and children were spared, but only to be taken to the Palace, where they subsequently met the same fate. Was there no God in heaven to forbid such revolting cruelties? The day smiled and nature remained unmoved at the horrible massacre.

The fate of[1] Mr. Davis, Mr. Tommy Davis, Mr. Nixon, Mr. Sendly, and Mr. Nickball was one. The pen grows dry and refuses to write. How impossible it is to fight against the hand of destiny! It is more than probable if the request of Mr. Davis had reached the King's ears sooner, he would have saved him, but the pen of the Omnipotent had already written his fate, and such a request was mere vain words. Each man's life is a history, and when the inevitable has been written of each, the ink becomes dry; for the purposes of God are immutable.

[1] N.B.—The above names are given as found in the Diary.

Incidents connected with the Movements of CAPTAIN DOUGLAS.

Scene at the Quarters of the Commandant of the Palace Guara.

Very early in the morning of the 11th of May, the attention of Captain Douglas was called to the burning bungalow across the river. Information of the arrival of troopers from Meerut had reached the Commandant, as also of the disturbances in the city. Boorun "Chobdar" (a silver stick in waiting) Bukliar Sing, Kishen Sing, messengers, reported that the residence of the Toll-Collector had been fired, and the officer in charge killed, and that the mutineers were making for the city, killing people here and there. At this moment one of the Sowars presented himself at the foot of the stairs, and told the sentry he wished to speak to Captain Douglas.

It was reported that the man was waiting below. Captain Douglas then came to the top of the stairs and inquired what he wanted. The man replied: "We have come from Meerut, where we have killed our officers, because they insisted on our using cartridges smeared with the fat of cows and pigs, and an attempt has been made to destroy our caste. Hindus and Mahommedans conjointly have created a mutiny (*bulwa*). There has been a fight; both Europeans and natives have fallen, and we have come here as complainants, seeking justice from the King. Advise us what we shall do, otherwise as we have been ordered, so we must do."

Captain Douglas' orderly states that the man spoke as if he were in a fury, and the gleam of bloodshed was in his eyes. Captain Douglas replied: "You have committed a great crime in killing your officers, and unless you at once cease from bloodshed in the city, you will be severely punished, as I have four companies of Gúrkhas."

As the Commandant ceased speaking the Sowar mounted his horse, and rode off to join his companions. Immediately after this a "Chobdar" (an attendant bearing a silver-handled *chourie* to keep off flies) came running with a message from the King, requiring the attendance of Captain Douglas, who went to the Dewan-i-Khás, where the King awaited him. On the way he met Ahsanúllah Khán and the King's Vakíl. From them he learned that a large force of mutineers had arrived in front of the city walls and were gathered on the city sands, raising loud cries. They urged the Commandant at once to take steps to restore order, as in the very presence of the King they were threatening, and dangerous. Captain Douglas found the King in the Dewan-i-Khás (Hall of Private Audience), and in reply to the King's questions as to what all this meant, he narrated what he had heard that morning—that a few of the troops at Meerut had mutinied and had fled to Delhi. He begged the King not to be anxious, as European troops from Meerut would assuredly be pursuing the mutineers, and must shortly arrive, and there were the regiments at Rajpúr besides. His Majesty might rest assured that the authorities had already taken steps to dispose of these men. From time to time during the interview, the loud cries of the mutineers penetrated the Audience Chamber. Captain Douglas asked permission to open the Water Gate leading to the river, with a view to calling some of the men into the presence of the King. The Vakíl and Ahsanullah Khán advised that this should not be done, and that Captain Douglas should not expose himself to the fury of the soldiery, who were already inflamed with bloodshed, and moreover, if they once obtained admission, they might plunder the Palace.

It was agreed that Captain Douglas should speak to the men from the river wall of the Palace. He did so, and called towards him two of the officers from among the mutineers.[1] They saluted the Commandant, and said: "The English tried to make Christians of us, and gave us these cartridges with that object; for this reason we have come to the King for protection, as we have been attacked, and some of us killed, by the English soldiers." Captain Douglas replied: "This place is under the private apartments (zenana) of the King; it is not the place for you to make a disturbance. Encamp somewhere on the river-bed, and the King will afterwards listen to your complaints." The men moved off towards the Rájghaut Gates of the city. As Captain Douglas was about to leave, after giving assurances to His Majesty, the King expressed great anxiety for the safety of himself and his family, and claimed the protection of the British Government. Captain Douglas again assured him he had no grounds of apprehension, and hurried to his house. There he learned that the Commissioner, Mr. Simon Fraser, was waiting for him at the bastion of the Calcutta Gate of the city. Stopping the buggy of Captain Dildar Khán, which was passing at the time, he drove on in it to the river-side bastion, where he found Mr. Simon Fraser, Mr. Hutchinson, and Mr. Charles Le Bas, the judge, with other gentlemen. Having joined them, he produced a letter which he had in his pocket. He gave

[1] The native officers were called "Subahdars" and "Jemadars."

it to Mr. Fraser to read, who returned it. Captain Douglas again read it. They then all conversed in English. While so doing a chaprassie of the Camel Department delivered a letter from the wife of the Toll-Collector, who had been murdered, asking for some arrangements to be made for the burial of her husband. Captain Douglas replied: "Under the circumstances of this mutiny I can now make no arrangements." At this moment five troopers came galloping up and fired a volley from their carbines. One shot, striking Captain Douglas on the foot, quite disabled him. He then slipped down into the fort ditch, where some of the budmashes (scoundrels) attempted to attack him, but they were deterred by the presence of Kishen Sing, Kúrmi Jat, and others attached to the office of the Fort Commandant, who carried him safely to the door of the Fort on a roughly improvised litter of sticks. After reaching the Gate, Mukhun Sing and Kishen Sing and others who were present carried him upstairs. He asked for some water, which he drank. He addressed the soldiers at the Gate, and said: "If you will shut the gates and exclude the mutineers, and will stand by the Europeans, I will promote one of your number to be a subahdar." The chaprassie then carried him upstairs to his room, where there were Mr. Jennings, the chaplain, and two ladies—Miss Jennings and Miss Clifford—who helped to bandage the foot. Captain Douglas fainted several times. On regaining consciousness he called out: "I left my sword on the open plain." Mukhun Sing, under the orders of Captain Douglas and of the other gentlemen, then closed the doors. A noisy set of ruffians, chiefly sweetmeat-sellers and Mogul residents of the Fort, with other seditious and murderous persons, crying, "Yá Allah! Yá Allah!" rushed up the stairs and called to Mukhun Sing to open the doors, else they would kill him as well. Mr. Jennings ordered the door to be opened, when the murderers rushed in, and with their swords released the life of each. The ladies had taken refuge in a mahogany wardrobe, and were dragged out. Mr. Jennings charged the men, and fell outside on the landing. The only one spared was Munshi Rám Lál, who was wounded. He was an officer of the King's household. It is believed he was knocked down with the butt end of a gun out of malice by one of the shopkeepers, who then escaped.

NARRATIVE OF THE ESCAPE OF SIR THEOPHILUS METCALFE.

این خـانه تمام افتاب است
این سلسله جمله زرباب است

I'n khána tamám aftáb ast ;
I'n silsila jumla zarbáb ast.

A Persian couplet of which the literal translation is as follows :—

This house (or family) is altogether as the sun ;
This family (or descent) is altogether as splendid as gold.

Early in the morning of the 11th May, Sir Theophilus had driven to the Court House, and it was then reported to him that mutinous soldiers were attempting to enter the city. To prevent this he at once got into a buggy, and putting the horse into a gallop, drove to the Kotwáli and sent off men to guard and prevent the opening of the Rájghaut Gate, and to ensure the shutting of the other gates. He then drove towards the Calcutta Gate, where he found the whole place in an uproar. The mutineers had been reinforced by a considerable body of troops from the garrison in cantonments, and the riffraff of the city were every moment adding fresh recruits to the turbulent mob.

After hairbreadth escapes, in which Sir Theophilus had to abandon his buggy, and make his way partly on foot and afterwards on a horse whose rider he seized, and summarily flung to the ground, he succeeded in finding temporary refuge in the Paharganj Thána. Here he was courteously received by Main-u-dín Hassan Khán, who faithfully promised, without any hesitation, to do all in his power to assist him, and as a preliminary measure, put his wardrobe at the disposal of Sir Theophilus, who thereupon proceeded to adopt a native disguise. Deeming it too risky, both on the Thanadár's account and his own, to remain any time in such close proximity to the city, where the mutineers had already commenced a wholesale massacre of all the Europeans on whom they could lay their hands, Sir Theophilus, on the earnest advice of the Thanadár, was dissuaded from making an attempt to return to cantonments, as it would inevitably lead to nothing but a useless sacrifice of his life. Instead he accepted the safe custody of Main-u-dín to the Kullali Bagh, where he found shelter in the house of a Lambadar, by name Búra Khán, who at once recognized Sir Theophilus, notwithstanding his disguise. Sir Theophilus' first anxiety was to learn the fate of the Europeans in the city, and he directed the Thanadár to ascertain all he could on the subject, and let him know the result as speedily as possible; and he begged him to spare no effort to save any lives he could. But the time for saving lives had already passed.

Suspected of assisting in the escape of Sir Theophilus Metcalfe, the Thanadár, as it was, ran no small risk of losing his own life, and it was only by using many subterfuges, and by the exercise of the most careful precautions, that he succeeded in keeping secret the whereabouts of the refugee, and preventing the bloodhounds of the city getting on the trail. Meanwhile Búra Khán left nothing undone to secure Sir Theophilus' safety, and to minister to his wants.

By way of an additional safeguard a second place of refuge was provided in a neighbouring thicket. Thither the refugee could betake himself at night, should any sudden hue and cry be raised by those who were known to be seeking his life. Búra Khán, moreover, had arranged with a few trusty adherents for assistance, should matters reach a crisis. Amongst these were two Rajputs, Boran Sing and Himat Sing. As Sir Theophilus felt he was only exposing himself and his friends to needless risk by prolonging his stay in the vicinity of Delhi, he prevailed on Búra Khán to pass him on to Jajjar, the chief of which state was not only a personal friend, but indebted for many kindnesses both to Sir Theophilus Metcalfe himself and to his father before him. Here, therefore, he had reason to expect, if not a warm welcome, at any rate, safety and shelter. Thanks to the arrangements made by Búra Khán, and the fidelity displayed by him and the Rajputs, Boran Sing, Himat Sing, and others, Sir Theophilus was safely escorted to Jajjar. (The writer of this narrative here pauses to remark that these men who in this dire time of need had stood so staunchly and faithfully by Sir Theophilus Metcalfe, subsequently, when better times had come, and the British Government had reasserted its authority, were not forgotten, but received the rewards they so richly deserved.) Just at the time of Sir Theophilus' arrival at Jajjar, the first flame of the Mutiny, which was spreading through the country, had reached Jajjar. The town was in a condition of great excitement. A number of Hindus serving in the Nawáb's contingent at once deserted, while the Mahommedan soldiers anxiously awaited the moment when they, too, might join in the rebellion. From time to time they raised loud cries of "Dín! Dín!" ("The Faith! The Faith!") Great excitement consequently prevailed in the town. It was on the 16th May that it was reported to the Nawáb that a European dressed in native clothes demanded his hospitality.

The Nawáb sent Abdul Samad Khán, his father-in-law, and Imdad Ali, the judge, to interview him. Sir Theophilus at once declared himself to them. They thereupon returned to the Nawáb, who sent him a hundred rupees in cash, with a message to leave the place at once. It immediately became known to the populace that he was there, and crowds assembled to satisfy their curiosity. Later on in the day the Nawáb sent a message that the fugitive might go to the garden-house of Jujuk Dáss. Shortly after he reached this house a trooper rode up and ordered the gardener to tell the Sahib to leave the place. He took the hint, and started at once with a heavy heart, never expecting to reach Hissar or Hansi alive. After going a short distance, and fearing lest he should be followed, he turned off the road and concealed himself in a thicket in the jungle. Nor were his anticipations wrong, for in a short time a troop of the Nawáb's cavalry went galloping in the direction in which he was going, and did not return until sunset. Under cover of darkness, and under the protection of God's providence, he reached Mr. Skinner's house.

Both at the time when the story reached Delhi and since the Nawáb's conduct has been severely criticized in Native society, for hostility to a foe is one thing, disloyalty to a friend another thing :

ترا اژدها گر بود یار غار
ازان به که جاهل بود غم گسار

"Tura azdahá gar bawad yár-i-ghár
Azán bih kih jáhil bawad gham gusár."

"Cherish a dragon as a friend, before
You trust a fool, when fortune smiles no more."

It was said at the time, in defence of the Nawáb, that Sannu Sing, the commandant of the Nawáb's cavalry, sent the trooper to Sir Theophilus to order him to leave the city, with the intention that he should be killed on the road and not in Jajjar itself, and that the Nawáb was not aware of his having left; and that he had intended to have sent him to Bhawalgarhi Pargannah for safety, and had instructed Wazir Ali and Syud-u-dín, two of his retainers, to escort him there. Nevertheless, the fact remains that he took no steps to see him, or to protect him, and allowed his troops to plan his assassination. When the tide of fortune turned the Nawáb was tried, and the above plea was put forward by Nabhi Khán, who wrote his defence. I have no doubt the Nawáb was afraid to implicate himself by protecting a European, although he was a personal friend. The pursuit of Sir Theophilus after he left Jajjar was, I think, most probably the doing of Sannu Sing, the Resaldar of the Rájah's contingent, regarding whom Munshi Jewan Lál has furnished me with the following note:—

"The Jajjar contingent was at this time commanded by one Sannu Sing. Feeling he was extremely unpopular with the Nawáb's troops, and fearing in their excited state he might fall a victim to their hatred, he quietly left Jajjar, immediately after his attempt on the life of Sir Theophilus, and went off to his own village. As soon as the contingent became aware that the Resaldar had disappeared, it deserted in a body, but a number of men, who had old scores to pay off, rode hard for Sannu Sing's village, intending to kill him and plunder his house.

"Anticipating some such attempt, Sannu Sing gathered all the members of his family around him, and assisted by his brother Súji Sing, deliberately murdered every female member of his family; then, locking the door of his house he and his brother rode away in disguise. When the troopers from Jajjar arrived and attacked the house, they found a heap of dead bodies. This brutal custom of killing the women of a family in cold blood was not uncommon among the Rájputs. In their eyes dishonour is worse than death. In the case of Sannu Sing the act was more unjustifiable, for it was quite possible for him to have concealed his women amongst his own kinsmen, but the brutal savagery of the man showed itself in the excitement of the moment. In place of dying bravely fighting his enemies, having placed his family in safety, he was guilty of a cold-blooded and unnecessary act of brutality, and then added to his guilt by avoiding his enemies by flight as a coward. Of such an one the Poet has said [translation]:—

"'He dared not face a deadly strife,
To die courageous as a man should die;
By bloody deed he rent each holy tie,
To live accurst a few more days of life.'"

INDEX.

E.

F.

G.

H.

K.

L.

M.

N.

S.

T.

U.

Stephen Austin and Sons, Printers, Hertford.